Trauma Room One

The JFK Medical Coverup Exposed

CHARLES A. CRENSHAW, M.D.

with J. GARY SHAW,
D. BRADLEY KIZZIA, J.D.,
GARY AGUILAR, M.D.,
and CYRIL WECHT, M.D., J.D.

Foreword by OLIVER STONE

PARAVIEW PRESS

NEW YORK

This is a revised and expanded edition of *JFK: Conspiracy of Silence* by
Charles A. Crenshaw with Jens Hansen and J. Gary Shaw, originally
published by Signet in April 1992.

"On the Trail of the Character Assassins" by D. Bradly Kizzia is a version
of a chapter originally published in James H. Fetzer, ed., *Assassination
Science* (Chicago, IL: Open Court/Catfeet Press, 1998); "The Medical Case
for Conspiracy" by Gary Aguilar and Cyril Wecht is a greatly expanded
version of a chapter originally published in James H. Fetzer, ed., *Murder
In Dealey Plaza* (Chicago, IL: Open Court/Catfeet Press, 2000).

Cover photograph: Trauma Room One, Parkland Hospital
Book design by smythtype

ISBN:1-931044-30-9

Library of Congress Catalog Card Number: 2001092684

To all of the dedicated scholars who have searched for the truth about JFK's assassination for the American people, especially those who have become friends and defenders of my observations in Trauma Room One.

Contents

Foreword *by Oliver Stone* / 7

Author's Note: Why This Book Was Updated / 9

Preface to the 1992 Edition / 11

CHAPTER 1   The Beginnings / 21

CHAPTER 2   Friday, November 22, 1963 / 29

CHAPTER 3   Saturday, November 23, 1963 / 106

CHAPTER 4   Sunday, November 24, 1963 / 120

CHAPTER 5   Twenty-Six Years Later / 140

CHAPTER 6   The Empire Strikes Back, 1992 / 146

CHAPTER 7   On the Trail of the Character Assassins / 156
             by D. Bradley Kizzia

CHAPTER 8   The Medical Case for Conspiracy / 170
             by Gary L. Aguilar, MD and Cyril Wecht, MD, JD

Photographs, Illustrations, and Tables / 265

About the Contributors / 287

Foreword

BY OLIVER STONE

I have obviously offered my perspective on controversial issues
through the medium of film. One such effort was the movie, *JFK,*
which hypothesized that there was a conspiracy behind the assassination of President John Kennedy on November 22, 1963. The movie
depicted actual evidence in a way that supported a controversial conspiracy theory.

Dr. Charles Crenshaw is a true eyewitness to the historical event that
was the subject of my movie. Unlike many conspiracy theorists, he was
actually in a position to know critical facts when he participated on the
Parkland Hospital trauma teams that endeavored to save the lives of
President Kennedy and his accused assassin. When Dr. Crenshaw's book
was first published in April of 1992 (shortly after release of my movie
JFK, for which he served as a technical consultant), he made a significant contribution to the historical record pertaining to the JFK assassination.

It seems incredible that the awesome power of the media, including *Journal of the American Medical Association* (*JAMA*) and those that
reported on its New York City press conference in May 1992, could be
employed so irresponsibly in an attempt to damage Dr. Crenshaw in the
eyes and minds of millions of people—damage which can never be
totally undone. Most private individuals obviously do not have the power
or resources to adequately respond to attacks in the mass media. The
legal system only provides a partial remedy. Because of the freedom
provided to the media by the First Amendment to the United States
Constitution, no court can legally order publication of a correction or
apology; but consider the chilling effect on an individual's exercise of

free speech about a controversial subject that vilification in the mass media (or fear of same) can have. As philosopher Joseph Hall once said: "A reputation once broken may possibly be repaired, but the world will always keep their eyes on the spot where the crack was."

One wonders whether *JAMA* and its former editor and writer really believe that their handling of this matter served to dignify that allegedly prestigious, scientific medical journal. Do they really think that trying to destroy the reputation of a distinguished and honorable medical professional who merely offered his opinions on a controversial subject was appreciated by its readers? The potentially devastating power of a free press requires that it be responsibly exercised, a notion that *JAMA* apparently either failed to learn or merely decided to ignore and abandon in the case of the JFK assassination.

Why This Book Was Updated

The book I originally wrote with Jen Hansen and J. Gary Shaw, *JFK: Conspiracy of Silence,* was published in April, 1992 and was well-received across the nation by the American public. I had broken the "edict of silence" thrust upon us, those who tried to save President John F. Kennedy, and, two days later, his accused assassin, Lee Harvey Oswald. My observations contradicted the "official" version of the assassination, as reported in the Warren Report. I stated that President Kennedy was shot at least once, and I believe twice, from the front, and Oswald could not have been a "lone gunman." I had anticipated criticism from some, but I never expected the vicious attack from my medical colleagues.

In May 1992, the editor and a writer for the *Journal of the American Medical Association (JAMA)* called a press conference in New York to promote a *JAMA* article which attacked me both personally and professionally. They quoted some of my fellow physicians who had been in the Parkland Emergency room on that tragic day, with statements that varied significantly from the testimony that they had sworn to before the Warren Commission.

I repeatedly asked *JAMA* for a retraction and correction and received correspondence denying our request. My coauthor Gary Shaw and I were advised to sue *JAMA,* and on November 22, 1992, exactly 29 years since that fateful day in Dallas, we filed suit for "slander with malice." In October, 1994, we agreed to court-ordered mediation and accepted a monetary settlement offered by *JAMA*. The litigation details and exposure of *JAMA*'s unethical publication are included in this book in the section written by our attorney, D. Bradley Kizzia.

The House Select Committee on Assassinations (HSCA) concluded in 1979 that President Kennedy's death was the result of a probable conspiracy, but their records were sealed until the year 2029. The 1992 President John F. Kennedy Assassination Records Collection Act (JFK Act) was a unique solution to nearly thirty years of government secrecy, and the government was required to release whatever information it had concerning the assassination. The JFK Act created an independent board that would oversee the government's implementation of the Act, the Assassination Record Review Board (ARRB).

Many of the revelations from the ARRB have substantiated my allegations in the original book. According to Saundra Spencer, the autopsy photographs of President Kennedy that she developed at the Naval Photography Center in 1963 were different from those in the National Archives since 1966. The ARRB Report also suggests that Dr. Humes, one of three autopsy physicians, appears to have changed his Warren Commission testimony when his deposition was taken under oath by the ARRB. Additional testimony questioned the autopsy and brain photography that are now in the National Archive and Records Administration.

I have no idea who shot President Kennedy or why. What I do know is that somehow and for some reason, there was a medical cover-up. The "official" autopsy photos do not depict the same wounds I saw in Trauma Room One at Parkland. The wounds I saw were wounds of entrance, and thus they could have not come from the rifle of Lee Harvey Oswald.

Preface to the 1992 Edition

My name is Charles A. Crenshaw. I have been a surgeon for thirty years. Throughout my career I have watched thousands of gurneys slam through swinging doors of emergency rooms carrying the old and the young, the rich and the poor, the broken and the dying.

Without exception, every time I have ever walked into an emergency room, I have encountered a victim of some unexpected calamity, the course of his life abruptly, sometimes permanently, interrupted. Terror, fear, remorse, shock, anger, and disbelief are but a few of the emotions that characterize trauma patients and their families. Helping these people is my business.

Trauma is ignored by most people, especially the young and rich who have no concept of life-threatening measures when they are well, when life is going their way. As the greatest killer of America's youth, trauma viciously and ruthlessly takes lives by stealth. Every day, each of us is exposed to a myriad of conditions that can subject us to severe injury, whether it be from an automobile accident, a fall on the ice, an injury in a sporting event, or a knifing or shooting. Trauma is not respectful of age, race, sex, occupation, or status.

Over the years, the faces of the many victims I've treated have blended into an indistinct obscured visage of pain, fear, and death. After so many cases, all my trauma patients seem as one, except for two—John Fitzgerald Kennedy and Lee Harvey Oswald.

The assassination of President Kennedy, the wounding of Governor Connally, and the murder of Lee Harvey Oswald were, in medical terms, classic cases of devastating trauma, specifically, hemorrhagic shock caused by profuse bleeding. One moment, the President and Governor were riding in a motorcade through downtown Dallas on a beautiful, sunny day, waving happily to the crowd. Only minutes later, they were at Parkland Hospital, mortally wounded, fighting for their lives. It was sudden. It was unexpected. And it was life altering. As for Oswald, he believed that he was securely in the custody of the Dallas Police Department. Then, in a fraction of a second he felt a sharp pain in his abdomen, and the American people had witnessed their first-ever murder live on their television sets.

Enormous damage was done to these men by the bullets that ripped through their bodies. The occipital parietal portion of the right hemisphere of President Kennedy's brain was obliterated, almost every organ in Oswald's abdomen was ravaged, and Governor Connally almost died from the missile that traversed his chest, arm, and leg.

Trauma can attack psychologically as well as physically. When it does, its effects can be paralyzing and long lasting. Today, families of the assassination victims, the citizens of Dallas, the medical personnel at Parkland Hospital, and those of us who remember still feel the sting and the reverberations from the hail of gunfire that lasted for only a few seconds that Fall day in 1963.

Compared to other events and incidents in my life, treating the President of the United States, as he lay fatally wounded, and then operating on the man who allegedly shot him, is like matching a magnificent ocean against an insignificant pond. Never, in my wildest imagination, did I consider that as a resident surgeon at Parkland Hospital in Dallas, Texas, on that fateful November day in 1963, I would experience the most poignant moments of my entire life. Ironically, feverishly struggling to save the dim spark of life remaining in President Kennedy's dying body was only the beginning of a harrowing weekend that ultimately introduced me to a level of discretion we seldom discover, one that I have had to practice to protect my medical career, and possibly my life.

Southwestern Medical School, Parkland Hospital, and the United States government have never been overly subtle about their desire for us doctors to keep quiet and not divulge what we heard, saw, and felt that November weekend in 1963. From the time President Kennedy was wheeled into the emergency room, until the recent filming in Dallas of Oliver Stone's movie, *JFK*, the doctors who witnessed President Kennedy's death have always felt the necessity to continue what has evolved over the years as a conspiracy of silence. Just recently, a gag order was issued from Southwestern Medical School warning those doctors still on staff there not to confer with Oliver Stone about President Kennedy's condition when he was brought into Parkland. Despite the fact that President Kennedy was neurologically dead when he was taken from his limousine, both Parkland Hospital and Southwestern Medical School, partners in academic medicine, will always be defensive about losing the most important patient they had ever had.

Through the years, there have been a thousand instances when I have wanted to tell the world that the wounds to Kennedy's head and throat that I examined were caused by bullets that struck him from the front, not the back, as the public has been led to believe. Instinctively, I have reached for the telephone many times to call a television station to set the story straight when I heard someone confidently claim that Oswald was the lone gunman from the sixth floor of the Texas School Book Depository, only to restrain myself—until now.

The hundreds of similar cases involving gun shots that I have seen and treated since 1963 have further convinced me that my conclusions about President Kennedy's wounds were correct. I know trauma, especially to the head. To this day, I do not understand why the Warren Commission did not interview every doctor in President Kennedy's room. The men on that commission heard exactly what they wanted to hear, or what they were instructed to hear, and then reported what they wanted to report, or what they were instructed to report.

Had I been asked to testify, I would have told them that there is absolutely no doubt in my mind that the bullet that killed President Kennedy was shot from the front. I would have also informed the Warren Commission about the call I received from Lyndon Johnson while we were operating on Lee Harvey Oswald. President Johnson told me that a man in the operating room would get a death-bed confession from Oswald. The incident confounded logic. Why the President of the United States would get personally involved in the investigation of the assassination, or why he would take the inquest out of the hands of the Texas authorities was perplexing.

Not until two years ago did I seriously consider writing a book on this subject. While I was attending an open house at a friend's home in Fort Worth, I was visiting with my friend, Jens Hansen, a writer who was completing his first book. We had previously discussed the assassination of President Kennedy and the other events of that weekend, but this discussion was more intense. We were speculating as to the long-term effects of President Kennedy's death.

I told him that I believed the Warren Report to be a fable, a virtual insult to the intelligence of the American people. Having read almost every book that had been published on Kennedy's death, in addition to having had an intense personal experience with the case, I considered myself one of only a few men who could make that claim. He asked me if I had ever considered letting someone help me write a book on the subject. I explained to him that we doctors who had worked on President Kennedy, whether out of respect or out of fear, had agreed not to publish what we had seen, heard, and felt. It was as if we were above that, as if what we knew was sacred, as if to come forward with our account would in some way desecrate our profession. To a degree, I think we were afraid of criticism. And if one of us had started talking, the others would have gotten into the act, and sooner or later, the finger-pointing would have begun.

Jens looked at me and said, "I know you've heard this a million times, and I don't want to sound like I'm preaching, but the American people have a right to know exactly what went on in Trauma Room One, and exactly what you saw. Moreover, they have the right to know that their government was changed, that the course of history was dramatically altered in 1963, through a conspiracy to assassinate the President of the United States.

"You saw and experienced more that weekend at Parkland Hospital than most any other person. Every critical event and important moment involved you. If you go to your grave with this information, if you do not publish it, the people who did this thing to me and to you, and to every other American, will be that much more protected. As a witness to one of the United States' most significant events, you have a responsibility and a duty to record what you know.

"By doing so, there will have been at least one person who was there who will have helped to expose the greatest lie of our time. This is your chance to do something very meaningful with your life, something so important that it outweighs your thirty years as a physician. I promise you this," he said, smiling. "Eventually, one of your fellow doctors will break ranks and talk. It's inevitable, and it might as well be you."

"You may be correct," I replied. "I've heard that appeal about a million times, but not quite as convincingly as you just put it. I'll think about it."

For over a year, his words echoed in my mind. Since 1963, people had encouraged me to write about my knowledge of John F. Kennedy's death. But never before had I seriously considered doing so.

Night after night, in a dreaded rendezvous with the past, I graphically relived every moment of that weekend in 1963, in morbid detail. More often than not, I awakened in the dead of evening in a cold sweat, trying to drive away the horrible images that were becoming clearer and more disturbing as time went on.

I was having a recurring image. In slow motion memory, I walked by Jacqueline Kennedy, who was bloodstained and distraught, as I entered Trauma Room One. As I approached, Dr. Jim Carrico and Dr. Malcolm Perry were feverishly working on President Kennedy. Beginning at his feet, I remembered every hair, mole and wrinkle on the President's body. With each successive image, the bullet hole in his neck bubbling blood, and parts of the President's brain dangling from his skull increasingly took on more dimension and color. His struggle to breathe and the fading sounds of his failing heart tormented me.

Drops of his blood hitting the kick bucket beneath the gurney tolled the remaining seconds of President Kennedy's life, as the voices of Dr. Charles Baxter and Dr. Kemp Clark echoed those eternal words of doom. Looking into the somber faces of Dr. Malcolm Perry, Dr. Robert McClelland, and Dr. Ronald Jones as we all accepted the inevitable, then embracing Jacqueline Kennedy, who knew that her husband was dead, recomposed within me the emotional tenor of those terrible moments.

I relived the tactics of intimidation practiced by the Secret Service Agents. The "men in suits," as we referred to them, struck fear into Parkland's personnel as the Agents went about providing more protection and concern for a dead President than they had shown for a living President. I followed the heavily armed Agents as their entourage surrounding the casket escorted President Kennedy's body out of Parkland Hospital, their arrogance almost palpable, Jacqueline Kennedy walking alongside, her hand resting on the coffin.

As the months passed, I continued to read and study every available publication on the subject, increasingly becoming more and more outraged at the great lie that had been perpetrated. For the first time, I questioned whether I had actually entered into a contract with the other doctors to not write my story. I hadn't taken an oath or signed an agreement to that effect. All I had done was fail to openly object to the edict of secrecy proclaimed in Trauma Room One by Dr. Charles Baxter, professor of surgery and director of the emergency room, just after President Kennedy died. Silence cannot be taken to mean tacit approval.

Finally, on November 17, 1990, while sitting at my desk at Peter Smith Hospital, after reviewing the mounting evidence and my recurring memories one last time, I decided to tell my story. I realized that the compulsion to chronicle my account of that fateful weekend at Parkland Hospital in 1963 had begun to grow within me almost immediately after the assassination. I knew I had to speak out, if for no other reason, because the democratic process created by the greatest constitutional document ever written was being callously and maliciously circumvented by a handful of cowards. My silence has protected them. The choice of the American people was cast aside with one squeeze of a trigger. The work of men like James Madison, Alexander Hamilton, John Jay, Benjamin Franklin, and the sacrifice of the millions who have defended it, were rendered impotent by a few sorry criminals.

Efforts to suppress and distort the truth about the assassination on the part of government officials and agents, as well as certain representatives of the media, has been well documented in previous works on this subject. That this effort included threats, intimidation, falsification and destruction of evidence, and even death has played no small roll in my silence of the past twenty-eight years. I am fifty-nine years old. My medical career is over, and I no longer fear the "men in suits " nor the criticism of my peers.

Several days later, I invited Jens Hansen to my home to tell him of my decision. When he arrived at my home in Fort Worth in the early afternoon, he left the motor to his car running and came to my door. He asked me if I had time to make a trip to Dallas. Fifty-five minutes later we entered the JFK Assassination

Information Center on the third floor of the West End Marketplace, at 603 Munger, just three blocks from the Texas School Book Depository Building in downtown Dallas.

Meeting us there was a man named J. Gary Shaw, who I quickly discovered is one of the world's top authorities on the Kennedy assassination. He has invested twenty-seven years and a small fortune into research and the investigation of every aspect of Kennedy's death. Through it all, he has amassed a vast source of information, much of which he has produced through personal interviews.

After we had toured the Kennedy exhibit, we followed Mr. Shaw into a room that held the Information Center's archives. He reached into a file drawer and withdrew a manila envelope. From it he removed several 8 x 10 photographs, handed them to me, and asked "Does that look like the same body that you helped place in the casket at Parkland Hospital in 1963?"

I was amazed. They were pictures of President Kennedy's autopsy taken at the Bethesda Naval Hospital, Bethesda, Maryland. But the photographs showed a back of President Kennedy's head that was different from the wound I witnessed. They indicated a contrasting scenario, one that would support the theory of a lone gunman firing from the sixth floor of the Texas School Book Depository. One picture showed President Kennedy's neck at the point where the bullet had entered, the spot where Dr. Malcolm Perry had performed a tracheostomy at Parkland to help the President breathe. The opening was larger and jagged—significantly different from the way it had looked to me in Dallas. There was no doubt in my mind— someone had tampered with the body, or the photographs.

"Where did you get these? I asked while I examined them.

"I'd rather not say, Dr. Crenshaw," Shaw replied.

After studying the pictures several more moments, I said, "No, these aren't the same wounds I saw at Parkland. From these pictures it appears that someone changed the President's wounds when these photographs were taken."

"Doc," Hansen said, "Gary has the facts to corroborate your belief that there was more than one gunman, that President Kennedy was struck by at least three bullets, two of which entered the front of his body. If you're interested, he has agreed to provide us some critical information. For years, he's been waiting to work with one of the doctors in Trauma Room One. He believes that one of the missing links to proving the conspiracy is the medical side of the assassination. "

"It gets worse," Shaw said as he returned the photographs to the file drawer, then turned and faced me. "According to reports, you placed Kennedy in a bronze casket after he had been wrapped in white cloth. Witnesses have now come forward to state that when Kennedy's body was delivered to Bethesda, he was taken from a gray shipping casket, not swaddled in white cloth, but instead zipped in a body bag like the ones from Viet Nam."

"I'm aware of that," I said. "In addition, Commander J. J. Humes and his cronies made about twenty or so critical mistakes in their postmortem examination. None of them were forensic pathologists or experienced in examining bullet wounds. In my opinion, if Earl Rose, the pathologist at Parkland, had been allowed to perform the autopsy, and report the results to the Warren Commission, the outcome of that report would have been considerably different. And the photographs of President Kennedy would have reflected the true nature of his injuries. But of course, that is exactly why the "men in suits"' (members of the secret service detail) took President Kennedy's body out of Parkland at gun point. They had their orders—orders from a high official in our government who was afraid of the truth."

At that meeting, Hansen, Shaw, and I committed ourselves to writing a work that would impart to the reader both the emotions of those days and the facts as we could best relate them through my experiences. As the words quickly turned to page after page, years of fear turned to anger. I soon realized that this work had become a catharsis, releasing a lifetime of frustration. It soon became evident to us that my story is another piece to the mysterious puzzle, and that we should write this account in the context of the big picture.

As a result, we asked Gary Shaw to join us in this endeavor by providing historical facts based upon his years of research. By weaving threads of my personal and medical observations of those incredible events into the ever-growing fabric of historical truth, we hope that in some small way the veiled has become less obscured, the perplexing has become clearer, and the government's lone-gunman theory is exposed as a preposterous lie. Further, it is our wish that my story, presented in this format, contributes to the ongoing effort to expose the Warren Report as a feigned document.

The cover-up of the truth of that nightmare in Dallas has insulted all thinking Americans. By revealing details of the events that occurred, and the medical facts of the patients treated during those three days at Parkland Hospital in 1963, we hope to provide a new perspective on the assassination of President Kennedy, and the tremendous, yet frightening, efforts to cover it up.

From the beginning, writing this book has been a labor of love and an exercise in pride for all three of us. I was amazed at the vividness of the details of those days in 1963 that I had repressed all these interim years, and the emotions I had deeply buried. I cried from the sorrow. I laughed at the funny moments that had refused to surrender to the insanity of it all. And I cursed the men who had killed the President and the government that had covered it up.

Here is my account of those incredible three days at Parkland.

CHAPTER 1

The Beginnings

Many of us have dreamed that history's grand scheme will involve us in some far-reaching role or experience, thrusting us into notoriety and dramatically changing our lives. in 1963, such a fate took hold of me while I was a resident surgeon working out of a county hospital in a town struggling to become a city, and for four incredible days ruthlessly shook me. When it had let go, I had passed through the nucleus of the most mysterious murder in United States history, the assassination of President John F. Kennedy. From that moment on, neither Parkland Hospital nor I would ever again be the same.

While growing up in Paris, Texas, I aspired to be a doctor due to the strong influence of my father, Jack Crenshaw, and our family physician, John Arch Stevens. After completing high school, and with the commitment to study medicine burning deeply within me, I attended Southern Methodist University in Dallas, where I excelled in their pre-med program. After earning a Bachelor of Science degree, I entered Southwestern Medical School, a newly established institution that provided the doctors for its teaching partner, Parkland Hospital, also a relatively new facility. Never in my wildest imagination did I consider when I walked into that first class that I would one day be standing over the President of the United States lying in the Parkland Emergency room, with the right side and rear portion of his head blown off. Nor did I envision operating on his alleged assassin, Lee Harvey Oswald.

Although I could have attended any medical school in

Texas, I chose the University of Texas branch in Dallas, because, not only was Southwestern the closest medical school, it was the most affordable. Tuition was only one hundred-fifty dollars a semester, excluding books. There wasn't any ivy growing on the walls, but it was a damn good school, just the same. It was there that Dr. G. Tom Shires, professor and chairman of the Surgical Department at Parkland, who we referred to as "the little Caesar of surgery," inspired me to become a surgeon. Dr. Shires had told me that a surgeon is an internist who can cut.

When I finished medical school, I spent one year as an intern in internal medicine at the Dallas Veterans' Hospital. Then in 1961, I took one of the five residency positions at Parkland, which immediately distinguished me and my fellow residents as being among the "cream of the crop," firmly placing us on the coveted path to academic medicine. Through my association with the divine (Dr. Shires), I felt anointed—as all his staff believed themselves to be. Dr. Shires had a way of subtly conveying the message that if you were on his team, you were on the best squad in medicine.

I was a confident doctor, as we all were, even arrogant I suppose. Our lofty opinions of our abilities as surgeons were partly attributable to the way in which we had learned surgical procedures. The saying went, "See one, do one, teach one." There was a lot of competition among us, but we respected one another as physicians and surgeons and worked well as a team—esprit de corps. We believed we could provide the best medical care in the country.

But the hospital was nervous about the image of residents playing such a supreme role in its services, although it was true. As a result, certain med-school officials deliberately masked the major role that I and other resident surgeons played in the medical aspects of the Kennedy assassination, and the Warren Commission failed to obtain from us what would have been important testimony. I had experience with head wounds from high-powered rifles, and I definitely had an opinion about the trauma to Kennedy's skull that was in conflict with the doctors who performed the autopsy. I can't speak for my fellow physicians who were in Trauma Room One, but I wasn't about to rock the boat by broadcasting my thoughts on the President's death, which could have threatened my future in academic medicine, and as it now seems, possibly even my life.

Many people still hold to the misconception that President Kennedy was delivered to a group of ragtag, country doctors whose medical expertise was limited to suturing cuts and treating sore throats. We didn't appreciate doctors from the eastern medical establishment inferring that the President didn't get superlative health care. The truth was to the contrary, as evidenced by the impressive careers of the staff and resident surgeons who were at Parkland Hospital's emergency room that day in 1963.

Dr. G. Tom Shires, who until recently was chief of surgery and dean of Cornell University Medical School in New York, is now chief of surgery at Texas Tech Medical School in Lubbock, Texas. Dr. Malcolm O. Perry, who until recently was professor of surgery and chief of vascular services at Vanderbilt University Medical School in Nashville, Tennessee, is now professor and chief of vascular surgery at Texas Tech University Medical School in Lubbock, Texas. Dr. James "Red" Duke, the surgeon who operated on Governor Connally, is professor of surgery and director of emergency services at the University of Texas Medical School in Houston, Texas. Dr. Charles R. Baxter and Dr. Robert N. McClelland are professors of surgery at Southwestern Medical School. Dr. Charles J. ("Jim") Carrico is chairman of the department of surgery at Parkland Hospital and Southwestern Medical School. Dr. Ronald Jones is chief of general surgery at Baylor Medical Center. And I am now clinical professor of surgery at Southwestern Medical School and director and chairman of the department of surgery at John Peter Smith Hospital in Fort

Worth, Texas. If I had been wheeled into an emergency room, mortally wounded, I would have felt pretty confident knowing that a surgical team like this one was taking care of me.

I've often considered what would have happened if President Kennedy's motorcade had been traveling east when he was shot, because they would have gone to Baylor Hospital. Back then, Baylor wasn't a teaching facility, and its staff wasn't prepared for trauma. There would have been perhaps one resident surgeon there. Connally, who was closer to death than anyone actually realized, may very well have died. Today, Baylor is a fine trauma hospital with excellent surgeons.

During my first year of residency, I conducted research in a fellowship under Dr. Shires' supervision in which we made medical history by discovering that death from hemorrhagic shock (blood loss) can be due primarily to the body's adjunctive depletion of internal salt water into the cells. Research continued to be a paramount function at Parkland. Almost three decades later, Doctors Joseph L. Goldstein and Michael S. Brown at Southwestern Medical School would again make medical history by winning the Nobel Prize for their research into cholesterol metabolism. I consider Southwestern now among the top five medical schools in the country, and I believe Parkland Hospital to be one of the finest trauma facilities in the world.

In 1963, Parkland was a 550-bed hospital, located between Harry Hines Boulevard and Stemmons Expressway, five miles north of downtown Dallas. It served an area population of one million people. Out of the 300 residents and interns, there were 25 general surgical residents. Today, Parkland is a 760-bed hospital with 850 residents and interns.

Since its inception, Parkland has been a M.A.S.H. unit for Dallas County's war zone, primarily treating the indigent who have no health insurance and who lack the money to purchase health care from private hospitals. As such, many of the injured brought to Parkland's emergency room are drunk, belligerent, and sometimes violent. I knew when the moon was full by the number of victims that were brought in. On an average day 380 emergencies are treated. For years we doctors there referred to the trauma team as those who treated the "knife and gun club."

When John F. Kennedy came to Dallas, health care was very different from what it is today, especially in the treatment of trauma-related injuries. Ambulances were hearses equipped with a single tank of oxygen, and there were no emergency technicians. Blood from African Americans was not allowed to be transfused into whites, and vice versa. Other hospitals in Dallas didn't want to treat trauma cases because they were a money-losing proposition. A hospital's entire annual budget for such care could be, and many times was, spent on a few patients. And there were no such programs as Medicare or Medicaid. Mostly, we were treating the poor and underprivileged. Given the choice, a person of any means would never have chosen to go to Parkland because of its reputation— that is, unless he was in need of trauma care, in which case Parkland Hospital substantially improved his chances for survival. Otherwise, the selection would have been a private hospital.

The Dallas policemen were our best friends, because they protected us when we had to treat someone who was spitting, hitting, biting, or kicking. We could handle the abusive language, but not the physical attacks. Back in those days we got the violent patients under control very quickly and effectively. In some cases we used towel clips on their ears, and, of course, the scissor-like blades completely penetrated their flesh. Then we would attach the other end to the bed sheet. If they moved, it would pull their ears off. We did the same thing to their noses, but we weighted the clip with a one-pound ether can draped over an I.V. pole. It sounds cruel, but it was for the patient's protection, too. Sometimes there was no other way to keep someone still long enough to treat him. You can't suture a man's laceration if he's spitting in your eyes and jabbing his fist into your groin.

I shall never forget the man who pulled a pistol on me in Trauma Room No. 4, which was off the beaten path and where the worst behaved were taken. We had to run the gurney into his abdomen until he dropped the gun. It was the wild, wild west of the medical world.

Working at Parkland as a third-year resident, I was almost always exhausted, irritable, and often ill. I was so used to this condition that, at one point, it wasn't until my eyeballs turned yellow that I realized I had hepatitis. We called residency the "black hole" because the doctors in it were struggling to escape, and the young physicians desiring to become surgeons were working to get in.

In addition to working the emergency room every other night, we served on elective surgery teams A, B, and C, where we worked every third night. We always rotated every other day on trauma surgical teams 1 and 2. I worked thirty-six out of every forty-eight hours, seven days a week in an atmosphere of bedlam, all for a mere one hundred dollars a month, leaving little time for my wife and child.

To stay abreast of ongoing research, I, like my colleagues, would rise at four o'clock in the morning and peruse the medical journals. Then I'd rush off to the hospital to check on the progress of my own research projects before beginning my surgical day. Under those conditions, treating patient after patient in a web of blood, pain, and death, eventually became an academic exercise for me and my fellow surgeons. It was paradoxical. We were skilled surgeons fighting to preserve life, yet the conditions under which we saw it made us increasingly irreverent toward it.

I've always considered myself a conservative Democrat. I remember the political atmosphere on the eve of November 22, 1963. In 1960, Richard Nixon won Dallas County, something a

Republican presidential candidate hadn't done since Reconstruction. During the heat of that election, Bruce Alger, the first Republican congressman from Dallas since the Civil War, spat on Lyndon Johnson and his wife as they walked from the Baker Hotel to the Adolphus, while others screamed, "LBJ has sold out to the Yankee Socialists." In the ensuing melee it took thirty minutes for the Vice President to cross the street.

One month before President Kennedy came to Dallas in 1963, a housewife who was part of an extreme right-wing group hit United Nations Ambassador Adlai Stevenson in the head with an anti-U.N. sign. As he fled through the protesting mob to his limousine parked outside the auditorium, someone spat upon him. Even after he was in the automobile, the crowd rocked the car in an attempt to overturn it.

If John Kennedy came to Dallas today, the city would warmly embrace him as their President. But in those days, the influence of extreme political factions, like the John Birch Society, made it appear that Dallas hated President Kennedy, not so much the man himself, but the person it perceived him to be. It wasn't that Texans wanted him dead—they just didn't want him as their President. We knew our European history pretty well, and like the founding fathers, we didn't want a king. He came across as royalty with his money, his lifestyle, his family, and his charisma—oh, that charisma that literally flowed from him. As I remember, the only politician in Texas who liked him was Ralph Yarborough.

Robert and Jacqueline had warned the President not to travel to Dallas, but he came down here anyway to soothe the ruffled feathers of the state Democratic party. Lyndon Johnson, John Connally, and Ralph Yarborough were all at one another's throats over the growing movement to dump Johnson in 1964 as the Vice President. Conservative Democrats and Republicans alike were deeply suspicious of the rich, liberal, arrogant, and Catholic President.

Where were you on November 22, 1963? Almost three decades ago, early on the morning of that historic day, I was in surgery, beginning yet another round in the war of medicine against mayhem. But this tour of duty would be different. It would inexorably thrust me directly into the path of a spell-binding drama. It was an adventure of which most people can only dream. It was a life-changing experience. When I walked into Trauma Room One, I entered the halls of history.

CHAPTER 2

Friday, Nov. 22, 1963

Midnight
Hotel Texas—Fort Worth

President Kennedy and Jacqueline are at the Texas Hotel in Ft. Worth. They arrived from Houston late the previous evening, reaching the hotel at 11:50 p.m.

The President's Secret Service entourage has gone to the Press Club for drinks. Finding that Texas law prohibits the sale of liquor after midnight, they journey to an all night "beatnik" nightclub called The Cellar. This night spot, which has no liquor license, has a reputation for giving away drinks to lawyers, politicians, policemen—anyone the owner thought to be important or useful in a time of need.

The owner of the club, Pat Kirkwood, is a close acquaintance of Jack Ruby. Both men employ strippers Tami True and Little Lynn. Little Lynn will later become the recipient of Ruby's alibi-establishing Western Union money order, wired only minutes before the Oswald shooting. Kirkwood's father is a partner in a Fort Worth gambling establishment with a close associate of Ruby, Lewis McWillie. McWillie, according to FBI documents, was a murderer and was employed by Cuban mafia leader Santos Trafficante. Trafficante was a key figure in the CIA's plots to kill Cuban President Fidel Castro. Cellar owner Kirkwood is himself an interesting figure. A soldier of fortune and pilot of his own twin-engine plane, he will fly to Mexico a few hours after the assassination.

Ten agents of Kennedy's protection detail take advantage of the Cellar's free alcohol until approximately 3:30 a.m. Four of these agents will be in the follow up car behind the President at the time of the assassination. At the Cellar another three agents, assigned to guard the President's hotel suite, take their "coffee break" with their fellow agents leaving two Fort Worth firemen in their place. These agents are overheard laughing and joking about leaving the protection of the President and First Lady in the hands of two firemen. Later, as shots ring out in Dallas, only one of the President's detail makes any effort to protect the Chief Executive. Attempting to leave the follow up car and aid the wounded President, he is ordered back by the Special Agent in Charge.

Though Secret Service regulations governing a White House detail while in travel status prohibits the use of intoxicating liquor of any kind, and a violation or slight disregard is cause for removal from the service, none of the agents involved will receive any disciplinary action.

In significant contrast to this security breach on the part of the President's protective personnel, none of the Vice President's Secret Service detail are involved in the drinking at the Cellar. In fact, they are in their rooms resting for the next day. Immediately after the first shot, LBJ's personal agent shouts "Get down" and vaults over the backseat, forcing the Vice President down and out of the line of fire.

4:00 a.m.
Hotel Texas — Fort Worth

The President will soon rise to begin another busy day, continuing his Texas tour to ameliorate the bitter feuding among top state democrats. Scheduled events include a parade through downtown Dallas and a luncheon at the Trade Mart. There is still a degree of uncertainty as to whether Vice President Lyndon Johnson and Senator Ralph Yarborough, at odds over politics, will agree to ride in the same automobile.

Home — Dallas

When I opened my eyes, I still felt tired. I didn't need an alarm clock to awaken me every morning between 4:00 and 4:30, because I had become accustomed to doing it every day—every day that I slept, that is. Its amazing to me how I programmed myself to get up at that ungodly hour, day after day, although I was always exhausted. So much did it become a habit, that I still rise at that time every morning, some twenty-seven years later. Its like being on automatic pilot.

I knew President Kennedy was coming to Dallas, because I had read it in the *Dallas Morning News* the previous day. But I didn't think much about the President that morning. In my enclosed world at Parkland Hospital, I couldn't get out to see him. Parkland took the best of me and every other surgeon there, and threw back what was left of us to our families. Already, my marriage was showing signs of strain.

Politics, although interesting to me, was way down on my priority list. But my father and I knew Sam Rayburn, who was from Bonham, twenty-five miles from Paris, Texas. Through the newspaper I had kept up with the problems in the Democratic party at that time. Politically, Texas was a divided and hostile state. After witnessing what had transpired with other Democrats visiting Dallas, namely Lyndon Johnson and Adlai Stevenson, I feared that Kennedy's visit might also initiate an ugly incident.

After rubbing my eyes for several moments, I was able to focus on the bedroom window. The blinds were partially open, and I could see that it was still pitch black outside. I remember not getting to see the sun for days. Extended periods of arriving at the hospital before sunrise and leaving after it had set made it difficult to keep track of time. For a resident surgeon in a trauma hospital, working where there are no windows, there's no such thing as day and night—just periods of being on-duty and off-duty. It was going to be a very unusual day in that the surgical schedule was light—one cholecystectomy (gall bladder operation). Then I would take off in the middle of the afternoon, which was something even more unusual.

I struggled out of bed and staggered through the dark to the bathroom. My wife was still sleeping, as was my three-year-old son, Chad. I closed the door, turned on the light, threw some cold water on my face, squinted at the mirror through puffy eyes, and marveled at the thirty-year-old face that looked fifty that morning. "Oh, God! It's show time" I groaned.

In the Autumn of '63, I was off trauma and on elective surgery. As a resident, I headed surgical team B, which was on duty twenty-four hours every three days. When I was on trauma, which was six months at a time, I rotated every other day. Of course this was in addition to all my other duties, such as research and working with junior residents. During surgery, a staff surgeon, usually Dr. Shires or someone else on staff, assisted me. "Show time" simply meant that I was on stage every moment of every day, playing to the harshest critics imaginable. That's the way it was for a resident surgeon pursuing academic medicine. Unlike controlling a drunk in the emergency room, or practicing out of a private hospital, there was no privacy in the operating room of an academic hospital, especially for a resident surgeon in charge of a surgical team. The results of your work disseminated through the hospital's grapevine network so fast that there might as well have been a marquee posting it. If you screwed up, everybody in the place knew it before the patient was rolled into the recovery room.

At the root of this intense competition was the intense jealousy between the "town" and the "gown." Some doctors chose the town, which was private practice. But I preferred the gown, which to me meant being on the cutting edge of medicine. I'd rather command the "Pinta" than ride on the "Queen Mary."

I lived at 4714 Bradford Drive, apartment A, which was a two-bedroom, two-bath place in a low-income apartment complex across from a housing project, five minutes from the hospital. My rent was one hundred seventy five dollars per month.

Parkland paid me one hundred fifty dollars a month, and I received two hundred additional dollars each month from an NIH Research Fellowship. My parents supplemented my income to make up the difference so that I could feed my family.

In the apartment just across from our back door lived my brother-in-law, an orthopedic surgeon. Ronald Jones, my senior resident at Parkland, lived just down the street. Medical personnel were segregated from other renters across the street in the low-cost housing project.

Parkland Hospital—Dallas

I got to the hospital that morning, a little before five o'clock. I remember how foggy and miserable it was as I walked from my 1959 Mercury. It looked to be a bad-weather day. For the first time that morning, my thoughts focused on the President's visit, as I thought how lousy a day it would be for a parade. Once in the building I went to the changing room on the second floor, where we did all the surgery, and put on a scrub suit and a white coat. Then I moved across the hall to the doctors' lounge and had my first cup of coffee, which was brewing twenty-four hours a day next to the operating rooms.

I then stepped down that same hall, by the anesthesia room and the recovery area, through a set of double doors that led to the nurses' station in the surgical ward, which was 2-East. There, I pulled the charts on my patients to review their progress during the past few hours. I also examined the lab tests I had ordered the previous day. The interns and senior medical students assigned to surgery conducted the tests and were responsible for knowing the laboratory results. I wanted the data before they got to the hospital. Then I would thoroughly quiz them.

When it came to supervising interns, students, and junior residents, I was considered one of the meanest sons of bitches in the entire hospital, because I insisted that they know and understand the importance of what they were doing at all times. Also, I wanted to look good because of the competition among the resident doctors. We were reviewed each year, and our performance was a matter of pride and promotion. It was gamesmanship. Actually, I wasn't nearly as bad as they claimed I was until my last year of residency, at which time my nature almost became malignant. If making a critical mistake was made traumatic enough for the perpetrator, I reasoned, he would not only remember it, but he would learn from it. I know that's true because some of the most valuable lessons I learned during my career were etched into my memory with disturbing revelation. I shall always be indebted to my mentors who assiduously taught me surgery.

After writing orders and reviewing the lab results, I went down to the first floor and walked to the medical school, which is contiguous to the hospital. There I reviewed the progress on Doctors Shires' and Baxter's research projects. Then, before breakfast, I returned to the hospital and made rounds to look in on several critically-ill patients. At that point everything was going smoothly. With Dr. Shires, chairman of the surgery department, out of town, I felt relaxed and unpressured. I was looking forward to finishing the one surgical case and taking off that afternoon, which to me was tantamount to a Hawaiian vacation.

Having visited all my patients, I went to the dining room on the first floor, and was eating two hard-boiled eggs, toast, and coffee while reading the newspaper. The *Dallas Morning News* was full of information and stories about President Kennedy and the First Lady. In one of the articles there was a map showing the route of his motorcade through downtown Dallas. From Love Field he would be driven south down Harwood Street to Main, then west to Houston, back north to Elm, then out Elm to Stemmons Expressway, and back north to the Trade Mart for a scheduled luncheon.

With sickening clarity, I also recalled a handbill distributed by an extremist group that viciously attacked the integrity of President Kennedy by claiming he was a Communist. The President was posed in a frontal and side mug shot atop the message, "This man is wanted for treasonous activities against the United States." The article further claimed President Kennedy was "...turning the sovereignty of the U.S. over to the communist controlled United Nations." I didn't consider him a conservative Democrat, not in the southern style, anyway, but he was a long way from being a Communist.

When I returned to the second floor to prepare for surgery, I went into the doctors' lounge. Dr. Baxter, the staff surgeon who was to assist me that morning, was there smoking a cigarette and drinking coffee. Next, I walked down the hall to the anesthesiologist's call-room to speak to the doctor who would be working with us. The television was on, and I noticed that Dallas Police Chief, Jesse Curry, was on the air. I reached over, turned up the volume, and listened as he admonished the citizens of Dallas to behave themselves and to make the President feel welcome.

7:15 a.m.
Irving, Texas

Lee Harvey Oswald leaves for his recently acquired job at the Texas School Book Depository in downtown Dallas. He is given a ride by co-worker Buell Frazier. Oswald has in his possession a 24-27-inch long paper bag which he places in the back seat of Frazier's car, telling Frazier they are "curtain rods."

Oswald, born in 1939 in New Orleans, had lived in various cities including New York and Fort Worth. As a tenth-grade dropout, he had entered the Marines in 1956. He was trained in radar operations and stationed at a top secret base for U-2 spy plane operations in the Philippines. He was also schooled, and became proficient, in the Russian language. In September of 1959, he requested, and was granted, an early hardship discharge in order to take care of his ailing mother. He traveled to his mother's home in Fort Worth, where he remained three days before leaving for New Orleans. At New Orleans he boarded a ship and journeyed to Russia where met and married Marina Prusakova. While in Russia, Oswald attempted to renounce his American citizenship, defect, and turn over secret radar information to the Soviets. Soon thereafter, one of America's U-2 spy planes was shot down over Russia, an incident which effectively disrupted the planned summit conference between President Eisenhower and Premier Kruschev.

Oswald, upon returning to the United States with his Russian wife and new daughter in June of 1962, was never questioned by authorities about his attempted defection nor his passing of secret information to our cold-war enemy. That there were no charges of treason brought against Oswald is only one of the many strong indicators of his connection to some agency of this government.

7:55 a.m.
Texas School Book Depository — Dallas
Oswald and Frazier arrive for work. Oswald removes the package of "curtain rods" from the car and carries it with one end in his right hand, and the other end in his armpit. It is this package, authorities would later claim, that Oswald used to sneak the alleged murder weapon into the Depository.

8:06 a.m.
Hotel Texas — Fort Worth
President Kennedy and Larry O'Brien, his close friend and aide, look out the hotel window at the parking lot below, where the President will give a speech in a few minutes. Kennedy tells O'Brien, "If someone wanted to get you, it wouldn't be difficult, would it?"

In retrospect, there appears to have been good reason for this observation. The Protective Research Section, a preventive intelligence division of the Secret Service, had received information on over four hundred possible threats to the President during the period March through November 1963. Approximately twenty percent of these threats could be attributed to political motivation. In 1979, the House Select Committee on Assassinations reviewed computerized summaries of these threats and determined three of them to be significant.

The first was a post card warning that the President would be assassinated while riding in a motorcade. No other information was given by the committee except to simply say that the card resulted in additional protection being provided when the President went to Chicago in March. We do know, however, that a previous attempt on the President's life in Chicago was foiled on November 5, 1960. The then Senator Kennedy was the Democratic presidential nominee and was campaigning at a giant rally at Chicago Stadium. It was three days before the election. A twenty-three year-old Puerto Rican, Jaime Cruz Alejandro, was subdued and disarmed by six policemen as he shoved his way toward Kennedy's open convertible with a loaded pistol.

The second significant threat of 1963, as determined by the House Select Committee on Assassinations, again involved Chicago and possibly resulted in the cancellation of the President's planned visit to the city for a parade and to attend the Army–Air Force football game at Chicago Stadium. On October 30, 1963, the Secret Service learned that Chicago resident Thomas Arthur Vallee, an outspoken critic of Kennedy's foreign policy, was in possession of several weapons and had requested time off from his job on November 2nd, the date of the President's planned visit. Arrested by Chicago police, Vallee was found with an M-1 rifle, a hand gun, and three thousand rounds of ammunition in his automobile. He was released that evening.

More information about Vallee was discovered by the Secret Service prior to the President's trip to Dallas on November 22. The suspect, it was learned, was a Marine Corps veteran with a history of mental illness, a member of the John Birch Society, and a self-styled, expert marksman. None of this information was forwarded to the agents responsible for protecting the President during his trip to Texas. A Secret Service report, however, dated four days *after* the assassination noted the similarity between the background of Vallee and that of accused assassin Lee Harvey Oswald. Was Vallee the proposed fallguy in a Chicago plot as Oswald was in Dallas?

It now appears there was another plot in Chicago planned for the same day, one that was much more sinister and complex than the "lone-nut" scenario outlined above. Abraham Bolden, the first black to serve on the Secret Service's White House Detail, has shed some light on this probable assassination attempt. Bolden had been assigned to the Chicago office in 1963. He alleged that shortly before November 2nd, the FBI notified the Chicago Secret Service office that it had received a teletype message stating that an attempt would be made on the President's life by a four-man team using high-powered rifles. At least one member of the team, Bolden said, had a Spanish-sounding name. Agents assigned to the Chicago Secret Service office were questioned by the House Select Committee on Assassinations in the late 1970s and were unable to document Bolden's allegations. There is, however, no evidence of the committee having questioned the FBI about the existence of such a message.

After the assassination, an urgent report from the acting special-agent-in-charge of the Chicago Secret Service office detailed the receipt of reliable information about "a group in the Chicago area who may have a connection with the JFK assassination." A member of this group, a Cuban exile, Homer S. Echevarria, an outspoken critic of President Kennedy, reportedly stated that his group now had "plenty of money" and would soon be buying more military arms "as soon as we (or they) take care of Kennedy." The financial backers were reported to consist in part of "hoodlum elements" who were "not restricted to Chicago."

Further recognizing the need to investigate Echevarria and his group, the Secret Service discussed their information with the FBI. The FBI responded that Echevarria and his group, though affiliated with some of the more militant anti-Castro terrorists, were not likely to be involved in any illegal acts.

Reluctant to accept the FBI's representation in light of the evidence, the Secret Service prepared to continue its investigation. Their attempts were blocked when the new President, Lyndon Johnson, appointed the Warren Commission and ordered the FBI to assume primary investigative responsibility. The order came down, not only to the Secret Service, but also to the Dallas Police Department, that the FBI would take "full responsibility," not joint responsibility, for the post-assassination investigation of conspiracies. Secret Service agent Abraham Bolden's information was buried.

The last of the three significant threats occurred on November 9th when an informant for the Miami Police secretly recorded a conversation with a right-wing extremist named Joseph A. Milteer. Milteer outlined an existing plot to assassinate the President with a high-powered rifle from a tall building. The Secret Service was informed of this threat on November 12th. A scheduled motorcade for the President's visit to Miami on November 18th was canceled.

It is obvious from the transcription of the secretly recorded conversation that this plot to kill the President was ongoing and flexible. Milteer stated, "It's in the works...there ain't any countdown to it. We have just got to be sitting on go. Countdown, they can move in on you—and on go they can't. Countdown is all right for a slow prepared operation. But in an emergency operation, you have got to be sitting on go." Though this statement presented an existing and persistent plot—information which was in the hands of the Secret Service—no effort was made to relay this threat to the agent in charge of preparations for the trip to Texas. (Transcripts of this recording were given to the Warren Commission and are in the National Archives in Washington, D.C.)

In light of the quick arrest of Oswald, an obvious patsy, it appears Milteer's further statement that, 'They will pick up somebody...within hours afterward...just to throw the public off," was not guess work.

Five days after the Secret Service was informed of the Milteer threat, and only five days before the President's death, another FBI teletype was reportedly received in the New Orleans FBI office. FBI

Security Code Clerk William Walter received the message. It warned of a conspiracy "to assassinate President Kennedy on his proposed trip to Dallas, Texas, November 22-23, 1963," and that "a militant revolutionary group" were the plotters. Milteer was connected with several radical and militant right-wing organizations and traveled extensively throughout the United States in support of their views.

FBI Agent Walter's charge that the FBI received information of a Dallas plot was denied by Harry Maynard of the New Orleans office.

The failure of government agencies to heed prior warnings of assassination plots against the President's life is well documented. Their inaction, and almost total neglect of precautionary measures, is appalling—if not suspicious. These agencies, however, are not alone in this regard. It appears that Louisiana authorities must share some responsibility for the Dallas assassination. Two days prior to November 22, 1963, they received information that two men were on their way to Dallas to kill the President. Of all the prior warnings of plots on the President's life, perhaps none is more chilling than the one given by former Ruby employee Rose Cheramie.

On November 20, 1963, Cheramie was found bruised and disoriented, lying beside a road near Eunice, Louisiana. The state policeman who found her reported that, while driving her to the hospital, she described being abandoned by two men whom she perceived to be of Italian extraction. The men, she said, were on their way from Miami to Dallas to kill the President. The patrolman described her as lucid and her account as quite believable. Several employees of the hospital confirmed that Cheramie had stated before the assassination that the President was going to be murdered.

As bizarre as it may appear, Louisiana State Police did not report this revelation to the Secret Service or other officials until after the murder of Oswald. Only then was Dallas Police Captain Will Fritz notified of this information. Fritz replied that he was not interested, and Louisiana authorities dropped the matter.

Rose Cheramie was killed on September 4, 1965, one of more than fifty individuals associated with the investigation of the Kennedy assassination who died within three years of that event. Her death, like her allegations concerning two men planning to kill the President, is shrouded in mystery.

Again, she was found injured and lying beside a road, and was taken to a nearby hospital. Her death certificate read DOA (dead on arrival) in three places. Official hospital records, however, describe treatment of her injuries over a period of more than eight hours. Significantly, these records also describe a "deep punctate stellate" wound to her right forehead in addition to other injuries. The wound to Cheramie's forehead as described, according to medical text books, occurs in contact gunshot wounds—that is, when a gun barrel is placed against a victim's body and discharged. It is especially applicable to a gunshot wound of the skull in which the thin layer of skin overlying bone traps gases from the weapon and causes expansion between the skin and outer table of the skull, thus lifting up and ballooning the skin and producing tears of a stellate (starlike) or cruciform-appearing wound of entrance.

Unfortunately, the autopsy that would shed light on the cause of Cheramie's death cannot be found by the responsible authorities. Investigation of the alleged "accident" revealed no blood, flesh, or hair on the automobile involved. The driver charged with striking Cheramie swears that he did not hit her. He has also stated that upon stopping to render aid and to transport the victim to medical facilities, he saw a late model red Chevrolet parked nearby. Cheramie's sister confirms the red Chevy story. She was told by investigating authorities that they too had seen the automobile at the scene shortly before the accident as they made their usual patrol of the area.

Was the death of Rose Cheramie an accident or was it murder? We may never know. In either event, Louisiana authorities failed in their duty to report her warning to those charged with protecting the life of the President.

President Kennedy's philosophical approach to the prevention of his own assassination proved an accurate observation. He had scoffed at many of the measures designed to protect him, and his frequent travel and contact with crowds posed a major problem for the Secret Service.

His policies were liberal and sometimes innovative. None of these traits, however, caused his death. That burden of guilt rests squarely on the shoulders of the agencies and officials sworn to law and order and charged with the responsibility of protecting the nation's leader.

Perhaps the Secret Service's negligence is best summarized in the House Select Committee on Assassination's report which states, "President Kennedy did not receive adequate protection," and that the agency "was deficient in the performance of its duties," and "possessed information that was not properly analyzed, investigated or used…in connection with the President's trip to Dallas."

Parkland Hospital—Dallas

I was in the ready room reassuring a very groggy patient that the surgery would go well, and that he would be fine because he had the best surgeons in the country taking care of him. Of course, I wasn't kidding. The self-assurance of a surgeon is mandatory when literally holding a life in his hands—when critical decisions and quick, skilled action are essential. The saying went, "Every surgeon who's worth his salt is stuck for an answer to the question 'who are the three best surgeons in the country?'" The dilemma was coming up with names for the other two.

That morning Dr. Tom Shires was in Galveston, Texas, attending a meeting of the Western Surgical Association. Standing in his place to assist me with the operation was Dr. Charles R. Baxter, a legend in his own time. Dr. Baxter was four years my senior, and had, along with Dr. Shires, greatly influenced my decision to become a surgeon. We were both from Paris, Texas. He had played the role of a big brother to me while we were growing up.

While the junior resident and intern who were to assist me were completing their pre-op duties, Dr. Baxter and I were at the scrub sink in the hall just outside the operating room sterilizing our hands while we discussed the research we were conducting at the medical school on regional abdominal hypothermia.

Through ongoing research at Parkland Hospital aimed at reducing the number of deaths from shock due to trauma, we discovered that when chilled Ringer's Lactate Sluice (salt water) is poured into the exposed abdomen, significant physiological changes rapidly occurred improving the patient's chances for survival. When four or five liters of Ringer's Lactate enter the abdomen, it serves two important functions. First, the core temperature of the kidneys is abruptly reduced; preventing the death of the organs caused by oxygen starvation from reduced blood supply. This avoided acute renal failure, which usually carried a 90 to 100 percent casualty rate. Second, the Ringer's Lactate is quickly absorbed through the peritoneum, then passed into the liver where it emerges as plasma look-alike. This was added protection for the patient in hemorrhagic shock when there is substantial blood loss.

As the body goes into hemorrhagic shock, which occurs from an inadequate volume of circulating blood, the vessels constrict and a vacancy we called the third space develops. In such a condition, the body's sodium is lost into the cells. Sodium is necessary to maintain blood pressure and to expand cells for delivery of oxygen to the kidneys and other organs. Under trauma condition, with significant blood loss, Ringer's Lactate supplements this process to minimize the possibility of kidney destruction which brings on the renal shock. In 1963, there were only two kidney dialysis machines in the city of Dallas, and so, this medical breakthrough was especially invaluable.

Thanks to the research on Ringer's Lactate at Parkland Hospital and Southwestern Medical School, damage to the kidneys during trauma can still be prevented and lives are saved. This same medical technology was implemented all over the world as standard procedure when treating trauma patients. For this important breakthrough, Drs. Tom Shires and Charles

Baxter should have received the first Nobel Prizes at Parkland.

After Dr. Baxter and I had finished scrubbing, we entered the operating room where he loudly sang the Sugar Bear Cereal song he had heard while watching television with his sons. The nurses immediately broke into laughter, and whatever tension may have existed in that room instantly evaporated. Its easy to see why Dr. Baxter was the most loved man at Parkland.

We were wearing shoes with copper brads and the nurses didn't wear nylon undergarments, precautions taken so that a charge from static electricity or a spark from the floor would not blow up the operating room. We were still using cyclopropane, an explosive type of anesthesia.

As the scrub nurse helped Dr. Baxter into his surgical gloves, he asked her if she had gotten "any" the previous evening, referring to sex, of course. Again, all present broke up in laughter. At that point, a first-year surgical resident joined us in the operating room to assist in the surgery. The resident had the worst job of all that day, which was to hold the liver back with a toweled retractor while I performed the operation. Believe me, holding that liver for two hours is pure hell.

"Surgical 'B' now in session," I announced as Pat Schrader, the scrub nurse, handed me a scalpel.

When I made the incision on the patient's right side, just below the ribs, Dr. Baxter remarked that all bleeding ceases in the end, which was a sarcastic implication that the patient might bleed to death in the time it took me to clamp the blood vessels. I never saw anyone do it fast enough to escape Dr. Baxter's vicious tongue. I had cut through the layers of the muscle and was ready to enter the lining of the abdomen. After verifying that the bowel was not going to be punctured, as can occur when it rests just below this lining, I made a slice with scissors, exposing the abdominal cavity.

9:00 a.m.
Hotel Texas—Fort Worth

President Kennedy returns to the Hotel Texas for the Chamber of Commerce breakfast. As he crosses the street the President chats with Tarrant County Sheriff, Lon Evans. Several minutes later Jacqueline arrives with Secret Service Agents as the audience cheers. She is wearing a pink suit with navy lapels and a matching pink pillbox hat. The President looks irritated because her entry receives so much attention.

Meanwhile former Vice President, Richard Nixon, is at Dallas' Love Field awaiting his flight out of Dallas. He has been in the city ostensibly to attend a board meeting of the Pepsi Cola Bottling Company, which his firm represents. He was later to recall that his time in Dallas was November 20–21, 1963, and that he was not there on the day of the President's assassination. He, along with convicted Watergate burglar and CIA agent E. Howard Hunt, are the only two men encountered in subsequent years who do not remember where they were at the time of the assassination.

9:30 a.m.
Dallas

Night club owner, Jack Ruby, arises for the day and proceeds to downtown Dallas. Ruby, born Jacob Rubenstein in Chicago in 1911, had been a runner for mobster Al Capone in the late 1920s. Ruby's mob related activities continued when he moved to Dallas in 1947. As an antecedent to his move to Dallas, the Chicago mob attempted to bribe the Dallas sheriff and to take over gambling, prostitution, and other vices in Dallas. Ruby was to run these criminal activities and serve as liaison to Chicago's underworld. In 1952, Ruby and two other associates purchased the Bob Wills Ranch House and renamed it the Vegas Club. In 1959, Ruby and another associate purchased a private club in the heart of downtown Dallas. A year later the club was renamed the Carousel Club and began to feature striptease shows. During this same period Ruby also became an informant for the FBI, a fact kept well hidden from the American public for approximately ten years. The Warren Commission denied Ruby's strong organized crime ties despite overwhelming evidence. A later investigation by a Congressional committee confirmed these ties.

Julius Hardie, an employee of a Dallas electrical equipment company, is proceeding east on Commerce Street nearing Dealey Plaza's triple underpass. As was his custom when in that area, he attempted to get a glimpse of his father-in-law who often worked in the nearby railroad yard. He noticed three men on top of the underpass, two of which were carrying "long guns." Hardie called the authorities after the assassination and was visited by two FBI agents. He related his story to the two agents but never heard from them again. The FBI has no report of this incident in its files.

10:14 a.m.
Hotel Texas—Fort Worth

President Kennedy and Jackie return to their hotel suite, where the President calls former Vice President John Nance Garner, wishing him a happy 95th birthday. Moments later, Kennedy is shown the full page advertisement in the *Dallas Morning News*, which is extremely critical of his administration and attacks him personally.

Parkland Hospital—Dallas

"Keep the goddamn liver out of the way," I barked at the junior resident, his hand already tired from having to continuously apply pressure to the inside of the abdomen. The operation was progressing smoothly, and the patient was stable. As I continued through the procedure, I asked Dr. Baxter, "Are you going to take off early, go downtown, and watch Kennedy's parade?"

Dr. Baxter shook his head and replied that the only way he would see "that son of a bitch" would be if he came to the back door of the hospital. The back of Parkland was the emergency entrance, and Dr. Baxter was the staff surgeon in charge of the emergency room. His reference to the President of the United States wasn't as disrespectful as it might seem, considering Baxter called everyone a son of a bitch. It was the personal pronoun he used for man and objects alike.

Dr. Baxter continued by asking if I thought Jacqueline was as sensuous as she was (and still is) beautiful. My reply was in the Baxter tradition. "If she is, the President is the luckiest son of a bitch in this world."

10:30 a.m.
Dallas

At the office of the Dallas County Sheriffs Department, at the corner of Main and Houston overlooking Dealey Plaza, long time sheriff Bill Decker meets with his deputies. He instructs them to remain outside the building, but stresses that they are to take absolutely no part in the security of the motorcade. Reportedly, these unusual orders had been delivered to Decker via a phone call from a still unknown source in the nation's Capitol.

10:40 a.m.
Hotel Texas—Fort Worth

President Kennedy's motorcade leaves the Texas Hotel for Carswell Air Force Base in Ft. Worth for the short 13 minute flight to Dallas.

10:50 a.m.
Dealey Plaza—Dallas

Twenty-three year old Julia Ann Mercer, driving west on Elm Street enters Dealey Plaza, a small park-like area just west of the downtown section of Dallas. She passes the Texas School Book Depository Building while heading toward the triple underpass. In front of her, congesting traffic, is an illegally parked pickup truck in the right lane. The vehicle is stopped with its right wheels on the sidewalk and its left side blocking her lane. While Mercer is behind the truck waiting to pass, she observes a white male wearing a plaid shirt stepping out of the passenger's side and walking around to the truck's side mounted toolboxes. There he removes what appears to be a rifle wrapped in paper and proceeds afoot up the grassy embankment toward a wooden fence. Finally able to pull her car around the truck, she looks into the face and locks eyes with its driver.

Later that same day, after the assassination, Mercer gave an affidavit at the Dallas sheriff's office where she was interrogated for several hours by uniformed officers, as well as plain clothes personnel whom she believed to be federal investigators.

Early the following morning, FBI agents came to her apartment requesting that she accompany them back to the sheriff's office. There she was shown approximately a dozen photographs. They requested that she pick out any she recognized as being the men she had seen in the pickup truck. She selected two photographs from the group, but was given no information as to their identity.

On Sunday, the day following her identification, she viewed television coverage of the Oswald shooting. She immediately identified Ruby as the driver of the truck and Oswald as the man with the rifle; the same men she had previously selected from the FBI photographs.

When the subject of Mrs. Mercer's information came up before the Warren Commission, Secret Service Agent Forrest Sorrells testified he decided not to investigate her claim because "...this lady said she thought she saw somebody that looked like he had a gun case. But then I didn't pursue that any further because then I had gotten the information that the rifle had been found in the building and shells and so forth."

Parkland Hospital—Dallas

After we had finished suturing the incision and dressing the abdomen, the patient was transported to the recovery room. I smoked a cigarette and drank coffee in the lounge with Dr. Baxter. I then walked down the hall to the recovery room to make sure my patient was stable and to write post-op orders.

11:03 a.m.
Honolulu

Across the Pacific Ocean, six members of the President's cabinet leave Honolulu for Japan. The prior day, other members of the President's cabinet had been meeting in Honolulu for a nine-hour conference on Vietnam. This group of high level political and military policy makers had decided to step up military operations against communist insurgents in this Southeast Asia country. This was in direct conflict with the Presidential decision to reduce U.S. troop strength in the area.

It is highly unusual, if not unheard of, for so many members of the Presidential cabinet to be away from the nation's capitol at a given time.

Parkland Hospital—Dallas

The operation had been completed, and the patient was stable. I was in a good mood because in just a few hours I would be going home. We were closing the abdomen by carefully suturing the muscles in a layered manner as we worked our way to the surface of the belly. With the critical part of the operation completed, Dr. Baxter was ready to get out of there and smoke a cigarette.

During the two hours we had been in surgery, in excess of twenty patients had been treated in the emergency room.

11:40 a. m
Love Field—Dallas

Dallas Police Chief Jesse Curry meets President Kennedy at Love Field. The President is impressed with the turnout and exclaims, "This doesn't look like an anti-Kennedy crowd."

Five minutes later the limousine leaves Love Field for downtown Dallas. Secret Service Agent William Greer is driving the automobile.

Governor John Connally and his wife, Nellie, are in the jump seat. The President and Jacqueline sit together in the rear. Close behind the Presidential limousine is the Secret Service follow-up car carrying ten Secret Service Agents. Vice President Lyndon Johnson and Senator Ralph Yarborough are riding together in a convertible to the rear of the Secret Service.

Parkland Hospital—Dallas

After finishing in the recovery room, I stepped back down the hall to get a cup of coffee in the lounge and to thank Dr. Baxter for assisting me with the operation.

12 noon
Dallas Morning News Building—Dallas

Reporter Hugh Aynesworth sees Jack Ruby at the *Dallas Morning News* building. Ruby later uses the statements of Aynesworth and other employees of the newspaper as confirmation as to his whereabouts during the assassination. However, three days after the assassination, Aynesworth told the FBI that "Ruby was seen there…but was missed for a period of about twenty to twenty-five minutes," and that "he had no information as to where Ruby had gone during this interval of time, nor did other employees. Shortly after Ruby had been missed, people began to come to the office of the newspaper announcing the assassination of President John F. Kennedy, and Ruby appeared shortly thereafter and feigned surprise at this announcement and gave some show of emotion over the news that had been received." Aynesworth also advised that "in view of the fact that the *Dallas Morning News* building is removed only about four blocks from the point where the Presidential motorcade passed, he could not understand why if Ruby had a love and devotion to the President as he claims he has, he had not walked this short distance for the purpose of seeing the President pass by."

Dealey Plaza—Dallas

While the motorcade proceeds along its journey to the Trade Mart, suspicious activities continue to occur in Dealey Plaza. Railroad supervisor Lee Bowers, Jr., from his position in a railroad tower behind Dealey Plaza's wooden fence, observes three strange out-of-state cars cruise slowly in and out of his area. Each automobile is driven by a white male, one of whom appears to be talking over a handheld microphone.

Ed Hoffman, off work for a dental appointment, realizes he is near the parade route and stops his car on Stemmons Freeway west of the Depository, in hopes of seeing the President. From this vantage point he is able to view the area behind the wooden fence. There, he notices two men standing a few feet apart and looking over the fence.

Carolyn Walther, on her lunch break from a nearby dress factory, is standing at a position catty-cornered to the Texas School Book Depository in front of the Dallas County Records Building. She sees two men, one holding a rifle, in the southwesternmost window of the Depository's sixth floor. High-schooler Arnold Rowland, a few feet south of Walther, also notices the rifleman in that position. Meanwhile, unemployed steelworker Richard Carr is job hunting on the seventh floor of the new courthouse building being constructed at the corner of Houston and Commerce. He, too, notices two men on the sixth floor.

12:15 p.m.
Dealey Plaza—Dallas

It is approximately fifteen minutes prior to the arrival of the motorcade into Dealey Plaza as Jerry Belknap, dressed in army fatigues and standing on the west side of Houston Street, suddenly faints. An ambulance is dispatched to take the-twenty-three-year-old part-time newspaper employee to the hospital. Ten minutes later (and five minutes before the shooting), C. L. Bronson sees the arrival of the ambulance to pick up Belknap. From his position, at the corner of Main and Houston, he records this commotion with a home movie camera. In doing so, he also captures what appears to be the movement of two and possibly three people in the easternmost sixth-floor depository windows. Belknap is taken to Parkland Hospital, but disappears before treatment. His background is never checked, and Bronson's film is never analyzed.

Parkland Hospital—Dallas

After hearing another one of Dr. Baxter's over-ripe jokes, I finished my coffee and walked past the double doors into the surgical ward. I pulled some charts, entered the doctors' room next to the nurses' station, sat down at the desk, and began writing orders. I remember how upbeat I was as I wrote out those instructions, knowing all the while that I had the afternoon and evening free.

12:25 p.m.
Texas School Book Depository

Depository employee Carolyn Arnold sees Oswald on the first floor near the front door of the building.

12:29 p.m.
Motorcade—Dallas

Geneva Hine, the only employee in the Depository's second-floor offices, observes the electrical power and telephone system go dead.

The Dallas Police radio systems Channel One, reserved for officers participating in the security of the President, is suddenly immobilized.

President Kennedy's limousine passes the Dallas County Courthouse as the motorcade continues north on Houston Street. All along the street and from the windows of the buildings people cheer and wave to the President. The Texas School Book Depository is just ahead. Nellie Connally turns and remarks to the President, "Mr. Kennedy, you can't say that Dallas doesn't love you."

Of course, not all the citizens of Dallas loved the President, as could be said of any city. But Dallas has received undue condemnation for its perceived role in President Kennedy's death. While Dallas had its radical element, the city itself was incidental in the assassination. The executioners of John Kennedy were determined to eliminate him whether it be in Chicago, Miami, Dallas, or any other location. They were "sitting on go."

12:30 p.m.
Motorcade—Dallas

President Kennedy's limousine turns west onto Elm Street, passing the Texas School Book Depository on the right, and slowly proceeds down the grade leading to Stemmons Expressway. Seconds later, shots ring out. The President clutches his throat. Governor Connally flashes a look of anguish. To the horror of the people standing there, the President's head appears to explode as a bullet rips through his skull. People are running, screaming, and covering their children and loved ones to protect them from the hail of bullets. Jacqueline climbs out onto the back of the limousine to retrieve a piece of her husband's head. Secret Service Agent Clint Hill, who is following closely behind, jumps onto the trunk of the car and pushes her back into her seat as they speed away toward Parkland Hospital.

Pipe-fitter Howard Brennan and fifteen-year-old Amos Euins, from their positions on the south side of Elm Street, see a man fire from the sixth floor, easternmost window of the Depository directly in front of them. S. M. Holland, railroad track and signal supervisor, along with several fellow employees is standing on the triple underpass overlooking Elm Street. Each sees a puff of smoke from the area of the wooden fence, as does Lee Bowers in the nearby railroad tower. Cheryl McKinnon, a college journalism major planning to write about the president's visit, is standing on the north side of Elm Street, and schoolteacher Jean Hill, positioned opposite her across Elm, each witnessed the smoke from the area of the fence. Ed Hoffman, from his vantage point on Stemmons Freeway, watches a man fire a rifle over the fence toward the approaching motorcade.

Dress manufacturer Abraham Zapruder, from his position atop a low concrete pedestal located on the north side of Elm Street near the wooden fence, records the President's assassination with his home movie camera. He hears shots coming from in back of him. He watches in horror as the President's skull explodes in a shower of blood and brain matter and sees him slammed violently backward and to the left. (Zapruder's filming of this fatal moment was strategic. He recorded for history the President's reaction to the volley of shots which struck him in these few short seconds. Significantly, it shows the President's head and upper body being thrown backward toward the rear of the limousine at a speed estimated at 80 to 100 feet per second. This violent movement is consistent with a shot from the wooden fence to his right front—*not* the Book Depository—to his right rear.)

Nightclub singer Beverly Oliver is standing on the south side of Elm Street across from the wooden fence and films the entire assassination with her 8mm camera. She too observes the puff of smoke from the fence. Unfortunately, this valuable film evidence was confiscated by men identifying themselves as government agents. The film has never surfaced. A film taken from her position would have provided the most comprehensive coverage of the entire assassination, scanning the Texas School Book Depository and the wooden fence, at the precise time of the shots.

In all, 277 of the more than 700 witnesses to the shooting have been identified. 107 of these 277 have given their statements as to the origin of the shots which killed the President. Seventy-five percent, or 77 of the 107, reported that at least one shot came from the President's right front—the area of the wooden fence. Though the Warren Commission stated emphatically that all of the shots were fired from the Depository building, to the President's right rear, the majority of witnesses refute this conclusion.

Building engineer J. C. Price is on the roof of the Terminal Annex Building on the south side of Dealey Plaza. He sees a man run from the area behind the wooden fence. Price stated that the man had something in his right hand and "was running very fast, which gave me the suspicion that he was doing the shooting."

Richard Carr, still on the seventh floor of the new courthouse in the aftermath of the shooting, watches as two men run from behind the Texas School Book Depository. The men enter a waiting station wagon and speed off north on Houston Street. Twenty-year-old James Worrell, Jr., witnesses the assassination from the comer of Elm and Houston and panics as the shooting begins. He quickly races northward, up Houston Street and sees a man exit from the back door of the Depository and walk quickly south on Houston.

Meanwhile, teacher Jean Hill, who has just seen the President's head explode a few feet in front of her, notices a man running from the area of the wooden fence. (In her 1964 Warren Commission testimony she would state that the fleeing man looked like Jack Ruby.) She quickly crosses the street in pursuit, but is stopped by a man identifying himself as a Secret Service Agent and is told that she can go no farther. Hill is one of several witnesses encountering men producing Secret Service identification in that area.

Several feet west of Jean Hill, mail-service owner Malcolm Summers drops to the ground as the shots ring out. Then, crossing Elm Street to the area of the wooden fence, he is stopped by a man in a suit with an overcoat over his arm. The man reveals a small automatic weapon under the overcoat and tells Summers, "Don't you'all come up here further. You could get shot."

Dallas Policeman Joe Smith is directing traffic at the intersection of Elm and Houston at the time of the shooting. Believing that the shots came from the area of the wooden fence or overpass, he races past the depository. He, too, comes face to face with a man who identifies himself as Secret Service. Moments later, Police Sargent D. V. Harkness, while assisting in sealing off the area, observes several "well-armed" men dressed in suits who tell him they are with the Secret Service.

Though it is quite logical that Secret Service Agents would be present in the area of a Presidential appearance, the record firmly establishes that none of the twenty-eight agents present in Dallas that day were ever on foot in Dealey Plaza before, during, or immediately following the shots. All of the agents in the motorcade continued to Parkland Hospital and only one returned to the area later in the afternoon.

Parkland Hospital—Dallas

As I ordered additional lab tests for a patient with post-op complications, a nurse passing by stopped and spoke to me. I returned her greeting, and she disappeared around the door as she continued on her mission.

12:31 a. m.
Dealey Plaza—Dallas

Still on Stemmons Freeway, Ed Hoffman continues to watch as the rifleman behind the wooden fence runs westward, passing the weapon to another man, then turns, walks calmly in the opposite direction, and disappears. The man taking the weapon quickly breaks it down, places it in a case, and proceeds slowly northward along the railroad tracks. He, too, disappears.

Sergeant Tom Tilson, an off-duty Dallas policemen, and his daughter are in his car just west of the triple underpass. It is a few minutes after the shooting. They watch as a man in dark clothing comes down the railroad embankment to a black automobile. He throws something into the back seat, hurries around to the front, gets into the car, and speeds off westward. Thinking this suspicious, they pursue the vehicle but lose it in the traffic. The man, Tilson later says, looked and dressed like Jack Ruby.

12:32 p.m.
Texas School Book Depository

Building superintendent Roy Truly and policeman M.L. Baker race into the Depository immediately following the shots. They encounter Oswald in the second floor lunchroom drinking a Coke. It has been approximately 90 seconds since the last shot was fired. Oswald appears calm and unafraid. Later the Warren Commission is to conclude, rather illogically, that this is the man, who, after just having killed one of the world's most powerful men, now hides the weapon, races down four flights of stairs, pops a soft drink, then casually greets a police officer— not even out of breath—all in 90 seconds.

12:33 p.m.
Washington, D.C.

A breakdown in the telephone system in the nation's capital occurs. It will not be restored for almost an hour.

A short time later, aboard the military aircraft carrying six members of the President's cabinet to Japan, a teletype message reports that shots have been fired at the President. With specific procedures for such an emergency, officials attempted to reach the White House Situation Room. They were prevented from doing so because the official code book was missing from its special place aboard the plane.

12:37 p.m.
Parkland Hospital—Dallas

The telephone rings at Parkland's emergency room nurses' station. The Dallas Police Department advise Doris Nelson, head nurse in emergency, that President Kennedy has been shot and is en route to the hospital. Nelson immediately orders personnel to prepare Trauma Room One for the President's arrival.

12:38 p. m.
Parkland Hospital—Dallas

I had just completed writing instructions on the first chart when I heard the unbelievable over the public address system. "Paging Dr. Tom Shires. Paging Dr. Tom Shires," the voice urgently uttered. I couldn't have been more shocked. I simply couldn't believe I had heard it.

Two things never happened at Parkland—face-lift surgery and the chief of surgery being paged over the intercom. If someone needed Dr. Shires, a messenger was sent. Hearing Dr. Shires' name echoing from the ceiling speaker scared me. I was concerned that one of the patients Dr. Shires had entrusted to me in his absence was experiencing upper gastrointestinal hemorrhaging. I immediately picked up the telephone and dialed "0" to answer the page.

"Mert, this Dr. Crenshaw. Dr. Shires is out of town. What do you need?"

"'Dr. Crenshaw, the President has been shot"

After a moment of intense silence, I replied, "If you're kidding me, I'll kill you."

"This is no joke, Dr. Crenshaw.'"

Mert was a buxom woman in her fifties who liked to play practical jokes. But the panic in her voice told me she was serious.

A bone-chilling sensation rushed through my body as I thought of going down to emergency and treating the President of the United States. At that instant any lingering question of why I had become a surgeon was definitively answered once and for all.

I slammed down the phone, jumped from my chair, and bolted through the double doors into the surgical area toward the stairwell leading to the emergency room two floors below us. Dr. Robert McClelland was standing in the hall, perusing a lighted x-ray box located directly down the hall from the doctor's lounge. When he looked up and saw me approaching in a full gallop, a perplexed expression covered his face.

"Bob!" I exclaimed as I came charging up to where he was standing. "The President's been shot, you've got to come with me."

When Bob heard those words, his expression changed to

one of astonishment. Without breaking stride, I grabbed him around the waist and propelled him along until he was running with me. We sprinted past the operating rooms, through the anesthesia conference room, and through the doors into the stairwell. Dr. Ken Salyer, a first-year resident in neurosurgery, who had sensed the urgency of the moment by our unusual behavior, followed us down to the emergency room. He later told me that was the only time in his life that he had seen either Dr. McClelland or me run anywhere.

Two Secret Service agents burst through the swinging doors into the emergency room and asked for gurneys for the President and Governor Connally. Dr. Bill Midgett, a second year ob-gyn resident, who had delivered Marina Oswald's baby on October 20, 1963, only about a month earlier and two days before Lee Harvey Oswald's birthday, was the very first doctor to encounter the President outside the emergency room. Several moments later, Dr. Midgett and several nurses rolled the President into Trauma Room One with Jacqueline at his side. The President was logged into the register as patient No. 24740 at 12:38 p.m. Governor Connally was logged in as patient No. 24743, an indication that other patients were being admitted and treated in the emergency room during the time when the President was being wheeled in.

As I leaped down the stairs, Dr. McClelland at my side, I had a terrible fear that I would be the only resident doctor in the room. I didn't know it, but Bob had a similar thought, fearing that he would be the only staff doctor there.

With labored breath Dr. McClelland asked me what had happened. I remember hearing the coins jingling in his pocket with each step.

"I don't know. I took Shires' page, and Mert told me that Kennedy had been shot."

Once we reached the bottom of the stairwell, we opened the door and emerged into the emergency room. There is always commotion around trauma, but what I saw was sheer bedlam. As we flew by the nurses' station, I yelled, "Which room?" A nurse with tears streaming down her face raised one finger.

I looked to my left and saw a man in a suit running. To my amazement, another man in a suit jumped into his path and smashed a clip machine gun across his chest and face. The first man's eyes immediately turned glassy, and he fell against a gray tile wall, and slithered to the floor unconscious. When I heard that gun slam against his face, I just knew the man's jaw was broken. Normally, I would have rushed over and treated the poor guy, but the President of the United States was in Trauma Room One, and his condition was worse than broken bones. I was to learn later that the man with the gun was a Secret Service Agent, and the one who had been hit was an FBI agent. It was a goddamn madhouse in the Emergency room... people running, yelling. Everyone suspected everyone else—complete and utter paranoia—that's the only way to describe it.

As I turned to continue toward Trauma Room One, there was Lyndon Johnson, being ushered into one of the minor-medicine cubicles, which were located past the nurse's station and partitioned by sliding curtains. His face was ashen, and he was holding his chest. Only recently, he had had a coronary, and I was afraid he was having another heart attack. Behind the Vice President was Ralph Yarborough, crying.

12:40 p.m.
Dealey Plaza—Dallas
Back in Dealey Plaza, Patrolman J. W. Foster leaves his station atop the triple underpass and moves to the area behind the wooden fence. There he discovers footprints and cigarette butts near the spot where witnesses observed the puff of smoke during the shooting. Continuing around the fence to Elm Street, Foster crosses the thoroughfare to a manhole where witnesses have gathered and where the ground has been disrupted. He

is joined by Deputy Sheriff E. R. Walthers and an unidentified man wearing a suit and carrying an overcoat on his arm. The man is later identified by Dallas Police Chief Jesse Curry as an FBI agent but refused to reveal his name. As Foster squats near the manhole and points to the open southwesternmost sixth-floor window of the Book Depository, the "FBI agent" reaches down to the disrupted ground area, and retrieves a spent bullet. Standing and turning, the "agent" places the bullet in his pants pocket, and moves away, disappearing into the crowd. This "agent" has never been identified and the bullet never seen again.

Parkland Hospital—Dallas

Moments later, Bob and I entered Trauma Room One. The first person I came face to face with was Jacqueline Kennedy, who was standing just inside the door in pensive quietness, clutching her purse, her pillbox hat slightly askew. She turned and gazed at me, then refocused her attention on her husband. The look on her face forever marked my memory. Anger, disbelief, despair, and resignation were all present in her expression. I whispered, "My God, my God, it's true."

In 1963, President Kennedy and Jacqueline received the same kind of attention that Prince Charles and Lady Di do today. I had read stories in the newspaper and magazines that claimed the President and the First Lady no longer cared for one another, that the perpetuation of their marriage was a necessity because of the Presidency. Human tragedy strips away the facade, exposing the person's core of true feelings and emotions. In all the sentiments I have seen displayed and heard expressed in my thirty years of practice by people grieving and hurting over trauma victims, I never saw or sensed more intense and genuine love than Jacqueline showed at that moment toward her dying husband.

Drying blood caked the right side of Jacqueline's dress and down her leg. Her once-white gloves were stained almost completely crimson. If she hadn't been standing, I would have thought she had been shot, too.

As Dr. McClelland and I approached, Dr. Malcolm Perry, the assistant professor of surgery, blurted that he and Dr. Jim Carrico, the physician who had first entered the room, had already inserted a endotracheal tube (breathing tube) down the President's throat

In astonishment, I beheld the President of the United States lying before me. Blood was caked on his steel-gray suit, and his shirt was the same crimson color. Even in that condition, his charisma filled the room. He was a larger man than I had imagined him. In fact, he filled the entire gurney. For someone who had been sickly most of his life, the President looked strong and substantial, just what you expect in a man who had achieved that degree of success.

I was standing at about the President's waist, looking at his general appearance, still unbelieving. Blood was seeping from the wound in his head onto the gurney, dripping into the kick bucket on the floor below. Then I noticed a small opening in the midline of his throat. It was small, about the size of the tip of my little finger. It was a bullet entry wound. There was no doubt in my mind about that wound, as I had seen dozens of them in the emergency room. At that point, I knew he had been shot at least twice.

Other doctors were rushing in to help. Drs. Baxter and Paul Peters, assistant professor of urology, had come from the medical school, and Dr. Salyer had followed us from the second floor. When we saw blood frothing around the President's neck wound, it became clear that the endotracheal tube had failed to increase the air volume in his lungs. Dr. Perry decided to perform a tracheostomy on the President's throat, where the bullet had entered his neck, between the second and third tracheal cartilages. Dr. McClelland ran to the top of the table. After Dr. Perry made a small incision, Drs. McClelland and Baxter helped ease in the tube. The procedure requires more than one person because the endotracheal tube must be lifted slightly to allow the other tube to slide down the throat.

Instinctively, I took the right leg. Dr. Salyer was stationed at my side to assist me. Everyone, physicians and nurses alike, knew what to do, as we had been through this procedure hundreds, if not thousands, of times. But I believed, as I think every doctor in Trauma Room One thought, that the President was dead from the very beginning. But goddammit, he was the President of the United States, and we had to do something. After all, we were surgeons.

Drs. McClelland and Ron Jones were stationed at the left arm and chest, Drs. Baxter and Peters took the right side of his torso. With a sick look on his face, Dr. Baxter glanced at me and shook his head in amazement. There was no doubt in my mind that he was referring to his earlier comment about meeting the President at the back of the hospital.

Moments later, Drs. Baxter and Peters began inserting an anterior chest tube on the President's right side, and Drs. Jones and McClelland were doing the same thing on left side to further assist in his breathing by expanding his chest cavity.

The doctors inserted the chest tubes into the President's body by making incisions between the ribs on both sides of his chest in the mid-clavicular lines, into his chest cavity. The trochars were then pulled out, and latex rubber tubing with holes in the sides to allow air to pass were fed down through the metal which are located at the shoulder blade level. Trochars, which are blunt, oblong instruments surrounded by metal tubes, were then plunged through the incisions into his chest cavity. The trochars were then pulled out, and latex rubber tubing with holes in the sides to allow air to pass were fed down through the metal sheaths into the chest cavity. The other ends of the rubber tubing were put into water-sealed drainage to create negative pressure to expand the lungs.

Turning to my right, I noticed that Jacqueline was still standing in the room. I wasn't sure if there was anything we could do to save her husband, but I didn't want her to witness what we were about to do to him. "Mrs. Kennedy, I think you should step outside," Dr Baxter said. Without taking her eyes off the President, she turned and walked from the room, watching him until she disappeared through the door. I was relieved.

As I turned back to the President, I spotted another problem. Clint Hill, the Secret Service agent who had pushed Jacqueline back into the car, was rambling around the room in a wild-eyed, disoriented fashion, waving a .38 caliber pistol. There we were, getting ready to work on a man who had just been shot in the head, and we had a crazy man running around with a loaded gun. I didn't know what he was going to do.

Hill had failed to do his job, which was to protect the President of the United States. My concern at that moment was that he would prevent us from doing our jobs, which was to give the President whatever chance we could.

"Baxter," I said as the nurses rushed to wheel into place the portable tables that contained cut-down and chest-tube trays, "What are we going to do about him?" Before Baxter could say anything, nurse Doris Nelson, supervisor of the emergency room, a heavy-set, granite-faced, no-nonsense woman, turned to Hill and snapped, "Whoever shot the President is not in this room." Hill didn't respond. "Look, " she persisted, "he's okay, he's okay, he's okay, " she repeated as she pointed to each doctor. "Now, put away the gun so that we can get to work."

Hill simply vanished. I don't remember seeing him again.

While Nelson had been talking to Hill, I removed the President's shoes and right sock, and began cutting off his suit trousers, with nurses Diana Bowron and Margaret Hinchclifte assisting. Don Curtis, an oral surgery resident, was doing the same thing to the left limb. I noticed that one of the oxfords that I had tossed to the side of the room had a lift in the sole. The President's right leg was three-quarters of an inch longer than his left leg.

Articles of clothing were flying throughout the room as we disrobed him. His coat and shirt were simultaneously cut away. Usually, trauma victims are stripped of all clothing so that an injury will not be overlooked. But no one ever attempted to remove the President's briefs. I think it was out of respect for the man, the dignified position he held, and the principles for which he stood that we subconsciously didn't want him lying there naked. In addition, with the horrendous head wound he had sustained, we weren't concerned with the lower part of his body. If we could have stabilized him, there would have been plenty of time to check for additional injuries.

The President's skin had a bronze cast to it. At first look he appeared to have a golden tan. But his coloring was not sun related. Rather, it was a physiological phenomenon. Dr. Carrico remembered reading that the President had Addison's disease. Under such a condition, the skin develops a dark tint. For this problem the President took steroids to compensate for the hormones the gland failed to manufacture. Admiral George Burkley, Kennedy's personal physician, traveling with the Presidential party, gave Dr. Carrico three 100-mg. vials of Solu-Cortef from the President's bag.

Today, it is hard to fathom that as recently as 1963, the President of the United States could be brought to a trauma hospital and the attending physicians would not have the benefit of knowing prior to his arrival his blood type or medical history. That was exactly the situation when President Kennedy was wheeled into Parkland. As a matter of policy, the government did not furnish such information to anyone. One of the President's Secret Service agents, Roy Kellerman, informed a nurse that President Kennedy's blood type was 0, RH positive.

After the Kennedy assassination, the procedure changed drastically. Now, when a President travels, a designated hospital in the city where he is visiting must maintain fully equipped emergency and operating rooms with trauma and surgical teams ready to go. In addition, the President's complete medical history is immediately available. During the 1970's, when President Ford was in Fort Worth, I was advised by the government that John Peter Smith Hospital was to be on alert as the designated trauma hospital. The procedures we followed would have given us every conceivable advantage to take care of the President had there been an emergency.

After we had removed the President's clothing, we were ready to begin the ABCs of trauma care—A is for airway, B for breathing, C is circulation. I placed my hand on the femoral artery located at his groin. "No blood pressure," said a nurse who was monitoring the President's vital signs. "I've got a heartbeat here," someone else said. Except for an occasional observation or instruction, there wasn't much talking in Trauma Room One. Everyone was in awe of the President, and the eminence of his position had a silencing effect upon us all.

Kennedy was barely breathing. The bullet that entered his neck had pierced the windpipe. Dr Carrico had forced an endotracheal down his throat.

After Dr. Carrico performed this procedure, three cutdowns (insertion of a plastic tube in the vein to give rapid infusion of fluids intravenously), one arm and both legs, were to start Ringer's Lactate because of blood loss (hemorrhagic shock). Dr. Salyer was assisting me with the cutdown on the right leg, and Dr. Curtis began the same surgery on the left limb.

Depending upon the condition of the patient and the severity of his wounds, blood and Ringer's Lactate are administered through an IV by sticking a needle into the vessel without doing cutdowns. But when massive amounts of these fluids are needed, an eighteen-gauge catheter (about the size of a pencil lead) is surgically placed directly into the vein by a cutdown procedure in that area.

After I had put on surgical gloves, a sterile sheet with a

small window hole was spread over the area that had been prepped, which was on the inside of the President's leg, about two inches above his ankle. I was handed a scalpel, and I made a small incision to expose the Saphenous vein. I then clamped off the blood flow and ligated the vessel leading to the foot. After making a small nick in the Saphenous vein, I inserted a catheter toward the heart, then tied the space between the vessel and the catheter to prevent leakage. I plugged the IV into the flange of the catheter, the clamp was removed, and Ringer's Lactate began flowing. During this ten-minute period, cutdowns had been completed on one arm and two legs, and fluids were moving through the President's body.

It had been almost twenty minutes since the President had been brought in. A tracheostomy had been performed, and he was on an automatic breathing machine (anaesthesia machine); the endotracheal tube which had been placed down his throat by Dr. Carrico had been removed after the tracheostomy; and two anterior chest tubes had been inserted to get air to his lungs so that oxygen would be available for his organs, especially his kidneys and brain. To transport the oxygen to the President's brain and organs, we had improved his circulation by making the three cutdowns. We had fluids, "0" negative blood, and Ringer's Lactate flowing into one arm and both legs through the enlarged portals. The ABCs of trauma care had been completed.

I walked to the President's head to get a closer look. The right occipital parietal portion of his brain appeared to be gone. It looked like a crater—an empty cavity. All I could see there was mangled, bloody tissue. From the damage I saw, there was no doubt in my mind that the bullet had entered his head through the front, and as it surgically passed through his cranium, the missile obliterated part of the temporal and all the parietal and occipital lobes before it lacerated the cerebellum. The wound resembled a deep furrow in a freshly plowed field. Several years later when I viewed slow-motion films of the bullet striking the President, the physics of the head being thrown back provided final and complete confirmation of a frontal entry by the bullet to the cranium.

When I saw the severity of the head wound, I thought that everything we had done for him during those twenty minutes was a complete waste of time. It was a four-plus injury, which no one survives. (In emergency medicine, injuries are described as one plus, two-plus, etc. A four-plus injury is a worst case scenario.) Correspondingly, we made a four-plus effort to change that statistic. If President Kennedy had, in some miraculous way, survived the attack, he would have remained in a perpetual vegetative state. Never again would he have uttered another sound or opened his eyes.

Dr. Kemp "High Pockets" Clark, a six-foot six-inch-tall neurosurgeon and associate professor and chairman of the Neurosurgery Division, entered the room, put on a pair of rubber gloves, and examined the President's cranium. I remember Dr. Clark frowning while shaking his head in despair as he looked on.

"Kemp, tell us how bad that head injury is," Dr. Baxter said, "because we are losing him."

"My God, the whole right side of his head is shot off," Dr. Clark replied. "We've got nothing to work with."

Dr. M. T. "Pepper" Jenkins, professor and chairman of the Anesthesia Department, and other anesthesiologists hooked up a torpedo (a machine which measures heart beats) to the President. When it was switched on, the green light moved across the screen in a straight line, without a hint of even the slightest cardiac activity. Dr. Clark noted that the President's eyes were fixed and divergent. Glancing at us, Dr. Clark again shook his head, indictating that it was too late.

Dr. Perry, bless his heart, just wouldn't give up. He began closed chest cardiac massage on the President, while Dr.

Pepper Jenkins continued to administer pure oxygen. None of us wanted to quit. When Dr. Perry's hands got tired, Dr. Clark took over. But in a few moments, it became clear that absolutely nothing could be done to save the man, and all efforts ceased. Dr. Fouad A. Bashour, associate professor of internal medicine, quickly connected a cardiotachy scope, which was a more sensitive machine than the torpedo, to the President. Again, the straight green light traversed the scope. Jenkins reached over and closed the valve to the anesthesia machine. We had just witnessed the most tragic event imaginable, the President's death.

As I panned the room, it took on a coldness, an ugliness it never had before. The gray wall tiles looked impersonal, almost offensive. Against the somberness of the black-rubber floor, bloody gauze and bandages, empty bottles, boxes, paper, pieces of tubing, and the President's clothing—were strewn everywhere. The artifacts of pain and death underscored the darkness of the moment, the sorrow within our hearts. Forever lodged in my memory was the dispassionate visage of that chamber.

Having minored in history and being a Civil War buff, I couldn't help thinking of Abraham Lincoln, another President brutally killed, shot in the head. Suddenly, I identified with the helpless feeling Lincoln's physician had surely experienced. I felt sorry for him, because I was feeling sorry for myself and everyone else in the room.

I later considered other bizarre similarities in the deaths of the two presidents. Among many, both had Vice Presidents named Johnson and both were slain in the presence of their wives.

Down the hall, doctors had just rescued a man who had been injured when he drove his truck into a concrete pillar. We could help a drunk, but we couldn't save the President of the United States. I felt cheated, because we never had a chance to use on the President the medical technology that was developed at Parkland to save trauma victims. The only thing that would have saved John F. Kennedy that day was a quick acting Secret Service agent or a bullet-proof bubble on his limousine. Even with the medical advancements of the last twenty-seven years, there is still nothing that can save a victim with such a severe a brain injury. The combined hemorrhagic shock and loss of neurologic functions are too great to overcome.

From a humanitarian standpoint, it shouldn't have made any difference whether it was the drunk or the President lying there. We always give an all-out effort, because as Dr. Baxter so insightfully put it, "A life is a life is a life." But that man on the gurney was different. He wasn't just another trauma victim. He was the President of the United States of America.

My perceptions of my country and its principles were forever altered that day. We all proceed through life with a degree of bravado, especially those of us in medicine. But I never believed I would feel fear and vulnerability like I did at that moment. Surgeons are not supposed to get caught up in the emotions of death, but this one gave me the chills. I was gazing at a corpse that to me represented the Constitution, the Bill of Rights and every other democratic tenet that has descended to us through hundreds of years of human genius, effort, and sacrifice. And I was frightened at the thought of someone trying to deny that magnificent heritage with a bullet.

The room was in dead silence, except for the muffled sounds of weeping. Then I looked down into that kick bucket, and I nearly lost my control. There, mingled with the President's brain tissue and his life's blood, were someone's red roses. Tears welled up in my eyes, and a lump the size of a baseball seized my throat. To me, the contents of that can represented our country—broken, bloody, and hurting. It symbolized the beauty of nature against the destruction caused by a madman or madmen. It showed what was left of a Presidency, a marriage, and a family, the memory of his two children. Never had the stench of murder filled my nostrils as strongly as it did at that moment.

As I stood there looking at the man, blood still oozing from his head, I wasn't a Democrat; I wasn't a Republican; I wasn't a liberal, wasn't a conservative. I was an American, who had just lost my President. Sure, I had been caught up in regional cynicism, that relic of pride manifesting in North vs. South, Rebel vs. Yankee, us vs. them, which is ingrained into us from childhood as part of our culture. But there's a plateau of decency that rises above all of that, and nothing evokes quicker change in one's perceptions than a tragedy. Suddenly, the scope of our lives was bigger than Texas, the Southwest, or the Nation.

We had discovered, as I believe most people do, that witnessing history being made can be almost as unpleasant an experience as making it. I took a deep breath and let it out slowly. I don't remember who shut the President's eyes, but when I helped Dr. Jenkins and Dr. Baxter cover the President's body with a sheet, they were closed. It was over. I looked at my wrist watch—it was 12:52 P.M.

12:52 p.m.
Dallas

The news of the President's death has not yet been announced. But someone in Dallas knows that the job has been done. An emergency telephone call is made from a Riverside 8 exchange to a Pablo Brenner or Bruner in Mexico City. The caller states, "He's dead, he's dead." Obviously the operational capacity of "sitting on go" had become "go"—mission accomplished.

12:55 p.m.
Garland, Texas

In the Dallas suburb of Garland, the phone rings in the court of Dallas County Justice of the Peace Theron Ward. The judge's secretary is still out to lunch, and he answers the call himself. On the other end of the line the excited voice of a Parkland Hospital nurse exclaims her relief at being able to reach him. "The President," she says, "has been shot." Could you come to the hospital as soon as possible?" The Judge immediately dismisses court and hurriedly proceed by automobile, red lights and siren, to the hospital.

In Texas, it is the duty of a justice of the peace to hold inquests, with or without a jury, in all cases of unlawful death. Because the murder of a President was not a federal crime in 1963, responsibility for its investigation and prosecution legally belonged to officials of the state of Texas. How this responsibility was usurped by the federal government has become one of the major questions in official rulings concerning the President's death.

The thirty-nine-year-old Judge Ward, a man with a ninth-grade education, was a Navy veteran of World War II in the South Pacific. Shot nine times, he carried a steel plate in his head. Following the war, he served five years as a Dallas deputy sheriff and five years with the Dallas police. Having been only recently elected as justice of the peace, and with minimal legal background, Ward is about to be forced to make one of the most controversial and critical decisions in the aftermath of the assassination of the President.

Parkland Hospital—Dallas

During the twenty minutes we had been working on the President, everyone in the emergency room remained in utter bewilderment. In the confusion, FBI and Secret Service agents, as well as Dallas policemen, were everywhere trying to identify one another and secure the hospital. News reporters were trying to get the story, and the medical personnel were endeavoring to process other patients in the midst of mania. Parkland's switchboard was shut down to most incoming calls so that all available telephone lines could be used by the authorities. Other injured patients arriving at the emergency room continued to filter through the mayhem for treatment. Through the thick of it all, the hospital managed to care for the public, as was the Parkland way.

When Jacqueline Kennedy wasn't standing outside Trauma Room Two, peeking in to get a glimpse of what was happening each time the door opened, she was at the nurse's station talking by phone to Robert Kennedy and other family members. She had also asked that a priest be sent to the hospital. Drs. James "Red" Duke and David Mebane were stabilizing Governor Connally in Trauma Room Two by inserting a chest tube and starting intravenous infusion of Ringer's Lactate before taking him to surgery. Under heavy guard, Lyndon Johnson remained hidden behind a curtain in the minor medicine room just across the hall from the President.

Once the sheet had been placed over the President, it was almost as if all fifteen doctors didn't want to be there. Dr. Baxter and I walked out of the room, and there, to our right, was Jacqueline with Admiral George Burkley, the President's personal physician, standing beside her. She had been in Trauma Room One, and she knew the President was gone.

Her head tilted downward with saddened eyes fixed on a world without her husband. I ran my arm around her shoulders. So broad were they, that I didn't think my hand would ever reach her arm. I asked her if she would like to lie down in the resident's lounge, which was at the end of the hall next to Trauma Rooms Three and Four. Back then we didn't have Valium, so I offered her a phenobarbital tablet. She hesitated, then said that she wanted to remain there, just outside Trauma Room One. Although she looked very composed, I believed she was still in shock, but who wouldn't be? She sat down in a chair and asked a passing aide for a cigarette.

I glanced down at the purse she was still holding, and noticed that some of the President's brain tissue had not been removed. In a subtle manner, I motioned for her aide to step aside. When he did, I asked him to clean the purse. I looked at my wrist watch. It was 12:55. Out of the corner of my eye I saw the priest walk up and stop by the nurse's station. I walked back into Trauma Room One to make sure everything was ready for the ceremony.

One of the several doctors and nurses still in the room was Dr. Fouad A. Bashour, chief of cardiology. He was Catholic, and he understood the significance of giving last rites to the President before he was officially pronounced dead, which had not yet occurred. With everything in order, I opened the door to the room and stepped aside. All of the President's clothes had been neatly folded and placed at one end of the room. I again looked at my wrist watch. It was 12:57 p.m.

1:02 p.m.
Oak Cliff Section of Dallas

Housekeeper Earlene Roberts watches as Lee Harvey Oswald enters the rooming house at 1026 North Beckley and goes to his room. While Oswald is in his room, Roberts hears a car honk outside—two quick short blasts. She peers out the front window and sees two officers in a Dallas police car drive slowly away. Oswald comes out of his room, leaves the house, and is last seen by the housekeeper standing at the bus stop a short distance away.

1:05 P.M.
South of Dallas

A few miles south of Dallas, on Interstate 45, a black automobile is stopped for speeding by the Texas Highway Patrol. Witnesses to the incident observe at least three men in suits in the car. One of these men identifies himself to the officer as a Secret Service Agent and states, "We're in a hurry to get to New Orleans to investigate part of the shooting." There is no record, however, of Secret Service personnel being dispatched to New Orleans on the day of the assassination.

Parkland Hospital—Dallas

With the exception of his feet, which were exposed, the President's body was covered with a sheet. Jacqueline Kennedy and Admiral Burkley returned to Trauma Room One. She went to the end of the gurney, leaned over and kissed her husband's great (big) toe. Father Huber, the priest who had been summoned, stepped to the head of the cart and carefully uncovered the President's head so as not to display the wound. Jacqueline approached, took the President's right hand and pressed it to her cheek. At this point I was blinking back tears and trying to swallow the lump in my throat. The priest began intoning the last rites.

"John Fitzgerald Kennedy, if you are living, I absolve you from your sins in the name of the Father, the Son, and the Holy spirit."

Tears spilled from my eyes and trickled down my face. The baseball in my throat had turned into a basketball, and I was not alone in that feeling.

As Father Huber dipped his thumb into the holy oil and tracked a cross on the President's forehead, he said, "Through this holy anointing may God forgive you whatever sins you have committed. By the faculty given to me by the Apostolic See, I grant to you a plenary indulgence and remission of all your sins, and I bless you in the name of the Father, and the Son, and the Holy Spirit, Amen." I again looked at my wristwatch. It was 1:01 P.M.

When the priest concluded, Jacqueline left the room. Most of us followed, except for several nurses, who immediately began preparing President Kennedy to be moved. I joined

Baxter, Perry, Jenkins, and Clark, who had congregated by the nurse's station. They were deciding upon the time of death to be posted on the death certificate that still had to be signed. Although it was 1:10 p.m., the document would show 1:00 p.m. as the time of death, because the administrating of last rites had begun just prior to that moment.

Normally, the job of signing the death certificate was relegated to the least ranking physician on the trauma team. Staff doctors didn't want to fool with it. In this case that would have been Dr. Salyer or Dr. Carrico. But for the President of the United States, everyone thought it appropriate that Clark sign the certificate, since President Kennedy had died of a neurological wound.

Once Dr. Clark had officially recorded the death of the 35th President, the doctors rushed to Trauma Room Two to help with Governor Connally. I stayed with Trauma Room One, because when there is a death, one of the duties of a resident on the trauma team is to make the arrangements to process the body, especially if there is a crime involved. Under Texas law, a homicide automatically requires an autopsy.

I opened the door to Trauma Room One and stuck my head in to check on the progress of the nurses who were preparing the President's body. When I turned around, I saw a group of people who I believed to be presidential aides and Secret Service agents, Dr. Vernon Stembridge, chief of surgical pathology, and Dr. Sidney Stewart, resident in pathology. The doctors were explaining, politely but forcefully that, pursuant to Texas law, they would be performing an autopsy on President Kennedy's body before it was taken from the hospital. In tones of equal forcefulness, but with greater determination, the men in suits responded that they had orders to take the President's body back to Washington, D. C. just as soon as it was ready to be moved, that there would be no Texas autopsy.

As both sides became more entrenched in their positions,

talking turned to shouting and hand waving escalated to finger pointing. Unable to prevail in their mission, Drs. Stembridge and Stewart angrily wheeled and stomped away. Not only were they outnumbered, but the men in suits had guns. My impression was that someone, who had given explicit instructions to these men, wanted Kennedy's body out of Parkland, out of Dallas, and out of Texas in a hurry. I also thought it unusual to hear Stembridge raising his voice, as he was a quiet, mannerly man.

I again checked on the progress being made on the President's body, then briefly stopped in Trauma Room Two hoping that a death certificate wouldn't have to be signed for Governor Connally also.

Since the assassin's bullet had passed through his body shattering his wrist, and lodging in his thigh, Governor Connally was experiencing difficulty in his breathing and was losing blood. To stabilize the Governor, Drs. Duke and Mebane had started an intravenous injection of Ringer's Lactate and placed a tube in his right chest to prevent his lung from collapsing. Just after I arrived there, the doctors and nurses were preparing to take the Governor to surgery.

1:15 p.m.
Oak Cliff Section of Dallas

At the corner of Tenth and Patton, nine-tenths of a mile from Oswald's rooming house, Dallas Police Officer J. D. Tippit is shot and killed beside his patrol car. Eyewitnesses at the scene give conflicting accounts of the crime. One report, broadcast over police radio, describes a man fleeing the scene as a white male, twenty-seven, 5 feet 11 inches, 165 pounds, black wavy hair, fair complected, white Eisenhower-type jacket, dark trousers, and white shirt—a description that does not match that of Oswald or his clothing. The man is said to be carrying a ".32 caliber dark finish automatic," far different weapon than the revolver in Oswald's possession at the time of his arrest. Spent cartridge shells found at the scene are reported by a veteran officer to be from "an automatic .38 rather than a pistol." The vast difference between .38 revolver and .38 automatic cartridges are too great for a veteran officer to misidentify.

Also, it was later discovered that bullets removed from the officer's body did not match the Oswald revolver. Neither did these bullets match the spent cartridge shells which were turned in as evidence. Of the four bullets taken from Tippit's body, *one* was a Remington-Peters manufacture and *three* were of Winchester-Western make. On the contrary, of the spent cartridges, *two* were made by Winchester-Western and *two* by Remington-Peters.

Aquilla Clemons, another eyewitness, sees *two* men at the scene. These men, she reports, converse with hand signals and then depart in different directions.

Only two witnesses, Domingo Benavides and Helen Markham, claim to have seen the actual shooting. Benavides, who had perhaps the best view, could not identify Oswald as the killer and was not called to testify before the Warren Commission. Markham, however, was called and gave, at best, flimsy testimony. Six times, under questioning, Mrs. Markham denied recognizing any of the four men—which included Oswald—in the police lineup. Undeterred by her denials and after continued badgering, Commission counsel finally gets the desired response as Mrs. Markham states, "…I looked at him. When I saw this man I wasn't sure, but I had cold chills just run all over me."

Even though the evidence, as can be seen, is conflicting and jerry-built, the Warren Commission eventually uses it to establish Oswald as the murderer of Officer Tippit. They do so in order to bolster their case for Oswald having shot the President. Oswald's shooting of Tippit, they propose, demonstrates his propensity to kill.

1:25 p.m.
Parkland Hospital—Dallas

Justice of the Peace Theron Ward arrives at the emergency entrance of Parkland Hospital. He attempts to enter but is prevented from doing so by men in suits he assumes are Secret Service agents. Making his way quickly around to the front entrance, he is recognized by a woman at the front desk who tells him the doctors are waiting for him and leads him back to the emergency room. Upon entering the area he is immediately confronted by Dallas Coroner Dr. Earl Rose. The frantic Rose, right arm upraised and finger pointing to the ceiling, shouts, "Ward, you are on the line!" Referring to the time in which a forensic examination could be made of President Kennedy, he continued, "We can have him out of here in forty-five minutes."

Instructions from pathology has already been given to operating room assistant supervisor Jane Wester for the preparation of a craniotomy (surgical cutting or removal of part of the skull for exploration) to be performed on the President. Dr. Rose is trained in forensic pathology (medical-legal examination preparatory to courtroom testimony) and was ready to carry out the laws of the state of Texas. It was his duty to examine the President's body, his clothes, the scene of the crime, determining the number of shots, as well as the direction from which they came.

Judge Ward is escorted to the door of Trauma Room One by Secret Service Agent Kellerman. Viewing the President's body from the doorway, he never enters the room. He notices a "plug" out of Kennedy's head, as well as the tracheostomy opening in his throat. Kellerman requests Ward to release the body into Secret Service custody. The Judge replies, "I will have to consult with Dallas District Attorney, Henry Wade." Calling Wade, Ward is told that, in Wade's opinion, a "missile" (bullet) must be taken into evidence and that Dallas Police Chief Curry should be queried on this point. Wade, in turn, calls Curry, confirming the opinion, and relays the information back to Ward. The judge mysteriously ignores the advice of the two Texas officials (to take possession of a bullet that may have killed the President) and releases the body to Kellerman. Without saying a word, Ward simply points to the exit, allowing Kellerman to begin removal of the body and all evidence associated therewith. Texas law was breached and a critical link in the investigative process violated.

1:26 p.m.
Love Field — Dallas
Police Chief Curry drives Lyndon Johnson to Love Field, where he boards Air Force One as the 36th President of the United States.

Parkland Hospital
When I walked back into the hall, Evalea Glanges, a medical student, was standing by the nurses' station. She told me a most peculiar story. While we had been working on President Kennedy, she was outside in the emergency room parking lot. Standing beside the President's limousine, she pointed out to another medical student that there was a bullet hole in the windshield. Upon overhearing her comment, a Secret Service agent nervously jumped into the car and sped away.

The limousine had been at least partially cleaned while parked at Parkland Hospital. There is no record of any evidence being found during this time.

The limousine was driven to Love Field and placed aboard a plane by Secret Service Agent Kinney. It arrives in Washington at 7:00 p.m. and is driven to the White House garage, where it is covered by a plastic sheet and guarded by agents.

At 9:10 p.m. the vehicle is inspected by representatives of the President's chief physician.

At 12:00 midnight, FBI agents, assisted by the Secret Service, examine the limousine. Several bullet fragments, and a three-inch triangular piece of the President's skull are removed as evidence. A small hole just left of center in the windshield as well as a dent in the chrome moulding strip above the windshield are noted. FBI agents state that the dent was made by a bullet fragment.

The bullet fragments taken from the limousine are not marked for identification. Six months later a Secret Service agent and a White House staffer were shown the crumpled fragments and were able to identify them as those found in the President's car shortly after the assassination. Of course, these fragments are linked to the Oswald rifle—a linkage that would never hold up in a court of law because of the broken chain in handling and marking this evidence.

Three days after the assassination, Carl Renas, head of security for the Dearborn Division of the Ford Motor Company, drives the Presidential limousine, helicopters hovering overhead, from Washington to Cincinnati. In doing so, he noted several bullet holes; the most notable being the one in the windshield's chrome molding strip which he said was clearly "a primary strike" and "not a fragment."

The limousine was taken by Renas to Hess and Eisenhart in Cincinnati where the chrome molding was replaced.

The Secret Service told Renas to "Keep his mouth shut."

Renas recalls thinking at the time, "Something is wrong."

The limousine was eventually rebuilt, bullet-proofed, and had incorporated into it every protective device known. President Johnson however, refused to use the car until its color was changed from its midnight blue—Kennedy blue—to standard black.

It is a shame and disgrace that evidentiary-gathering procedures were not followed with respect to the Presidential limousine. More shameful, however, is the fact that a vehicle of such historical significance—a virtual Ford's Theater—was not preserved. This was not a thoughtless act.

Dr. Glanges also had witnessed President Johnson and Ladybird leaving for the airport. After they were rushed to an awaiting station wagon, the President crouched down in the back seat as the automobile left for Love Field. The front seat of the vehicle was loaded with worried Secret Service agents. Men in suits were everywhere. But they had good reason to be on edge. For all they knew, there was a plot to eliminate the entire hierarchy of the United States government, and the new President could be attacked at any moment. I must admit that the Cuban missile crisis popped into my mind more than once that day.

The Secret Service's one and only job was to protect the President of the United States and other government officials around him, especially the Vice President. Having miserably failed at that task by allowing one Presidential assassination that day, the agency's message was abundantly clear to everyone—they wouldn't allow another one.

1:30 p.m.
Parkland Hospital—Dallas

Veteran newsman Seth Kantor, radio newsman Roy Stamps, and housewife Wilma Tice see Jack Ruby at Parkland Hospital. Both Kantor and Stamps have known Ruby for years. (In his testimony before the Warren Commission, Ruby denies his presence there. The commission chose to believe Ruby in spite of evidence to the contrary. To do otherwise, smacked of conspiracy.)

1:33 p.m.
Love Field—Dallas

President Johnson boards Air Force One and tells Col. James B. Swindal that the aircraft will not leave for Washington without President Kennedy's body.

Oak Cliff Section—Dallas

A Dallas Police radio dispatch reports, "He is in the library, Jefferson, East 500 block, Marsalis and Jefferson." Minutes later, a follow up dispatch says, "We are all at the library." Again, minutes later, "*it was the wrong man.*"

Who is this suspect, so quickly apprehended and just as quickly dismissed as "the wrong man"? At this early stage, the only way they could have known it is the wrong man would be for them to know the *right* man.

The library, located at the intersection of East Jefferson Street and Marsalis Avenue, is six blocks from Oswald's rooming house and within only one block of Ruby's apartment. Oswald is known to have frequented this library three to four times a week.

Just as it has never been clear as to exactly how Oswald was so quickly known to be in the Texas Theater, it is still unclear why the police were so quickly dispatched to this library. Was some unknown hand guiding authorities toward Oswald?

Parkland Hospital—Dallas

A distraught Malcolm Kilduff, White House Press Secretary, holds a press conference at Parkland Hospital. He announces the time of the President's death as 1:00 and says that, "He died of a gunshot wound in the brain." When asked by a newsman to elaborate on the cause of death, Kilduff points to his right temple and replies, "Dr. Burkley told me it, it's a simple matter…of a bullet right through the head."

As Dr. Glanges and I continued to talk, a bronze casket was being wheeled toward Trauma Room One by two male employees from the O'Neal Funeral Home. I opened the door, allowing them to enter, then followed them in. I was the only doctor in the room. All of the tubes had been removed from the President, his body had been cleaned, and he had been wrapped in two white sheets. The casket was opened, and two nurses placed a clear plastic sheet and then a plastic mattress covering over the green-satin lining to keep any blood that might seep from the wounds from staining the inside.

The door opened again; Jacqueline Kennedy entered with Dr. Burkley and walked to the side of her slain husband. She carefully lifted his right hand and placed her wedding ring on his little finger. She stood in silence, looking at the man with whom she had shared so much of her life. As she turned and left, I stood staring. The finality of the moment was almost more than I could accept.

Before I directed that the body be moved, I turned down the sheet and took one long, last look at President Kennedy's head wound. I was the last doctor at Parkland Hospital to see it. After making my final examination, I lightly stroked his reddish-brown hair. I felt so terribly sorry for him. He was handsome, intelligent, charismatic, young—but dead.

The President was lifted into the casket. As the two men sealed the coffin, it seemed strange to feel such a closeness to a man whom I had never known, other than through the news media. As I watched the handles being slowly turned to tighten the lid, I wondered who had done this to the President, and what effect it would have on our country.

It wasn't until 1991, when I saw the autopsy pictures of John Kennedy that had been taken at the Bethesda Naval Hospital, that I realized there was something rotten in America in 1963. The very last and most alarming thought one wants to have of his government is that he cannot trust the people who run it. But that is exactly what I believed when on January 19, 1991 I examined the official autopsy photographs taken in Maryland on November 22, 1963.

The doctors there had recorded the condition of John F. Kennedy's cranium, a state that had substantially changed during the period of six hours and over a distance of fifteen-hundred miles. Great effort had been made to reconstruct the back of the President's head, and the incision Perry had made in his throat for the tracheostomy at Parkland had been enlarged and mangled, as if someone had conducted another procedure. No doubt, someone had gone to a great deal of trouble to show a different story than we had seen at Parkland.

More disturbingly, there were two eyewitnesses present at the autopsy, James Jenkins and Paul O'Connor, who swear that President Kennedy arrived at the naval medical facility zipped in a gray body bag inside a different coffin—one of cheap material. And even more astounding, these men, who have gone through numerous tests and substantial harassment to be proclaimed credible, claim there was no brain when the body came out of the gray bag. As the last doctor to see President Kennedy before his body left Parkland, I can unequivocally report that there was no gray body bag, and that he still had the left side of his brain.

The Warren Report is also mysterious to me. As I watched the President's loosening grip on life, I had absolutely no doubt that I was viewing two frontal entry bullet wounds. Had we turned him over, we would have discovered a third entry wound in his back, between the shoulder blades. And beyond absurdity is the "magic bullet" theory, postulating that a missile traveled through President Kennedy's neck, then traversed Governor Connally's torso, whereupon it shattered his wrist, and finally lodged deeply within his thigh.

Macabre and tabloid-style stories have purported that John Kennedy is alive in the basement of Parkland Hospital. As a physician, I know life from death, and when we placed President Kennedy in that casket, he was dead.

1:40 p.m.
Oak Cliff Section—Dallas

Lee Harvey Oswald enters the Texas Theater on East Jefferson Street in the Oak Cliff section of town.

1:45 p.m.
Parkland Hospital—Dallas; The "Magic Bullet"

Hospital engineer Darrell Tomlinson discovers an intact bullet on a stretcher and turns it over to hospital security director O.P. Wright. Wright attempts to turn over custody of the bullet to an FBI agent, who refuses to accept it. He then gives it to Secret Service Agent Richard Johnsen. (Both Tomlinson and Wright, when later shown a bullet alleged to be the one discovered at Parkland Hospital, declined to identify it as the one they handled that day. Only Tomlinson was ever questioned by the Warren Commission about this strategic piece of evidence found a short time after Jack Ruby's appearance at the hospital.)

This bullet, defying all logic and flying in the face of all rules of evidence, was to become the major link between the assassination and suspect Oswald. The Warren Commission, in its haste to label Oswald as the sole rifleman firing from a position behind the President, created the following impossible scenario:

Oswald fires from the sixth floor southeasternmost window of the Book Depository. The missile strikes the President in the upper back near his spine, exiting his throat just below the Adam's apple. Then, while pausing in mid-air, it turns right, then left, then downward, entering the Governor's back below the right shoulder blade near his armpit. The bullet continues on its fabricated path through Connally's chest, shattering his fifth rib and exiting just below his right nipple. The missile then enters the outer forearm near the wrist, splintering the large radius bone, exiting the inner forearm and finally embedding itself in Governor Connally's left thigh. From here, this miracle working missile disengages itself, cleans itself of any trace of blood or tissue, and in unmutilated, almost perfect condition, buries itself under the mat of an emergency room stretcher.

This implausible theory was presented to the American people as fact and portrayed Lee Harvey Oswald as the lone, unaided killer of the President. In doing so, the Warren Commission had to ignore the missile's broken chain of evidence, utilizing an illusionary bullet trajectory, and approve obvious wound fabrication or alteration of the President's body.

1:50 p.m.
Texas Theater—Oak Cliff Section of Dallas

Lee Harvey Oswald is arrested at the Texas Theater and taken to the Dallas Police Station. The circumstances of his apprehension are intriguing.

Johnny Brewer, manager of a shoe store near the theater, observes Oswald go into the movie house without paying, and notifies the theater cashier. The cashier, Julia Postal, did not see Oswald enter the theater but relates the incident to concession operator, W. H. Burroughs. Burroughs states that he heard the front doors open but saw no one come past him through the lobby. Assuming that the Oswald had taken the stairs to the balcony, Postal calls the police.

Within minutes, several cars of police (about fifteen officers), FBI Agents Robert Barrett and Bardwell Odum, along with Dallas Assistant District Attorney Bill Alexander, converge on the theater—all to capture a man suspected of entering the theater without paying. The house lights are turned up and the authorities enter the theater. Ten to fifteen people are scattered throughout the room. One of them, a man sitting near the front, tells officer M. N. McDonald, "The man you want is sitting in the third row from the rear, not in the balcony." McDonald moves cautiously down the aisle, crouching low, gun drawn, toward Oswald. However, he stops about midway to talk to two people. Oswald stands up as McDonald approaches and a scuffle ensues. Other officers join in subduing Oswald and drag him, protesting, from the theater and place him in an awaiting police car.

Johnny Brewer witnesses the arrest and sees, "Fists flying...they were hitting him," and hears some of the police holler, "Kill the President, will you." Julia Postal allows a police officer to use her box office phone and hears him remark, "I think we have got our man on both accounts." S. L. Reed, taking pictures of the incident outside the theater, overhears an officer state that Oswald "killed the President."

George Applin not only witnesses the arrest of Oswald, but also sees Jack Ruby inside the theater.

Many questions arise regarding the quick apprehension of Lee

Harvey Oswald. Why did so many officers respond to a one man gate crasher? Why did an assistant district attorney leave the Book Depository murder site to accompany officers to the theater? Why did an FBI agent participate in the arrest, which at that time could only be surmised as a local misdemeanor? Why were the arresting officers already proclaiming the capture of the murderer of both President Kennedy and Officer Tippit? More importantly, was Jack Ruby at the scene? And if so, why? Could it have been Ruby himself who points out Oswald to arresting officers?

1:57 p.m.
Dealey Plaza — Dallas

Lee Bowers, still at his position in the railroad tower near Dealey Plaza, reports to Dallas officers that a man is hiding in a railroad car. Bowers had stopped the train after observing the suspicious acting man "hunkered down" inside the open top car. Several officers proceed to the area, and with arms drawn, apprehend three men. The three men are taken to the nearby sheriff's office and are later turned over to Captain Will Fritz of the Dallas Police Department. The men were never booked, and no official record exists of their having ever been questioned. (Later, when Fritz is questioned about the disposition of the three suspicious characters, he replies, "If you talk to the FBI they might help you…that's the only ones who'd have it.")

Parkland Hospital — Dallas

As though on cue, a phalanx of guards poured into Trauma Room No. I just as the coffin was being rolled out. They looked like a hoard of locusts descending upon a corn field. Without any discussion, they encircled the casket and began escorting the President's body down the hall toward the emergency room exit. A man in a suit, leading the group, left little doubt in my mind who was in charge. That he wasn't smiling best describes the look on his face. Just outside Trauma Room One, Jacqueline joined the escort and placed her hand on the coffin as she walked along beside it. I followed directly behind them.

When the entourage had moved into the main hall, Dr. Earl Rose, chief of forensic pathology, confronted the men in suits. Roy Kellerman, the man leading the group, looked sternly at Dr. Rose and announced, "My friend, this is the body of the President of the United States, and we are going to take it back to Washington."

Dr. Rose bristled and replied, "No, that's not the way things are. When there's a homicide, we must have an autopsy."

"He's the President. He's going with us," Kellerman barked, with increased intensity in his voice.

"The body stays," Dr. Rose said with equal poignancy.

Kellerman took an erect stance and brought his firearm into a ready position. The other men in suits followed course by draping their coattails behind the butts of their holstered pistols. How brave of these men, wearing their Brooks Brothers suits with icons of distinction (color-coded secret service buttons) pinned to their lapels, worn with the pride of the German's SS, willing to shoot an unarmed doctor to secure a corpse.

"My friend, my name is Roy Kellerman. I am Special Agent in charge of the White House detail of the Secret Service. We are taking President Kennedy back to the capitol."

"You are not taking the body anywhere. There's a law here. We're going to enforce it, " said Dr. Rose.

Admiral George Burkley, White House Medical Officer, said, "Mrs. Kennedy is going to stay exactly where she is until the body is moved. We can't have that... he's the President of the United States."

"That doesn't matter," Dr. Rose replied rigidly. "You can't lose the chain of evidence."

For the second time that day, there was little doubt in my mind as to the meaning of what was happening before me.

"Goddammit, get your ass out of the way before you get

hurt," screamed another one of the men in suits. Another snapped, "We're taking the body, now."

Strange, I thought, this President is getting more protection dead than he did when he was alive.

Had Dr. Rose not stepped aside, I'm sure that those thugs would have shot him. They would have killed me and anyone else who got in their way. A period of twenty-seven years has neither erased the fear that I felt nor diminished the impression that that incident made upon me.

They loaded the casket into the hearse, Jacqueline got into the back seat, placed her hand on top of the coffin, and bowed her head. As they drove off, I felt that a thirty-year-old surgeon had seen more than his share for one day. My wristwatch read 2:08 p.m.

2:15 p.m.
Love Field — Dallas

President Kennedy's body is placed aboard Air Force One. Jacqueline Kennedy accompanies the casket, remaining with it at all times except for the short period she is in attendance while Johnson is given the Presidential oath.

City Hall — Dallas

Officers arrive at the jail with suspect Lee Harvey Oswald. Oswald's forehead shows a fresh abrasion and his left eye is bruised and swollen. His clothes and hair are disheveled. It is apparent that his arrest had come only after a fight. He is taken to the interrogation room by Detectives Richard Sims and Elmer Boyd.

Upon the announcement that the President's killer had been apprehended, and that his name was Lee Harvey Oswald, FBI agent James Hosty quickly heads to Dallas police headquarters. Oswald was well known to the agent and had been assigned to him upon Oswald's move to the Dallas area. In the weeks prior to the President's visit, Agent

Hosty had made two unsuccessful attempts to contact Oswald. He had only been able to speak with Oswald's wife, Marina, and her close friend, Ruth Paine. Oswald, on the other hand, had attempted to make contact with Hosty and had delivered a note to the agent's secretary at FBI headquarters.

As Agent Hosty races up the stairs toward the interrogation room where Oswald is being held, he is joined by Police Lieutenant Jack Revill. Hosty tells Revill, "We knew that Lee Harvey Oswald was capable of assassinating the President of the United States, but we didn't dream he would do it." The meaning of this cryptic comment has never been adequately explained. On the surface, however, it appears to be another attempt to quickly place the blame for the murder on the "lone nut," Lee Harvey Oswald. Agent Hosty was eventually forced to deny making the statement to Revill or face the question, why, if Oswald was a known threat to the President, did the FBI never alert the Secret Service? Hosty must have known from his previous contacts with Oswald's wife and her friend Ruth Paine that Oswald was employed at the Texas School Book Depository, overlooking the motorcade route. Mrs. Paine had been instrumental in helping Oswald acquire this job.

2:20 p.m.

Captain Fritz has Oswald brought from the interrogation room to his office in the Homicide and Robbery division. Present in the office with Fritz are Detectives Sims and Boyd, FBI Agents James Bookhout, James Hosty, and Joe Meyers, and a Secret Service Agent. Oswald is asked if he worked for the Texas School Book Depository. He replied that he did. When asked what part of the building he was in at the time the President was shot, he stated that he was having lunch on the second floor.

2:30 p.m.

Captain Fritz orders three of his detectives to meet Sheriffs deputies at the home of Ruth Paine in the nearby city of Irving. This is the location where Oswald's wife had been staying. The officers are to search the premises.

Parkland Hospital

I went up to Operating Room No. 5 on the second floor to watch Drs. Robert R. Shaw, professor of thoracic surgery, and James Boland and James "Red" Duke, residents in thoracic surgery, operate on Governor Connally's chest. Diagnosis of his thoracic condition was a single gunshot wound to the chest with comminuted fracture of the fifth rib, laceration of the middle lobe, and hematoma of the lower lobe of the right lung. After one hour and forty-five minutes of surgery, Drs. Charles F. Gregory, professor of orthopedic surgery, and William Osborn, orthopedic resident, operated on the arm. Simultaneously Drs. Shires, Baxter, McClelland, and Don Patman, senior resident in surgery, worked on the left thigh. I observed Dr. Osborn remove at least five bullet fragments from the Governor's arm and handed them to nurse Audrey Bell. A bullet fragment in the Governor's left thigh was not removed, as it was not a threat at this location.

Total operating time was three hours and fifty minutes. All surgery on Governor Connally ceased at 4:45 p.m. From surgery, he was taken to the recovery room, where an intensive-care area was established by partitioning the room with sheets. This was well before the sophistication of modern intensive care units and equipment.

2:38
Love Field—Dallas

Aboard Air Force One preparations have been made to give the oath of office to Lyndon Johnson. Dallas Federal Judge, Sarah T. Hughes, a Johnson appointee, has been called in to administer the oath. President Kennedy's personal Bible is removed from his private cabin and used in the ceremony. Mrs. Kennedy stands beside Johnson, still in her pink blood-soaked suit. Judge Hughes is shaking but manages to get through the twenty-eight second oath.

3:30 p.m.
Paine Home—Irving

Officers arrive at the residence of Michael and Ruth Paine at 2515 West Fifth Street in Irving. Mrs. Paine greets the officers at the door and indicates she has been expecting them. Inviting them in, she agrees to a search of the house. Officers do so and in the garage they find a blanket said to have been used to wrap a rifle, but the rifle is gone. Mr. Paine arrives home from work during this time.

There are many unanswered questions about the role of Michael and Ruth Paine in the lives of Lee and Marina Oswald. However, none raises more interest than an FBI report of a telephone conversation between the couple on the day following the President's death. Mr. Paine is heard to comment that he felt sure Oswald had killed the President but did not feel that he was responsible. Paine further stated, "*We both know who is responsible.*" This statement indicates that the Paines possessed knowledge that someone, with whom they were familiar, was manipulating or directing Oswald. Though this information was in the hands of the FBI, neither of the Paines was ever officially asked to name this mysterious "responsible" person.

4:00 p.m.
Aboard Air Force One

Somewhere high over the United States, the new President receives news that the assassination is the act of one lone individual and that NO CONSPIRACY EXISTS. The information comes, not from Dallas, but from the nation's capitol. Specifically, it came from either McGeorge Bundy or Commander Oliver Hallet in the Situation Room of the White House Communications Center.

4:35 p. m.
City Hall—Dallas
Oswald is taken by officers to the show-up room for the first of several line-ups. Oddly, though he had been searched at the time of his arrest, Detectives Boyd and Sims decide to search him again. In Oswald's pockets they find five live rounds of .38 ammunition and a bus transfer slip.

Tippit shooting witness, Helen Markham, views the lineup of Oswald and three others and gives her very shaky identification.

5:10 p.m.
Andrews Air Force Base—Bethesda, Maryland
At Andrews Air Force Base, the coffin is placed into an ambulance for its trip to Bethesda Naval Hospital, where the autopsy will be performed. Robert Kennedy, Jacqueline, and Gen. Godfrey McHugh sit in the rear of the automobile with the casket. President Johnson and his entourage leave aboard helicopters for the White House.

Parkland Hospital—Dallas
Although I was technically off duty, I stayed with Connally to help change the Governor's dressings and monitor certain laboratory values. I had been closely following research into the coagulation problem of trauma victims. Because of my interest in this area of medicine, Dr. Shires allowed me to assist him on the Governor's case.

Prothrombin, a substance produced by the liver, is one of the factors that promotes clotting. When blood loss is extensive, this clotting agent can be depleted, requiring that the patient be given Vitamin K which is used by the liver to produce prothrombin. The Governor's' prothrombin time was prolonged, which might have exposed him to additional bleeding.

6:00 p.m.
City Hall—Dallas

WFAA radio and television reporter Victor Robertson, Jr., stands in the hall near the entrance of Captain Fritz's third-floor office. Two police officers are guarding the door. Robertson sees Jack Ruby approach and attempt to enter the office. He is prevented from doing so by one of the officers who says, "You can't go in there, Jack." Ruby makes a joking remark and heads back down the hall toward the elevator.

6:30 p.m.
City Hall—Dallas

Again Oswald is taken to the show-up room. Bus driver Cecil McWatters identifies Oswald as a passenger on his bus shortly after the assassination. Ted Calloway and Sam Guinyard state that Oswald is the person they saw running, gun in hand, from the scene of the shooting of Officer Tippit.

7:00 p.m.

Marina Oswald and Mr. and Mrs. Paine are brought into police headquarters. Shown the rifle allegedly found on the sixth floor of the Book Depository, Marina states that it is "like" her husband's but that she is "not sure." Officers take her affidavit.

7:00 p.m.
Bethesda Naval Hospital—Bethesda, Maryland

President Kennedy's body has been transferred from the casket to the eight-foot long autopsy table in the center of the morgue's main chamber. Present in the room are no less than twenty-eight people. Among those crowded into the area are the President's personal physician, agents from the FBI and Secret Service, the commanding officer of the Naval Medical Center, and the surgeon general of the Navy.

Commander J. J. Humes, the Director of Laboratories of the

National Medical School at the Naval Medical Center in Bethesda, chooses J. T. Boswell, M.D., chief of pathology and P. A. Finck, M.D., chief of wound ballistics pathology, Armed Forces Institute of Pathology at Walter Reed Medical Center, Washington, to assist him in performing the autopsy. None of the three men was a practicing forensic pathologist or had special expertise in examining bullet wounds.

In 1979, the House Select Committee on Assassinations investigated the records of the President's postmortem examination and reported it to be fraught with procedural errors.
They charged the following:

1. The President's body was taken out of the hands of those responsible for investigation of the death and autopsy—Texas Authorities.
2. Those performing the autopsy had insufficient training and experience to evaluate a death from gunshot wounds.
3. Physicians who treated the President at Parkland Hospital were not consulted before commencing the autopsy.
4. Circumstances at the time of autopsy were not controlled by the pathologist.
5. Proper photographs were not taken.
6. The President's clothing was not examined.
7. The autopsy procedure was incomplete because:
    a. External examination failed to accurately locate wounds.
    b. The bullet tracks were not dissected to determine their course through the body.
    c. The angles of the bullet tracks through the body were not measured relative to the body axis.
    d. The brain was not properly examined and sectioned.
8. The report was incomplete, inaccurate, and prepared without reference to photographs.
9. The head wound location was incorrect.
10. Other wounds of the President's body were not localized with reference to fixed body landmarks so as to permit reconstruction of trajectories.

These glaring procedural inaccuracies and errors are blamed on the inexperience of the autopsy team. But was inexperience and improper procedure the culprit—or was the autopsy purposefully falsified in order to frame Oswald as the lone assassin and declare NO CONSPIRACY? Much can be learned concerning this question by carefully analyzing the testimony of doctors and aides at Parkland Hospital. A comparison of what they observed of the President's wounds to those as reported by the Bethesda autopsy team reveals irreconcilable discrepancies. Consider the following:

1. At Parkland Hospital the wound to the right rear of the President's head is a large gaping hole extending from behind the ear all the way around to the back of the head. At Bethesda Naval Hospital, the back of the President's head is intact with only a small puncture just to the right of midline near the base of the skull. The large gaping hole is only on the upper right side with no damage to the rear of the head. [Figure 1B]

2. At Parkland Hospital, a small wound of entry is seen in the President's throat just below his Adam's apple and slightly enlarged to accommodate the tracheal tube. Upon examination at Bethesda, this wound has become a three inch wide gaping gash. [Figure 4]

3. At Bethesda, pathologists discover a wound in the President's upper back near the spine. Parkland Hospital doctors were not aware of this wound. In their frantic but futile attempt to resuscitate the President, they never turned him over to examine his back. [Figure 1C]

Another of the more important evidentiary aspects of any investigation involving gunshots are the bullets and bullet fragments connected with the crime. In this area, as with the post-mortem examination of the President, the evidence is incomplete, distorted and outright erroneous.

Cases in point are:

1. *The Stretcher Bullet:*

This so called "magic bullet" is covered elsewhere in this book. As has already been shown, this bullet could not later be identified by its finders, Tomlinson and Wright. Neither could it later be identified by the Secret Service agent who received it, Richard Johnson, nor the man

Johnson released it to, Secret Service Chief James Rowley.

There were *no* residues of blood or tissue on the bullet and it was obviously a "plant." At this late date, it is difficult to understand how such a fabrication could ever have been put forth as theory, let alone fact. But, the reality is, powerful and learned men *did* place this flawed theory into the public record as fact. Upon recognizing this, one is then forced to question the motive and intent of those responsible for such a fable.

2. Bullet Fragments

The Warren Commission received two bullet fragments which were "found in the front of the President's car." One fragment was from a portion of a bullet's nose area" while the second was from "a bullet's base portion." These fragments were badly mutilated, and it could not be determined whether they were portions of a single bullet or were two separate bullets. Both of these fragments did possess residues of blood.

Three small lead fragments are found in the floorboard of the rear of the limousine. One of these fragments is reported missing in 1970.

Though these fragments are said to be from the Oswald rifle, their finding, handling, and identification are questionable.

At the President's autopsy, three small fragments are removed from the President's head. X-rays show many minute fragments scattered throughout the skull.

3. Whole missiles:

Two FBI agents present during the President's autopsy, James Sibert and Francis O'Neil, receive and sign a receipt for a "missile removed during the examination of the body."

The receipt is in the official record though the missile itself has never been entered into evidence.

Captain David Osborne, chief of surgery at Bethesda, was also present at the autopsy. He recalls seeing an "intact slug" (a missile) fall out on to the autopsy table as the President's clothing was moved.

Back at Dallas, in Dealey Plaza just after the assassination, an FBI agent picks up a bullet in the grass just beyond the south curb of Elm Street a few feet from where the President was slain. Photographs at the time clearly reveal the agent bending to pick up the bullet and then placing it in his trousers pocket. The bullet is never seen again and no report is found in the official record. However, alert newsmen, as well as photographers, have documented its existence. The November 23 edition of the *Dallas Times-Herald* reports: "Dallas Police Lt. J. C. Day of the Crime Lab estimated the distance from the sixth floor window the slayer used to the spot where *one of the bullets* was recovered, at 100 yards. The magazine *New Republic* of December 21 stated: "...police officers were examining the area at the side of the street where the President was hit, and a police inspector told me *they had just found another bullet in the grass*."

4. *Governor Connally:*

As determined by X-rays, Governor Connally continues to have two small fragments in his body. They were never removed during his treatment at Parkland Hospital. Officially, only three very small fragments were removed from the Governor. This is disputed, however, by operating room nurse Audrey Bell. She states that four to six small- to medium-size fragments were handed to her by doctors treating Connally's wounds. Her statement is confirmed by Texas Department of Public Safety officer Charles Harbison, who received the fragments from Bell, then passed them on to the FBI. The House Select Committee on Assassinations' report concerning these fragments stated that "The method of labeling and handling this evidence was so poor that there might have been difficulty in having it admitted as evidence in a criminal procedure."

To further complicate matters, the Governor's clothes, of primary importance to the investigation, were laundered by person or persons unknown, prior to being turned over to authorities .

The House Select Committee on Assassinations, while reinvestigating the circumstances surrounding the assassination of President Kennedy, chose to verify the original Warren Commission findings concerning the medical and ballistics evidence. It did so despite missing and poor-quality autopsy photographs, unverified x-rays, missing tissue slides of the wound areas, lack of probe or dissection of the wounds, no sectioning of the brain, and the burning of original autopsy notes. (These original autopsy notes were burned by Commander Humes, the chief autopsy surgeon, in the fireplace of his home on Sunday morning following the assassination. There has never been a reasonable explanation for this act.) The Committee's conclusion, therefore, is based on tainted evidence, manipulated trajectories, and a false autopsy. It ignored, or labeled erroneous, all testimony and evidence that they found in conflict with the lone assassin scenario created by their predecessor, the Warren Commission.

Concerning the missing autopsy materials, the Committee reports "... evidence tends to show that Robert Kennedy either destroyed these materials or *otherwise rendered them inaccessible*." Could Robert Kennedy, the President's brother, have been making preparations to investigate his brother's death should he himself become President? Before an audience of students at San Fernando State College in California on June 3, 1968, three days before his own assassination, he stated, "Only the powers of the Presidency will reveal the secrets of my brother's death."

After Robert's death, Evelyn Lincoln, President Kennedy's personal secretary, became concerned about the disposition of the autopsy materials. To make certain that the family was aware of their existence, Ted Kennedy was contacted. He replied back that everything was under control.

7:03 p.m.
City Hall—Dallas

Oswald is arraigned before Justice of the Peace David Johnston for the murder of Officer Tippit. Captain Fritz signs the complaint. Assistant District Attorney Bill Alexander is present.

7:55 p.m

Jeannette and Virginia Davis, residents near the Tippit murder scene, are brought in to the show-up room. Oswald makes his third appearance in a lineup. The Davises identify Oswald as the man they saw unloading a pistol as he came across their yard immediately following the shooting.

8:55 p.m.

Detectives J. B. Hicks and Robert Studebaker take Oswald to the Homicide and Robbery Office for fingerprinting. A few minutes later, Detective Pete Barnes comes in, and the three crime lab men make paraffin casts of Oswald's hands and right cheek. (The tests came back positive for his hands and negative for his right cheek, indicating that Oswald may have fired a pistol but not a rifle.)

9:00 p.m.

Buell Wesley Frazier and his sister, Minnie Randle, are brought in to Homicide and Robbery and give affidavits. Oswald had ridden to the Book Depository with Frazier on the morning of the assassination. Both state that Oswald was carrying a package with him at the time.

9:30 p.m.
Downtown Dallas

An attendant at Nichol's Parking Garage next door to Ruby's Carousel Club receives a phone call from Jack Ruby. Ruby requests the attendant to give one of his strippers, Little Lynn, five dollars in cash, stating he will reimburse him when he comes to the club a short time later. The attendant complies with the request, but asks the stripper to sign a small piece of scratch-pad paper as a receipt for the money. This is the first time Ruby has ever made such a request of the attendant.

Approximately thirty minutes to an one hour later, Ruby arrives at the garage and reimburses the attendant. In doing so, he also makes an unusual request that the garage attendant stamp Little Lynn's signed receipt in the garage's automatic time clock. Again the attendant complies with Ruby's request and the receipt is dated and timed, "1963 Nov 23 PM 10:33." Ruby leaves the garage and heads for City Hall a few blocks away.

11:00 p.m.
Oswald is placed in a jail cell.

Bethesda Naval Hospital—Bethesda, Maryland
At Bethesda, the autopsy of President Kennedy continues. Nearby, Robert Kennedy and family friends await the results.

Parkland Hospital—Dallas
While we waited for test results, Dr. Duke and I drank coffee, smoked cigarettes, and compared notes on our most amazing day. I remember stopping in the anesthesia call room several times that night to watch the non-stop news coverage of the Presidential assassination. We had seen the undoing of many careers that day, especially those of Secret Service agents. And it was apparent to me that other people, mostly reporters, were capitalizing on the tragedy to further their professions. I do not believe that we at Parkland, and I in particular, fit into that category, as evidenced by my waiting twenty-seven years before writing this book. Most of the doctors who were there are nearing retirement age. If we had intended to use that experience to further our medial opportunities, we would have begun long before now.

When the lab results indicated that Governor Connally's prothrombin time had been reestablished and was within the normal limits, I decided to go home. As I emerged from the hospital and walked into the parking lot, my legs felt weak, and a blustery north wind chilled me down to my bone. But the rawness that troubled me the most had nothing to do with weather. Rather, it had to do with the abrupt change of our government in the time it took to squeeze a trigger.

Orderly succession or not, the United States of America would never again be the same. A new course for the country had already been set in the mind of the new President, who, although a Democrat, had different ideas, opinions, and

---

dreams than his predecessor. I sensed that a day would not go by that I wouldn't, in some way, relive the experience. Yet, I must determine if I was fortunate for the insight and sensitivity that comes from such an ordeal, or cursed with a scarred memory of the horror and fear of it all.

As soon as I arrived at the apartments, neighbors and friends descended upon me to learn what had happened at Parkland. I was very careful about what I told them, because I sensed there would be several accounts of the assassination. More than anything else, I wanted to learn the facts about who had done it and the way it was accomplished before I said too much, even to curious outsiders. The look on the face of the man with the machine gun still bothered me. I didn't want to cross paths with him ever again.

After several hours of giving an edited account of my day, everyone left and my wife went to bed. It was 2:00 a.m. I remember reading a medical journal for about an hour to get my mind off of the assassination. It is difficult to unwind after witnessing the death of the President of the United States. As I read, I asked myself over and over again, "How will you ever top this? Where do you go from here?" The answer that came roaring back each time was, "Back to work in three hours."

Before heading for bed, I turned on the television for a few minutes to find out what was happening. All three networks were still on the air. For the first time, I saw Lee Harvey Oswald and heard how he had allegedly shot the President from the sixth floor of the Texas School Book Depository Building. When they showed the President riding in his limousine, waving to the crowd, it was hard for me to believe that I had, only hours before, watched him die and then embraced his mourning wife.

As I shuffled to the bathroom in the dark, just as I had done twenty-three hours earlier, I was physically and emotionally exhausted. Too soon, I would rise to begin another surgical shift that wouldn't end until Sunday at 9:00 a.m. I stopped and kissed my son on his forehead. Life was zooming by, and I was missing being part of my son's life, but what could I do?

I closed the door, turned on the light, and looked into the mirror. The face staring at me looked ten years older than it had appeared the previous morning. Shaking my head, I mumbled, "Showtime," which now had an entirely new meaning. But little did I know that showtime had only begun.

11:20 p.m.
City Hall—Dallas

Buell Frazier, the Depository employee who had driven Oswald to work on the morning of the assassination, is arrested and brought in for questioning. His rifle, a British 303 Enfield with a fully loaded clip, is confiscated. He receives, and passes, a polygraph examination.

Oswald is removed from his cell and taken to the show-up room for the fourth time. On this occasion he is brought before the news media for a press conference.

Jack Ruby has arrived at City Hall from Nichol's Parking Garage and his strange escapade of having the attendant date and time stamp Little Lynn's five dollar receipt. (In retrospect, this action is an apparent attempt to establish an alibi that will support a lack of premeditation had he been able to murder Oswald at this time. This action is almost an exact duplication of his episode at the Western Union Office on the following morning just before he kills Oswald.)

Through his ownership of the Carousel Club, Ruby is friends with many of the Dallas police officers. This friendship allows him access to areas that are off- limits to other citizens. Now in attendance for Oswald's press conference, he stands on a table at the rear of the show-up room with a *loaded pistol in his pocket.*

Following a brief question and answer session with reporters, Oswald is taken back to his cell. District Attorney Henry Wade remains behind and outlines Oswald's activities and background to the reporters. While doing so, he erroneously states that Oswald was a member of the "Free Cuba Committee." He is quickly corrected by Ruby. From his position at the back of the room, Ruby tells Wade that he means "Fair Play for Cuba Committee." Only a person very familiar with Cuban politics of that period would know the difference between the Free Cuba Committee, an anti-Castro organization, and the Fair Play for Cuba Committee, a pro-Castro network. Ruby's close affiliation with Cuba-connected mobsters, as well as his Cuban gunrunning activities, made him knowledgeable of these politically-opposite organizations.

11:26 p.m.

Chief Curry and Dallas District Attorney Henry Wade decide to file charges against Oswald for the murder of the President. Captain Fritz signs the complaint and gives it to Wade and his assistant Bill Alexander.

CHAPTER 3

Saturday, Nov. 23, 1963

12:10 a.m.
City Jail—Dallas
For apparently the fifth time Oswald is taken to the first floor show-up room. On this occasion he is accompanied by all the detectives in the Homicide and Robbery office as well as numerous other detectives and uniformed officers. He remains there only five minutes. No explanation or reason is given for this action. Was this used as an opportunity to "bug" or search his cell? Or both? He is then taken by elevator to the fourth floor jail for searching (his third) and booking.

12:20 a.m
Oswald is taken to the fifth floor jail and placed in a cell for the night.

1:35 a.m.
According to Police reports, Lee Harvey Oswald is arraigned for the murder of President John F. Kennedy before Justice of the Peace David Johnston. Hours earlier, a complaint against Oswald for the murder of Officer Tippit was processed. Formal arraignment followed just minutes later. However, in the case of the President's murder, formal arraignment does not occur until two hours after the complaint was signed. There is considerable doubt whether he was actually arraigned at all.

If Oswald was arraigned at 1:35 a.m., what was the reason for this long delay? And why was he taken from his cell in the middle of the night? Normal procedure would be to hold the arraignment when court opened on Monday. Of course, Oswald would have been dead by then and Dallas authorities made to look even more inept, their suspect deceased prior to formal charges being filed.

Perhaps Oswald's midnight press conference can shed some light on this puzzle. At that time Oswald was asked by a reporter, "Did you kill the President?" Oswald replied, "I have not been charged with that. *In fact nobody has said that to me yet.* The first thing I heard about it was when the newspaper reporters in the hall asked me that question." Is Oswald feigning ignorance, or had he truly not been informed of his being a suspect in the President's murder?

Dallas police attempted to leave no doubt that they had quickly and efficiently solved the case and that Oswald had been arraigned for President Kennedy's murder. This self-serving effort is categorically disputed by an FBI document that states, "No arraignment of the murder charges in connection with the death of President Kennedy was held inasmuch as such arraignment was not necessary in view of the previous charges filed against Oswald and for which he was arraigned."

3:40 a.m.
White House—Washington, D.C.

The President's body finally arrives at the White House and is taken to the East Room. The original time of arrival had been 10:00 p.m., some nine and one-half hours after the assassination. The scheduled arrival had been moved to 11:00, then 12:00, then 1:00 a.m., then 2:00, then 3:00, before finally reaching the White House at 3:40 a.m. It has been fifteen hours since the shots rang out in Dallas. Queried about the delay, the slain President's chief physician, Dr. George Burkley, responds, "It's taking longer than expected." He was not asked, nor did he offer, to explain what "It" was.

Jacqueline Kennedy accompanies the President's flag-draped casket into the East Room. She is still wearing her blood-stained pink suit, though she has been urged by several people on several occasions to change. She had replied, "No! I want THEM to see what THEY have done."

7:30 a.m.

Oswald awakens to eat breakfast and to resume questioning by various authorities.

Parkland Hospital—Dallas

"What is your name, sir?" a deep, polite voice boomed from the tall policeman.

"Dr. Charles Crenshaw," I replied. "I'm a surgeon at this hospital"

As I reached into my pocket to produce identification, Parkland's assistant administrator, who was standing beside the officer, nodded at him in confirmation, and I was allowed to pass. When I walked through the doorway, the scene in the hallway verified what I had suspected as I had driven into the Parkland's parking lot that it was to be another unusual day.

Automobiles bearing the markings of news organizations, law enforcement departments, and state and federal agencies were everywhere, as were the officials, roaming between the hospital and the medical school vigilantly patrolling the area. Still looming in the minds of the police was the concern of a conspiracy to kill Governor Connally.

Newsmen were frantically perusing the premises for an interview with anyone wearing a white coat. Police worried about security. Medical personnel were trying to provide health care. And the men in suits were still lurking about, cultivating an aura of trepidation and intimidation. They always had the "game face" look of being perpetually pissed off.

"Dr. Crenshaw, tell me about the procedures that you performed on the President," a reported asked, intentionally blocking my path toward the emergency room. Apparently, the news media had identified every doctor who had been in Trauma Room One, and we were being searched out for interviews.

"Did he say anything before he died?" another reporter immediately asked.

"How many times was he shot?" someone else shouted, while more news men gathered around me.

"What is the condition of Governor Connally?" a voice demanded to know.

"Do you believe Oswald shot Kennedy in the back of the head from the Texas School Book Depository Building?" a man with CBS inquired as the cameraman behind him shone lights in my eyes.

The question shocked me. Instantly, a scenario began to form in my mind, and the thought was terrifying. If Lee Harvey Oswald was the lone assassin, they have a lunatic, a madman. But if I tell them the medical truth, that President Kennedy was shot from the front, they have more than one gunman, they have a conspiracy, I thought to myself.

Then I remembered Agent Hill, and how the men in suits had moved the President's body out of Parkland before an autopsy could be performed—how they would have shot Earl Rose and anyone else who had gotten in their way—how the President's limousine had been rushed out of view when the bullet hole in the windshield was noticed by the medical student. The people involved in this game played for keeps. For the first time, I sensed the presence of the pervasive influence of corruption, and it chilled me to the bone.

Just as the film was about to roll, I replied, "An official statement was made yesterday. I have nothing to add. Now, if you would excuse me." With that, I turned and threaded my way through the crowd of people toward the emergency room. At that moment I entered the "conspiracy of silence." I wasn't asked or told to do so, nor was any overt pressure ever placed upon me. I was acting from an instinctive survival feeling, the one that had gotten me through medical school, through internship, and into one of the best surgical residency programs in the country. To do otherwise would have meant saying, "Hell, no, Oswald didn't shoot him in the head, because the President was shot from the front." None of us doctors was willing to do that. We all valued our medical careers too much.

At a news conference in the hospital the previous day, Drs. Malcolm Perry and Kemp Clark suggested that the President must have been turning to his right when he was shot. The reason was that they also believed that the bullet that ripped through President Kennedy's head had entered from the front. When the films showed that the President was not turned when he was shot, nothing more was said, as I remember. I didn't blame Drs. Clark and Perry one bit. They, too, had observed the men in suits, and had heard about the scene with Dr. Earl Rose. Every doctor who was in Trauma Room No. I had his own reasons for not publicly refuting the "official line."

I believe there was a common denominator in our silence a fearful perception that to come forward with what we believed to be the medical truth would mean considerable trouble. Although we never admitted it to one another, we realized that the inertia of the established story was so powerful, so thoroughly presented, so adamantly accepted, that it would bury anyone who stood in its path. I had already witnessed that awesome, dictatorial force in the Earl Rose incident, the same fierceness that I would, for years to come, continue to recognize in the tragedies awaiting those people who sought the truth. I was as afraid of the men in suits as I was the men who assassinated the President. Whatever was happening was larger than any of us. I reasoned that anyone who would go so far as to eliminate the President of the United States would surely kill a doctor.

It wasn't that we doctors had an interest in disputing the one rifle, one man, one assassin theory. We're physicians, not police investigators, and detective work is not our business. But in this case, the medical evidence I saw overwhelmingly disputed what the Warren Commission claimed was the direction from which two of the bullets came that struck the President.

Dr. J. J. Humes, the physician who performed the autopsy

at Bethesda, called Dr. Perry, inquiring about the President's neck wound. Until informed, Dr. Humes was not aware that a bullet had entered the President's throat—only that a tracheostomy had been performed at that spot. After that discussion, we questioned the ability and qualifications of the team that performed the autopsy on the President. We heard reports that those doctors hadn't conducted an autopsy for years. And when I finally saw the official autopsy pictures many years later, I knew something had been askew. If a post-mortem examination had been conducted on President Kennedy at Parkland, more questions would have been raised and the autopsy pictures would have shown a different story, one that would have led the investigation in other directions.

I've often wondered what would have been the consequences of looking directly into that camera and boldly stating, "President Kennedy was shot in the head and in the throat from the front." Now, after all these years, I realize that such courage would have been utterly ineffective and suicidal. The truth, staring directly into the face of our government, stood about as much chance of coming to light as a June bug in a hail storm, and I wouldn't have fared any better.

Already, the eastern press had begun to discredit us as physicians and Parkland as a hospital. If you had any association with Dallas, you were suspect. To come forward and give an unwavering, professional opinion that was contradictory to the official story would only have given them a personalized target. I never understood why the government didn't behave in the same manner, why the press wasn't equally critical, or why the American people didn't condemn Los Angeles when Robert Kennedy was killed as they had Dallas when President Kennedy was assassinated.

The hospital administration was paranoid about publicity, especially at a time like that. In view of all I had heard, seen, and sensed, I wasn't about to appear on the six o'clock news, giving an interview about the death of the President. A nursing student had already fallen into disfavor, and was later thrown out of school, because she informed the press of the number of blood units Connally had received.

Although no official instructions had been issued by the hospital administration, there was a tacit implication, an unspoken warning in their general attitudes that said that anyone who was intelligent enough to pursue a medical career was also smart enough to keep his mouth shut. Failure to do the latter would result in foreclosure on the former. We were all young doctors who for years had struggled and sacrificed to achieve that level of success. And we had a fortune in money and time tied up in our professions. The thought of throwing all that away weighed heavily on my mind.

Avoiding several more reporters, I rushed through the emergency room, past the Obstetrics and Gynecological section, and entered the stairwell that Dr. McClelland and I had descended the previous day on our way to Trauma Room One. I was in a hurry to see how Connally's blood work looked since midnight, and I still had other patients to care for. Newsmen were even camped out on the stairs, waiting for doctors to pass. Two of them followed me up to the second floor.

The scene in the surgical suite was equally chaotic. A Texas Ranger wearing boots and a ten-gallon hat was stationed in the hall just outside the anesthesia call room. He looked eight feet tall. One riot—one Ranger—that was their reputation. Again, I was identified and allowed to pass. I immediately went into the doctors' dressing room and changed my clothes. But looking like doctors didn't exclude us from having to clear every security check point as we moved about the hospital.

Several minutes later, Dr. Shires and I went in to see Governor Connally. His wife was still inside the make-shift, intensive care area. Doctors Shaw and Duke had seen Connally earlier that morning. They had checked his chest tube to make sure his lung was not collapsing. The Governor also was made to cough, to expand his lungs and prevent pneumonia, which was extremely painful because of his shattered rib. Usually, the chief of surgery observes while the resident changes a dressing. But Dr. Shires did it for Connally, and I thought that was appropriate. If I were the Governor, I would expect that level of care. Governor Connally was alert and seemed to be doing well. Each day, he was moved to a different room within ward 2-East to prevent another attempt on his life from a window. But nothing ever happened at Parkland that indicated anyone wanted to harm him. Apparently, his only misfortune had been catching a stray bullet while riding in the same limousine with a man marked for death.

After I looked in on the rest of my patients, I went into the doctors' lounge. All the physicians in there were drinking coffee and talking about the assassination. Down the hall, other doctors were watching as the networks continued to condemn Dallas on television. Everyone was melancholy, in slow motion, still in shock. Parkland had lost the most important patient it would ever have, and Dallas had earned a dubious place in history.

10:30 a.m.
City Hall—Dallas

Oswald is removed from his cell and taken to Captain Fritz's office for his second of five official interrogations. Also present, in addition to Fritz and other homicide officers, were Secret Service Agents Forrest Sorrels and James Bookhout as well as US Marshall Robert Nash.

11:30 a.m.
City Hall—Dallas

Detectives Elmer Boyd, C. N. Dhority, and Ray Hall obtain a search warrant from Justice of the Peace Joe B. Brown, Jr. for Oswald's rooming house. They proceed to the residence and again search Oswald's room.

11:33 a.m.
The second interrogation complete, Oswald is returned to his cell.

12:30 p.m.
Detectives Gus Rose, Richard Stovall, John Aclamcik, and Elmer Moore obtain a search warrant from Justice of the Peace Joe B. Brown, Jr. for the home of Michael and Ruth Paine at 2515 West Fifth Street in Irving. Marina Oswald and the two children have been residing with the Paines since moving from New Orleans. Oswald had spent the previous Thursday night in their home visiting his family. After her husband's arrest, Marina and the children were whisked away into protective custody by the FBI. First, they were sequestered in the Hotel Adolphus, then in the Executive Inn Motel, and finally in the Inn of Six Flags in nearby Arlington. They were not present for this search. The officers seized several articles belonging to Oswald.

12:35 p.m.
Oswald is brought back to Captain Fritz's office for the third interrogation since his arrest. FBI Agent Bookhout and Secret Service Agent Kelly are present as are homicide officers and a man named George Carlston. For the first time Oswald is shown a small snapshot of the soon to become famous photograph of himself holding a rifle, communist newspapers, and with a revolver on his hip. He had no comment.

1:10 p.m.
The interrogation of Oswald is halted and he is taken back to his cell. His wife Marina and mother Marguerite visit him for twenty minutes.

2:15 p.m.
For the final time Oswald is taken downstairs to the show-up room. On this occasion two taxi drivers, William Whaley and W. W. Scoggins,

identify Oswald. Scoggins says that Oswald is the man he saw running from the scene of the shooting of Officer Tippit. Whaley claims Oswald was the passenger he drove from downtown Dallas to Oak Cliff following the assassination of President Kennedy.

3:30 p.m.
Oswald's brother, Robert, arrives at the jail and visits him for five minutes.

3:30 p.m.
County Records Building—Dallas
District Attorney Henry Wade continues working on the Oswald Case.

Parkland Hospital—Dallas
With only three hours sleep since Friday morning, I felt exhausted. So, I was lying down in the resident's call room, dozing. It was the lightest day I could ever remember having at Parkland. The whole city was in shock over the President's death. For the moment, people had quit drinking, stabbing, and shooting.

Just as I was beginning to enter a deeper sleep, the telephone rang. It was the emergency room requesting a doctor come down and examine a man who appeared to be having an attack of appendicitis. The trauma team was in surgery, so they called me because I was in charge of elective surgery "B." I sent a first year resident down to examine the patient. In a few minutes, the resident called me to report that he believed the man needed to be taken to surgery for an appendectomy. I struggled out of bed and trudged down to the emergency room.

The patient was having abdominal pain, but I wasn't convinced that he needed surgery. I decided to observe him for several hours and let his body tell us what to do. Many times at private hospitals, the procedure is to first get the patient comfortable by giving him a pain shot—that's what he's paying for, and that's what he expects. But at an academic hospital, we allow the patient to endure a reasonable amount of pain, if it's necessary, to give us an accurate diagnosis. Pain medication camouflages symptoms, which can waste valuable time and result in incorrect medical treatment, both of which are dangerous to the patient.

6:00 p.m.
City Hall—Dallas

Captain Fritz holds the fourth interrogation of Oswald in his office. Present for this interview are other homicide officers, Secret Service Agent Kelly, and FBI Agent Bookhout. On this occasion Oswald is shown an enlargement of the photograph of himself holding the guns. This time he repudiates its authenticity declaring that the "face is his," but the body was not, and the photo was a composite. He understood photography real well, he said, and in time he would be able to show that it was not his picture.

7:15 p.m.

Oswald is returned to his cell.

9:30 p.m.

Michael Paine gives Detectives John Adamcik and Elmer Moore an affidavit saying he had observed a rifle wrapped in a blanket in his garage on a few occasions prior to the assassination.

Parkland Hospital—Dallas

It took at least five rings for the telephone to penetrate the heavy state of sleep that had gripped me. As I struggled to find my ear with the receiver, I stepped out of my dream and back into Parkland.

"Dr. Crenshaw, I would appreciate your coming down and reexamining the patient with the abdominal pain," came the resident's voice from the black plastic pressed to my head. "His temperature is beginning to rise."

I'll be right there," I uttered lethargically.

Once on my feet, I ran my hands through my hair and splashed some cold water on my face. When I walked from the resident's call room and into the hall, people were wandering around as if they were at an amusement park. Parkland was still in shock and moving in slow motion, just as I was. The hospital remained abuzz with talk about Kennedy. Members of the press continued to roam the halls, looking for interviews and stories.

On my way to the observation area in the emergency room, I stopped in on Governor Connally to make sure he was comfortable and to check the dressing on his leg. As a security measure, all the rooms in ward 2-E had been vacated.

My patient in the Emergency room was still having pain in his right lower quadrant, had a slight temperature, and his white count was increasing, but not yet in the dangerous range. It was still too early to determine if he needed surgery. Many times, patients with these symptoms will suddenly improve without further treatment. If he was having an attack of appendicitis, the signals from his body were not conclusive. Being in pain is not in itself a sufficient reason to cut open the abdomen. First, I must have a confirmed diagnosis.

Before I went back to the second floor, I walked around the Emergency room, marveling at the number of people who were being treated. With so few cases, the chances of getting a good night's sleep were excellent. The President's death had almost brought Dallas to a complete halt.

On my way back to the resident's call room, I took a quick detour into the anesthesia call room and again saw Oswald on television. A reporter was speculating that President Kennedy had been shot three times by Oswald from the Texas School Book Depository Building, and that one of the bullets had gone through Kennedy's body and then hit Governor Connally. When I heard that, I looked at Dr. Red Duke and shook my head in amazement. He returned the gesture. Again, I thought of the opening in the President's throat that was an entry wound. Later, when the "'magic bullet" theory was propagated by the Warren Commission, I immediately concluded that a bullet wouldn't have had the energy to go through that much tissue, cartilage, muscle, and bone of two men, and remain intact. We knew that theory was ridiculous. But that was the story that was being disseminated. It later became the official story.

11:00 p.m.
City Hall—Dallas

Dallas Homicide Captain Will Fritz receives a person-to-person telephone call from new President Lyndon Johnson. He is ordered to stop his investigation. Fritz had been steadily attempting to thoroughly investigate the President's murder despite interference and opposition from Federal authorities. He had received several phone calls urging him to cease the investigation because, "You have your man." Fritz had thus far ignored these cajoles and had continued his investigation. He halted the inquiry only after receiving the President's order. (Years later, reflecting back, Fritz tells close friends, "But when the President of the United States called...what could I do?")

11:44 p.m.
Downtown Dallas

Jack Ruby leaves his Carousel Club and goes to the Pago Club to visit a friend.

Parkland Hospital—Dallas

I called down to the Emergency room to get a report on my patient. The resident informed me that he was asleep, and that his temperature was the same as the last time we had checked. I told him that unless our patient's condition worsened, if he didn't need surgery by nine o'clock in the morning, elective surgery "C" would be on duty and they could take over his case.

CHAPTER 4

Sunday,
Nov. 24, 1963

2:15 a.m.
Dallas Sheriff's Office

Sheriff's officer Perry McCoy receives a phone call from a "white male," who tells McCoy that Oswald is going to be killed during his transfer from the city jail to county jail. The reason for calling, McCoy is told, is that the caller wants the department to have the information so that none of the deputies would get hurt.

2:20 a.m.
City Hall—Dallas

Police Lieutenant Billy Grammar, working in the communications room, also receives a message from an unidentified caller. The caller specifically requests to speak with Grammar after inquiring of another officer as to who is on duty. Refusing to identify himself, the man tells Grammar, "You know me." He then begins to describe the plans for Oswald's transfer in detail and tells the Lieutenant that other arrangements should be made or, "We're going to kill Oswald right there in the basement." The voice of the caller is familiar to Grammar but he is unable to put a face to it. The threat is taken seriously and a report is filed with Chief Curry.

2:30 a.m.
FBI Office—Dallas

An unnamed employee of the local FBI office receives a telephone call from an anonymous male. Speaking in a calm and mature voice, the caller advises that he represented "A committee…we are going to kill the man that killed the President."

3:20 a.m.
City Hall—Dallas

Dallas Police Captain W. B. Frazier receives a call from FBI Agent Milton Newsom informing him that an anonymous threat to kill Oswald was received at the Dallas FBI office.

Parkland Hospital—Dallas

All was quiet at Parkland Hospital, and I was getting some much needed sleep.

6:00 a.m.
Parkland Hospital—Dallas

I awakened at six o'clock that Sunday morning, feeling rested, a sensation that seldom came my way. For a resident surgeon, getting six hours of uninterrupted sleep ranks up there with a raise in salary.

The reporters had already returned to Parkland, and security was still tight. And of course, the ever present men in suits were still there. I put on a fresh scrub suit, went down to the Emergency room, and checked on my patient. I saw no real change in his condition.

I rushed to the cafeteria and ate breakfast, then returned to the second floor to see more of my patients and meet Shires to check on the Governor's condition. He was still being moved from room to room, and protective devices were placed in front of all windows to prevent snipers from shooting into the room.

6:30 a.m.
City Jail—Dallas
Captain Fritz arrives at City Hall in preparation for further questioning of Oswald.

7:00 a.m.
The Dallas police begin preparations for transferring Oswald out the Dallas city jail. The basement is cleared and guards are stationed at the ramps leading into the garage.

9:00 a.m.
Chicago
An officer of the Chicago branch of the American Guild of Variety Artists (AGVA) sends a message intended for Jack Ruby in Dallas. The message reads, "Tell Jack not to send the letter today, it would be awkward in Chicago." AGVA is an entertainer's union long dominated by members of organized crime. Coded language is a common tool of the underworld, and the meaning of this cryptic order has never been adequately explained nor investigated. Whatever its meaning, the orders were never delivered to Ruby.

9:30 a.m.
City Jail—Dallas
At the Dallas Police Department, James R. Leavelle, a homicide detective, recommends to Dallas Police Chief Curry that additional precautions be taken by making Oswald's transfer on the first floor, rather than the basement; that double-crossing the news media will create an effective diversion. Curry tells Leavelle that the television people will be

allowed to document the transfer of Oswald to show that he has not been abused or beaten.

Detectives Leavelle and L. C. Graves are told that they will transfer Oswald to the Dallas County jail. They then remove Oswald from his jail cell and take him to Captain Fritz's third-floor office for further questioning. Present are Captain Fritz, several homicide detectives, Secret Service Agents Forrest Sorrells and Thomas Kelly, and US Postal Inspector Harry Holmes. Chief Curry sits in briefly at the beginning of the interrogation.

Minister Ray Rushing arrives at City Hall and takes the elevator to the third floor. While on the elevator, Rushing meets and talks with Jack Ruby. The minister is one of four witnesses who testified that they had seen Ruby in or near the police building at various times between 8:00 a.m. and 11:00 a.m.

Parkland Hospital—Dallas

Officially, my surgical team was off duty, and elective "C" had begun. I had finished making rounds to see all my patients, including the man in the observation room with the abdomen pain, who I had just turned over to elective "C." We were in the doctor's lounge, drinking coffee, smoking cigarettes. Depending upon one's rank, a doctor very often had to stand while his superiors occupied the limited seating. As a third year resident, I was sitting that morning, along with Drs. Shires, Perry, Jones, and Duke.

Had I not gotten so much sleep the previous night, I would have gone home. But feeling rested, I stayed to talk with my colleagues about the assassination and how Parkland had been taken over by law enforcement officials and the news media. With an air of suspicion and excitement hovering over the hospital, none of us wanted to leave. We felt that Parkland was under siege, and we wanted to protect it. I don't believe Dr. "Red" Duke left the hospital for three days. It was almost as if we sensed that something else would happen, and we residents didn't want to miss it. At that point, nothing would have surprised us.

Also high on the discussion list was Kennedy's autopsy at Bethesda. After Dr. Perry's conversation with J. J. Humes, the doctor who performed the post-mortem examination, we had doubts as to whether they had ever conducted such a procedure. And, although carefully and quietly stated, we were expressing the same views on the direction from which the bullets had been fired that struck President Kennedy and Governor Connally. We never knew if the men in suits might be listening.

10:35 a.m.
City Hall—Dallas

Ira Walker, a WBAP (Fort Worth) television technician, is inside the station's news van at the audio board awaiting Oswald's transfer. The van is located just outside City Hall. Jack Ruby comes up to the window and asks Walker, "Has he (Oswald) been brought down yet?"

11:00 a.m.
Dallas

Rev. William A. Holmes, pastor of the Northaven United Methodist Church, delivers a sermon critical of Dallas. He poignantly states, "President John Kennedy was killed two days ago in Dallas, and the one thing worse than this is that the citizens of Dallas should declare unto the world, 'We take no responsibility for the death of this man'...There is no city in the United States which in recent months and years has been more acquiescent toward its extremists than Dallas, Texas."

After Holmes' discourse was broadcast on "The CBS Evening News" two days later, he receives telephone calls that threaten his life. Agents advise him that he should leave Dallas for several days.

Parkland Hospital—Dallas

Parkland Hospital officials are notified by Bob Struwe, hospital controller, that large crowds have gathered to watch Oswald's transfer.

Before leaving his cell for the basement, Oswald puts on a black sweater to disguise himself since everyone has seen him on television in his clothes. He turns to Leavelle and says, "There ain't nobody gonna shoot me."

11:17 a.m.
City Hall—Dallas

Jack Ruby leaves City Hall, walks a half-block to the Western Union office, and sends a $25.00 money order to Little Lynn, one of his strippers, in Fort Worth. The timing of this transaction, in light of his appearance and disappearance at the *Dallas Morning News* Building at the time of the President's shooting, seems to be another alibi producing maneuver. It eventually served to establish Ruby's lack of premeditation for Oswald's murder. In reality, since the announced transfer time was 10:00 a.m., it also appears likely that Ruby possessed inside knowledge of when Oswald would be moved.

Upon returning the short distance to City Hall, Ruby enters through an unguarded door, proceeds down one flight of stairs to the basement, crosses the parking area, and joins the group of policemen and reporters awaiting Oswald's transfer. His timing could not have been more perfect. As if on cue, Oswald, handcuffed to Detectives Leavelle and Graves, enters the basement area from the adjoining jail office. As an unmarked car backs into position to pick up Oswald and transport him to the county jail a few blocks away, the sound of a car honking echoes through the basement. As Oswald nears Ruby position he appears to glance quickly toward him, then turn away.

Detective Leavelle, cuffed to Oswald's right arm, notices Ruby holding a pistol by his side. He sees Ruby crouch, extend the pistol, and quickly move in on his prisoner, but has no time to react. Ruby, gripping a .38 Colt Cobra pistol tightly in his right hand in an "assassins grip" (a Chicago term for the grip used by an assassin to prevent the weapon from being wrenched from his hand; this grip utilizes the middle finger on the trigger and the index finger on the cylinder above), he fires one shot point-blank into Oswald's left mid-section. Oswald cries out loudly in pain and collapses to the floor.

Detective Graves, escorting Oswald by his left arm, catches only a glimpse of Ruby passing in front of him to deliver the fatal shot. Grasping Ruby's wrist and gun simultaneously, he spins around with the assailant while other officers converge to assist. Together the officers subdue Ruby and wrest the weapon from his hand. In the midst of the struggle Ruby blurts out, "You all know me, I'm Jack Ruby."

Standing nearby, Detective Don Archer witnesses the shooting and assists in apprehending Ruby. He and other officers place Ruby in a fifth-floor cell. Archer, staying behind to guard the prisoner, observes Ruby's strange behavior. Ruby was "very hyper" and "sweating profusely." He had been stripped down for security purposes and his rapid heart beat could readily be seen. Ruby requested and was given a cigarette. Later, word came that Oswald had died as a result of the shooting. Archer conveys this information to Ruby, telling him that, "It looks like it's going to be the electric chair for you." Instead of becoming more agitated, Ruby became calm, ceased perspiring, and his rapid heart beat slowed to normal. Archer then asks Ruby if he would like another cigarette. Ruby replied, "I don't smoke." Ruby's behavior, Archer noted, was a "complete turnaround." It was apparent that his life depended on his getting Oswald.

Parkland Hospital—Dallas

The first year resident on my surgical service called me from the emergency room, advising that the patient with the apparent appendicitis could wait no longer for an appendectomy, that his temperature and white count had increased considerably during the past hour. I told him that if someone would staff "C" service, and would allow him to operate, I had no objections. Several minutes later, they were in surgery. Like most first and second year surgical residents, he was hungry for action.

11:21 a.m.
City Hall—Dallas

Detectives Leavelle and Billy Combest carry Oswald back inside the jail. Fred Bieberdorf, a medical student and city jail medical attendant who is in the basement, gives a cardiac massage when no heartbeat is detected.

Parkland Hospital—Dallas

Elective surgery "C" was operating on the appendectomy patient, and Dr. Jones was staffing the trauma team in surgery. Dr. Shires had just left the hospital, and I was still sitting in the doctor's lounge, talking with Dr. Perry. The telephone rang, and I answered it. On the other end of the call was the hospital administrator, C. J. (Jack) Price. When I identified myself, he asked me who had a free operating team. I told him that there were no available surgical services, that the one that had just come on was in surgery. In a strained voice, he imparted to me that he needed an operating team down in the emergency room immediately. I had never known the hospital administrator to call the doctor's lounge and request a surgical team, and especially in such an anxious voice. So I agreed, and took what was left of surgical service "B," and Drs. Gerry Gustafson and Dale Coln, both residents, and went downstairs. Dr. Perry and the others remained in the doctor's lounge. At that point, none of us knew that Oswald was on his way to Parkland.

11:24 a.m.
City Hall—Dallas

The ambulance arrives at the jail. Oswald is thrown onto a gurney and shoved into the back of the vehicle. Bieberdorf accompanies Oswald to

Parkland, giving heart massage the entire way.

Jack Ruby is taken upstairs at the city jail for interrogation. He reveals that it was his intention to shoot Oswald three times.

Parkland Hospital—Dallas

We were standing in the hallway, just outside Trauma Room One, when Jack Price told us that Lee Harvey Oswald had been shot and was en route to Parkland. I simply could not believe that we were about to treat the alleged assassin of President Kennedy.

I noticed that several nurses were readying Trauma Room One. In perhaps, the most perceptive moment of my life, I turned to the nurse and exclaimed, "In deference to President Kennedy, we will not treat this patient in Trauma Room One. When Oswald arrives, put him in Trauma Room Two." At that time we all assumed that Oswald was the killer of our President.

Price's face lit up in agreement. Immediately, he recognized the long-term significance of that decision. For years, Jack Price has repeatedly expressed to me his appreciation that I had the presence of mind to make that distinction.

Word of Oswald's impending arrival traveled the hospital halls faster than a staph infection. Dr. Ronald Jones was called out of surgery. He rushed down to join me and the rest of our group while we waited for the ambulance to arrive. Dr. Perry remained on the second floor to assemble a surgical team while the operating room was being readied. Having seen the shooting on television, Dr. McClelland rushed out of his Highland Park home and drove to the hospital. And when Dr. Shires heard the news on his radio, he turned his car around and headed back toward Parkland.

11:30 a.m.
Dallas

Dallas police lieutenant Billy Grammer is at home asleep after his night shift duty at police headquarters. He is suddenly awakened by his wife who tells him that a man named Jack Ruby has just shot Lee Harvey Oswald while in the basement of the police station. Only now does a face appear to go with that familiar voice who called earlier, while he was on duty, to warn of Oswald's impending death. He also recalled having unexpectedly met, and talked, with Ruby in a restaurant near the station only a week before. This recollection served to cement his identification of the voice on the phone as being that of Ruby.

11:32 a.m.
Parkland Hospital—Dallas

Lee Harvey Oswald is wheeled into the Emergency room at Parkland Hospital.

As Oswald was rolled into Trauma Room Two, he was deathly pale. I observed that he had dilated pupils, was unconscious and unresponsive, had no palpable pulse, but did have a heartbeat. The bullet had entered his left thorax, traveled through his body, and could be felt just under the skin on his right side. From his bloated abdomen, it was evident that his injury was causing him to continue to lose blood internally.

We quickly cut away Oswald's clothing, underwear and all. Then, while Dr. Jenkins inserted the endotracheal tube, Drs. Coln, Gustafson, and I performed three venous cutdowns, one on each leg and one on the left forearm. I did the one on the right ankle. Without delay, we initiated Ringer's Lactate, then got "O" negative blood flowing into two cutdowns. In violation of hospital policy, but as a measure he believed he had to take if Oswald was to have a chance of surviving, Dr. "Red" Duke had sprinted to the blood bank and collected an armful of "O" negative blood, and returned to the Emergency room without documenting the withdrawal. "O" negative blood is a universal type, and can be given to anyone. I believe that demonstrated the effort we all made to save the man.

Simultaneously, Jones inserted a chest tube and connected it to a closed waterseal drainage bottle to prevent Oswald's left lung from collapsing. A blood sample was sent to the blood bank for immediate typing, the front of the gurney was lowered to help get blood to his heart and brain, and Dr. Bill Risk catheterized him. In record time, only seven and one-half minutes, we had completed the resuscitation procedure and had him on his way to surgery. We all sensed the significance of saving Oswald.

Getting him up to surgery was like a fire drill. At least a dozen of us, entangled in tubes and equipment, pushed the gurney, plus IV stands, and an anesthesia machine down the hall and squeezed into a small elevator. On our way up to surgery, we suddenly stopped on the first floor. As the doors opened, two of Oswald's friends, who were on their way to the emergency room, came into full view. They never knew it was Lee Harvey lying on that cart, because all they saw was a mass of humanity and equipment.

Once on the second floor, we rushed Oswald into the operating room. Drs. McClelland and Shires had not yet arrived, but did so just minutes after the operation began. As we prepared to open Oswald's abdomen, Dr. Duke arrived with a pasteboard box full of type-correct blood units (A-1 Rh negative), which were administrated under pressure through the three cut-downs.

I shall never forget "Red" Duke continuously circling the operating table, carrying that box of blood. Around and around he went, IV pole to IV pole, replacing empty bottles with full ones, while tube bulbs were being squeezed to increase the volume of fluids going into Oswald's circulatory system. If we hadn't had large amounts of blood entering him through the cut-down veins before his abdomen was exposed, his remaining blood volume would have quickly emptied when the incision was made, and he would have bled to death in only seconds.

At 11:44 a.m. twelve minutes after Oswald had been admitted to Parkland, Dr. Perry made a midline abdominal incision that began just below the sternum and extended almost to his pubis. When the peritoneum, an envelope-like lining in the abdomen, was cut, three liters of liquid and clotted blood, three-fourths of Oswald's volume (almost one gallon) gushed from his abdomen like water from a bursting balloon. It went everywhere—on the sheets, on the floor, on us. When the pressure in the abdomen was released, the remaining blood in Oswald's body began rushing into his abdomen through numerous portals.

As I held a retractor with one hand, and suctioned blood from the abdominal cavity with the other hand, Dr. Shires assessed the internal injuries. In a split second, a piece of lead smaller than a thimble had done no less harm to Oswald's abdomen than would several blows with an ax. The bullet had lacerated the aorta and vena cava, shattered the spleen, and slashed through the stomach, pancreas, kidney, liver, and finally lodged in the right lateral body wall. It did about as much damage to the vital organs as one shot can do. I later named it the Parkland shish kebab.

Blood was running and squirting into the abdomen through each of the wounds, especially the spleen, aorta, and the vena cava, which is the large vein running from the abdomen to the heart. Drs. Shires, McClelland, Perry, and Jones were attaching clamps and applying finger pressure to the arteries, veins, and organs to stop the bleeding before they could begin repairing the damage. The scene that day was equivalent to preventing a boat from sinking when it's taking on water, with part of the crew bailing and the others plugging holes.

After the major bleeding had been brought under control,

I looked up and took a deep breath. When I did, I spotted a large man across the room whom I didn't recognize. He resembled Oliver Hardy in a scrub suit with no mask. Most alarming, there was a pistol hanging from his back pocket, and if it had fallen to the floor, it could have discharged and killed someone. I never knew how he got into the operating room or who gave him the scrub suit.

Just two days earlier, a Secret Service agent had rambled through the emergency room waving a gun as the President of the United States lay there, dying. Incredibly, the man who had been accused of shooting President Kennedy was now lying before me, fighting for his life, while another pistol-packing intruder looked on. I didn't know what to think, except that we had to get a cap and mask on the son of a bitch before he contaminated the entire room with bacteria.

I motioned for one of the other resident surgeons to relieve me. I scrubbed out and got the proper attire for the guy. I wanted to throw his ass out of the operating room, but I was afraid he would shoot me. Without saying anything, I handed him the cap and mask. He put it on without comment. As I was turning around, a nurse tapped me on the shoulder and asked if I would take a telephone call in the supervisor's office. She had chosen me to take the call because I was the head of Surgical "B," the team that began the operation. I agreed to answer the call and left the operating room.

When I entered the office, the receiver was lying on the desk.

"This is Dr. Crenshaw, may I help you?"

"This is President Lyndon B. Johnson," the voice thundered. "'Dr. Crenshaw, how is the accused assassin?"

I couldn't believe what I was hearing. The very first thought that I had was, how did he know when to call?

"Mr. President, he's holding his own at the moment," I reported.

"Would you mind taking a message to the operating surgeon?" he asked in a manner that sounded more like an order.

"Dr. Shires is very busy right now, but I will convey your message."

"Dr. Crenshaw, I want a death-bed confession from the accused assassin. There's a man in the operating room who will take the statement. I will expect full cooperation in this matter," he said firmly.

"Yes, sir," I replied and the telephone went dead. I almost laughed in the President's face. If he could have seen the mess in the Operating Room and the condition of our patient, he wouldn't have asked.

As I stood there in a state of disbelief, my mind was racing. First, "death-bed confession" implies that someone is going to die. If Oswald doesn't die on the table, is "Oliver Hardy" or someone else going to kill him?

Second, anyone who knows anything about Texas politics is familiar with the 1948 U.S. Senate race when Johnson defeated Coke Stevenson, and the election improprieties that were documented in South Texas. It occurred to me that if a dead man could vote in Duvall County then, and they were documented as having done so there again in 1960 during the presidential election, why can't a dead man confess to a murder in Dallas County?

And finally, why would the President of the United States personally call the operating room at Parkland Hospital and ask for a death-bed confession? That question still puzzles me now. Why wouldn't someone with the Dallas police or the FBI make that request? Then, more questions followed, inquiries that had frightening, inconceivable answers.

I rushed back into the operating room and approached Dr. Shires. There was blood everywhere, and five sets of hands were working in Oswald's belly.

"You won't believe who I just talked to," I said to Dr. Shires.

He looked at me with a "What's next" expression.

"President Johnson would like for us to allow that man over there to get a statement from our patient."

Shires glanced at "Oliver Hardy," shook his head in disbelief, and returned his attention to the operation. I wish that I could have taken a picture of him as he stood there, covered in blood. It would have been worth an entire library of words in expressing our efforts to save Oswald.

Under the best circumstances, it would have been days before Oswald could have spoken lucidly to anyone. It was ironic. We had a patient on the table under oxygen anesthesia, bleeding to death from a bullet that had penetrated almost every organ in his body, and the President of the United States wanted the intruder with the gun to conduct an interview. The fact that a stranger was in the operating room during surgery, something that would have never been tolerated, best illustrates the hospital's state of confusion at that time.

Only moments later, at 12:37 p.m., almost one hour into the operation, Oswald's heart began to fail. Dr. Akins, the anesthesiology resident reported to the operating team that Oswald's cardiac condition was weakening, and that his pulse rate was slowing. Electrical impulses on the cardioscope confirmed the sudden development. Dr. Shires placed his hand under Oswald's diaphragm to detect heart activity. As everyone looked on in still silence, Dr. Shires shook his head and told Dr. Perry that Oswald's rhythmic cardiac activity had stopped.

I walked over to our visitor with the gun and remarked, "There won't be any deathbed confession today." Like Clint Hill, "Oliver Hardy" disappeared, and I never saw him again. Dr. Perry grabbed a scalpel and cut open Oswald's chest by making an incision between his ribs, exposing the heart. Two injections were immediately administered directly into the heart, as additional drugs were added to the IVs. To overcome the adverse effects of the acid of anaerobic metabolism that had invaded the blood from hemorrhagic shock, we were perfusing

Oswald's system with medication. Only moments later, he went into ventricular fibrillation. His heart was quivering like Jell-O.

While waiting for the voltage to build on the defibrillation machine, Dr. Perry began manual cardiac massage. To no effect, Dr. McClelland pressed the paddles to Oswald's trembling organ and administered a jolt of electric current. Again, he embraced the heart with the conductors and applied a shock, this time stronger than the previous one. The muscle jumped, but it was to no avail. In spite of escalating the voltage each time, Dr. McClelland could not restart the heartbeat. Dr. Perry again administered manual cardiac massage, but Oswald's color had turned blue because of the lack of oxygen. Dr. Shires examined his eyes. His lenses were opaque. It was 1:07 p.m., and Lee Harvey Oswald was dead.

For several moments we stood there in silence, gazing at a dead man who had possibly taken the secrets and evidence of Kennedy's assassination to the grave. Outside of President Kennedy, this was the one patient we did not want to lose. We thoroughly believed that we had a chance to save Oswald. Had the ambulance that brought him to Parkland been furnished with equipment and emergency medical technicians to administer oxygen through an endotracheal tube and dispense Ringer's Lactate through IV's, resuscitation could have occurred at the scene of the shooting.

Oswald did not die from damaged internal organs. He died from the chemical imbalances of hemorrhagic shock. From the time he was shot, 11:21 a.m., until the moment fluids were introduced into the body through cutdowns, 11:40 a.m., there was very little blood circulating in Oswald's body. As a result, he was not getting oxygen, and waste built up in his cells. Then, when the fluids were started, the collection of waste from the cells was dumped into the bloodstream, suddenly increasing the acid level, and delivering these impurities to his heart. When the contaminated blood reached the heart, it went into arrest, then cardiac arrhythmia, and finally fibrillation. The drugs that were injected directly into Oswald's heart were intended to stabilize the muscle, but the damage couldn't be reversed. His heart had stopped and couldn't be started again.

If Ringer's Lactate had begun flowing into Oswald when the ambulance arrived at the police station, he would not have been without circulation for twenty minutes, the waste would not have built up in his cells, and his heart, in all probability, wouldn't have stopped. If today's emergency care had been available in 1963, Lee Harvey Oswald could have lived, because he would have been brought into the hospital in a more stable condition. All the damage caused by the bullet could have been repaired with every expectation of a full recovery.

While the bullet was removed from Oswald's right side and turned over to the legal authorities waiting outside the operating room, we began preparing to go downstairs to a conference room packed with journalists eagerly waiting to get word on Oswald's condition. I gave Dr. Shires a clean, white coat. His was covered with blood.

We dreaded going into the news conference and reporting the death of President Kennedy's accused assassin. When we entered the room, our solemn glares told the story. Doctors are notorious for maintaining "game faces" (somberness) in the full view of adversity, but there must have been a clear message in the way we looked that afternoon. Those reporters knew Oswald was dead before a word was ever spoken.

Dr. Shires walked to the microphone. We were standing directly behind him. He announced that the accused assassin, Lee Harvey Oswald, had expired at 1:07 p.m., while in surgery; that everything humanly possible was done to save him, but that the adverse effects of hemorrhagic shock could not be overcome. Then Dr. Shires asked if there were any questions.

Of all that had happened during those three days, the very first inquiry by a newsman on the first row may have topped it all. He asked, "Doc, is he dead?" From that moment on, my impression of the press took a steep dive. Other, more intelligent, questions were along the lines of wanting to know if Oswald had said anything before he had died, and why he couldn't be saved.

It's amazing to me that, during those three days, we treated hundreds of people who were wheeled into the emergency room, so mangled and torn that death should have been certain. But someway, most of them managed to live. Yet, we could not salvage the life of the President or his accused assassin.

For years, I have replayed our performance that weekend in 1963, and I keep coming to the same conclusion—neither of them could be saved. Parkland had superlative surgeons, state-of-the-art equipment, and it was an early Mecca of medical research for trauma. I'm convinced beyond any doubt that President Kennedy or Lee Harvey Oswald, in the same condition that we received them in at Parkland, would have died in any hospital in the world.

When Dr. Shires had concluded the meeting, I ducked out a back exit and headed for the parking lot. All the way to my car, reporters were at my heels, requesting an interview and barking questions. Ignoring all their attempts to get a story from me, I jumped into my automobile and drove home. When I arrived at my apartment, I found the place full of people—more bedlam. All my neighbors, friends, and in-laws were there, waiting to quiz me on every detail of the previous three days. And again, I carefully chose my words to tell them almost nothing, for I never knew when one of the men in suits might be just outside my window, listening.

3:00 p.m.
Washington, D. C

Walter Jenkins, President Johnson's assistant and right-hand man, converses by phone with FBI director J. Edgar Hoover. Hoover tells Jenkins, "There is nothing further on the Oswald case except that he is dead…Oswald having been killed today, after our warnings to the Dallas Police Department, was inexcusable. It will allow, I am afraid, a lot of civil rights people to raise a lot of hell because he was handcuffed and had no weapon. There are bound to be some elements of our society who will holler their heads off that his civil rights were violated—which they were." (Emphasis added)

Dallas—FBI Headquarters

FBI Special-Agent-in-Charge J. Gordon Shanklin calls Agent James Hosty into his office. Shanklin is holding the note Oswald had delivered to the agency a couple of weeks before the assassination. He passes it to Hosty and says, "Here, get rid of it." Hosty, obeying his superior, takes the note to the toilet and flushes it down the commode. The existence of the note was kept secret until twelve years after the President's murder. Its contents have never been revealed. (Only two things can really be surmised about the contents of the note. One, it would not have helped point the finger of guilt at Oswald, and two, it would have caused the FBI great embarrassment.)

And it was this agency, the FBI, which was given "full responsibility" for the investigation of the murders of John Kennedy and Lee Oswald by the new President, Lyndon Baines Johnson.

Evening
Home—Dallas

I wanted to know what the networks were saying about Oswald, Parkland, and Dallas, but there were too many people in the house to turn on the television. By 10:30 p.m., everyone had left and the telephone finally stopped ringing. At last, I was sitting alone in my living room, my shoes off, and a cold beer in my hand. Earlier that day there had been advertisements for a program that was to air immediately after the late news and would be a synopsis of the events over the past three days. I turned on the Sylvania, propped my feet, and lit a cigarette.

The program opened with a film clip of President Kennedy and Jacqueline in Fort Worth at the Hotel Texas. From there, their path was documented to Love Field in Dallas. As the scene changed to show the motorcade traveling through downtown Dallas, I began to feel anxious. When I saw the Presidential limousine approaching the Texas School Book Depository, my body stiffened.

Several minutes later the focus of the program changed to Oswald. It showed him being arrested. He told a newsman that he hadn't shot President Kennedy. Then the camera switched to two men escorting Oswald into the basement of the Dallas city jail, the narrator explaining that the accused assassin was being transferred to the county jail. Suddenly, a man in a hat lunged from the crowd of people and shot Oswald. I simply could not believe what my eyes had witnessed. I remember the grimace on Oswald's face. He had good reason to exhibit pain. I had seen what the bullet from that gun had done to his abdomen.

Treating trauma victims is bad enough without also seeing the barbaric acts inflicted upon them. Having seen all I could stand, I turned off the television and went to bed. Even after closing my eyes, I continued to see the images and events of the past three days in vivid detail against a black background—insanity in silhouette.

CHAPTER 5

Twenty-Six Years Later

O ne summer evening in 1989 before I wrote this book, I was attending a medical meeting in downtown Dallas. When it had concluded, I began my drive back to Fort Worth. I was headed west on Elm Street, which ties into Stemmons Expressway that leads north to Parkland Hospital. Being almost midnight, there was very little traffic. As I approached the Texas School Book Depository Building at the comer of Houston and Elm, I got the same eerie feeling I always have when I pass by that location. I parked and got out of my car. Although I have driven by it hundreds of times, it was the first time that I had actually stopped and walked the journey. Perhaps I had avoided it because of the memories that had lingered for so many years.

Even at the late hour, several people were milling around that fateful spot. Day or night, someone is always there, going through the same routine, looking up at the sixth floor from where shots were fired, then staring at the grassy knoll, from where possibly more shots were fired.

I parked my car and began making the one-half block pilgrimage down descending Elm street until I reached the exact location where the President had been shot. I got a chill that began at the back of my neck and ran down to my toes.

Imagination took over. I looked up at that sixth floor and saw a man with a rifle. Turning to the grassy knoll, I heard shots, and saw the President clutch his throat and lean slightly forward. Then more shots ring out. Connally grimaces with pain, collapsing into his wife's lap, just before the President's head explodes and recoils backward from the force of the missile. In a second, in my minds eye, I saw the events unfold, people screaming, blood, brains, utter bedlam.

"Good evening," a young man standing beside me whispered, as if speaking at a normal volume would have been disrespectful.

Escaping the mirage of Kennedy's limousine disappearing into the triple underpass, I replied, "Hello, do you come here often?"

"No, this is my first time. I'm from Wisconsin." He hesitated for a moment as he glanced up at the sixth floor of the Texas School Book Depository Building. "I have to leave early in the morning, and I wanted to be here just for a few minutes."

"What do you think happened?" I asked.

"Lee Harvey Oswald shot President Kennedy from up there," he replied confidently, while pointing to the famous window.

"What about there," I asked while pointing to the grassy knoll area? He shrugged in indifference.

"Where were you on November 22, 1963," I continued.

"In a baby bed, probably," he answered, then chuckled. "Where were you?"

"Me?" I hesitated for several seconds. "I was working in a hospital, watching a man die. I'm a doctor."

"Who do you think really killed him?" he asked.

"I don't know."

The young man smiled and nodded good-bye, then turned and left. His question continued to reverberate through my mind. Who killed John F. Kennedy?

The passing of twenty-eight years have not softened the horror of those moments, nor diminished the troubling images of that weekend in 1963. A thousand times a thousand, I have relived that terrible hour when I stood, helplessly watching the last drops of life seep from the President's body. Then, two days later, we tried to save Lee Harvey Oswald after he had essentially bled to death before being rolled into the emergency room.

More disturbing than the images of President Kennedy are the questions about President Johnson. Why did he insist that Kennedy's body be placed on board Air Force One before returning to Washington? Why did he personally call Captain Will Fritz of the Dallas Homicide Department telling him that he had his man, and that no further investigation was needed? Why did he personally call Parkland about a confession from Oswald? Why would a President with the immediate and monumental task of taking over the United States government involve himself in a matter that should have been routinely handled by the law-enforcement agencies? Why did he usurp the authority of the Texas officials and place the responsibility for the investigation in the hands of a personal crony, FBI head J. Edgar Hoover? No doubt, the operations of murder and cover-up required no less than a sovereign figure who, first, had the influence, power, and knowledge to carry out the deed. Second, and more difficult, such a person must cover up the act through the manipulation of information. Only one man had such power on November 22, 1963, and he became President of the United States. Paramount to this operation of obscurity was the appointment of the Warren Commission and the locking up of vital information for seventy-five years—both of which were the acts of Lyndon Baines Johnson.

And above all, what was meant by Johnson's curious and perhaps prophetic pronouncement, seven months before the trip to Texas when he said "...the President of the United States is like a pilot and the election is when the Nation picks an airplane and a pilot for the next four years. Once you pick him, and you're flying across the water in bad weather, don't go up and open the door and try to knock him in the head. He's the only pilot you have, and if the plane goes down, you go with it. At least wait until next November before you shoot him down." November 1963 was not a presidential election year, and

Johnson, an extremely experienced politician, knew it.

Parkland Hospital was placed in the untenable position of bringing back to life two important men who had been afforded the most inept and incompetent protection ever provided. In the President's case, the Secret Service agents assigned to him had gotten drunk the evening before he was shot. As for Oswald, the Dallas police allowed a virtual gangster to stand within only a few feet of the man accused of assassinating the President of the United States.

We did all we could do for those two men. We did all anyone could do, but the dead cannot be made to walk again. President Kennedy was neurologically dead when he was wheeled into Parkland. In the case of Oswald, had the modern day emergency medical system been available, he could probably have lived. Now, ambulances fully furnished with state-of-the-art resuscitation equipment are dispatched to the victim within three minutes, the most critical time period for a trauma injury. Thanks to skilled paramedics and medical technicians, the patient receives the same treatment at the accident scene that he would at Parkland Hospital. Ringer's Lactate applied through IV's, electrocardiograms, shocks to the heart, and constant communication with a physician in the emergency room at the hospital enable the medical personnel to provide life-saving care that could have made the difference in Oswald.

More frustrating than the assassination itself was the behavior of the government and the people who blamed Parkland for both deaths. This, as well as the deceit of the Warren Report, are the reasons I decided to research and then write this book. Had I not been in those emergency rooms and experienced the subsequent intimidation and criticism, I would have never made the commitment to tell the story.

That the real story has not been told is a tragedy. The thought of a conspiracy to kill the President, plus the power to obscure it through the Warren Commission, led me to the obvious conclusion—people within our government, in concert with the "silverfish"' of our society, murdered the President of the United States. It was a coup d'etat—no better than a thirty-second revolution in a third-rate country, a thousand of which have been seen on the movie screen which bring thoughts of "never in America."

In the case of the physicians and medical personnel at Parkland Hospital, the conspiracy of silence was a mixture of fraternal doctrine, naïveté, fear and career-mindedness. This career-mindedness can best be summarized in Dr. Charles Baxter's decree that, "We made an opening statement to everybody concerned that if anybody on the medical side ever made a dime off the assassination, we'd see to it that they never went anywhere in medicine again, because that's how strongly we felt that this was a private thing."

The true conspiracy of silence and the fraternal doctrine that gives it life is found more explicitly in the action and inaction of other groups and individuals connected in some way to the President's death. Included in, but not limited to, this association are the President's family and aides, the new President and his aides, government employees, military officials, the FBI, the Secret Service, the CIA, Texas Law Enforcement personnel, local and national news media, Dealey Plaza witnesses, Jack Ruby's and Lee Harvey Oswald's friends and acquaintances, as well as the military pathology team and its witnesses.

Think of this collection of people, organizations, and events as a mass of spaghetti, each strand representing someone or something related to John F. Kennedy's death. So entangled and convoluted are they that it is almost impossible to trace any one element or person to a conclusion. There is no beginning or ending—no clear path progressing to a final resolution—just more leads twisted around dead ends that disappear into a pile of confusion.

Many of the people in these groups knew they were telling lies which were accepted as facts; they knew that their silence was ordered, they knew that the evidence was fabricated, falsified, and destroyed, and they knew that witnesses were intimidated, ignored, and inadequately interrogated.

On the Phil Donohue Show, Richard Helms, former CIA director, provided us with a rare and revealing glimpse into the reality of this phenomenon when he answered the question: Why don't people speak up? "People don't speak up at the time for several reasons," Helms said. "One, they don't know the facts at the time. Secondly, in all of these cover-ups—for example the Secret Service knew all about John Kennedy's womanizing—but they had a conspiracy of silence. Why? Because they worked for John F. Kennedy! It is very difficult in real time to get people to talk, particularly when there may be sanctions against them—and the young lady who is twenty-five, who wants to take on one of these powerful figures sometime by saying something she knows about them, does so at her own peril. Ahhh, I don't want to emphasize that anything damaging is going to be done to her, but by the time the newspapers, or somebody, gets through with her she'll wish she hadn't done it." (Emphasis added)

From the silence of the people involved came a great miscarriage of justice, and an almost complete loss of faith by the American people in their government and its agencies. Due to their active or passive participation in the continuing cover-up, we are faced, twenty-eight years after the fact, with the still unsolved murder of one of the world's leaders. The assassination was a brutal action that changed our domestic and foreign policy, and reshaped history. The individuals involved in this conspiracy of silence are neither heroes nor great Americans. At best, they may be considered cowards...at worst, co-conspirators or accessories after the fact. This conspiracy must end.

CHAPTER 6

The Empire
Strikes Back, 1992

When this book was first released in April 1992, it received immediate national attention. Television, radio and print media carried the story nationwide. My appearance on the ABC-TV show "20/20" alone was estimated to have reached into 19 million American homes. Because of this widespread publicity, the book quickly made the *New York Times* bestseller list. It would remain there for eight consecutive weeks, two of those as the number one seller.

Never in our wildest dreams had my two co-authors, Jens Hansen and J. Gary Shaw, and I anticipated such a reception. Personally, I had felt all along that my first hand account concerning that fateful and historic weekend was good human interest, and that my personal recollections and reflections—impressions I had struggled long and hard to make exact—would be warmly received by an American public tired of the same old rehash of events. We also strongly believed that the American people deserved that for a change. My two co-authors and I were elated about our work. Others, as we quickly learned, were not so excited.

When we wrote *JFK: Conspiracy of Silence,* as this book was originally called, we poked a pointed stick into the eye of a national lie. Little did we realize that we had so surprised and infuriated a sleeping, insidious monster, full of arrogance and rage. After twenty-nine years of cover-up, this book apparently represented one of the greatest threats to exposing at least part of the truth in what has become America's black eye—a wound that will never begin to heal until our government admits that Lee Harvey Oswald did not act alone, if he acted at all, in killing one of our greatest presidents. Still so protected are the perpetrators, as well as the spector of this timeless event, that not even the passing of three decades has lessened the viscousness with which they will assault anyone daring to throw light on this subject shrouded in darkness.

As Shakespeare so poignantly illustrated, perpetrating a lie is like spinning a web. As the desperation grows to conceal the deceit, so does the size and complexity of the snare, until it becomes increasingly difficult to escape the sticky convolution of untruths. And only by continuing to weave more lies can entrapment be avoided. Such was the John Kennedy assassination and the years of cover-up that followed.

The original plan of my co-authors and I was to present this true story concerning the events surrounding November 22, 1963 in a simple, inexpensive, easy-to-read book; one of which would be available to the great majority of the American public. Our general feeling was that the majority of the public were neither JFK assassination critics nor researchers, and that too many voluminous, heavily detailed and expensive works on the subject were already in print. What was needed, we postulated, was a simple approach to the subject, a book that everyone could read, understand, and afford. That this undertaking came to fruition following the theater run and attending publicity of Oliver Stone's popular and award-winning movie JFK can only be classified as nothing short of miraculous. More importantly, the book's contents had been kept relatively secret until right up to time for its publication. Therefore, its release, and immediate publicity and popularity, appeared to catch the defenders and apologists of the official version of the assassination completely by surprise.

The allegations and accusations leveled at me and the book

were fast and furious, and seemed to come from every direction. That some of these came from a few of my former colleagues was both surprising and personally disheartening. My co-author, J. Gary Shaw, had warned me several times during the preparation of the book that I should anticipate such an attack. "There is," he said, "a long history of this type of counter-attack with regard to the critics of the official version of the JFK assassination."

A Blueprint for Countering Critics

These attacks, I learned, were not uncommon. In fact, when it comes to criticism of the Warren Commission's findings, they are the norm. Anyone, it appears, who receives widespread media attention for a dissident view and believable alternative to the official line is quickly branded as a conspiracy theorist or "buff" who is capitalizing on a tragedy strictly for financial gain. These allegations and accusations follow an all too familiar pattern, one that was laid out and observed in detail over the past 30 years of dissent.

By late 1966, three years after the President's assassination and two years after the issuance of the Warren Report, several books had appeared challenging the government's official conclusions. It appears that the first agency to take note of this, and quickly order a counterattack, was the CIA. In early 1967, the agency, under Director Richard Helms, circulated a detailed memorandum to its various stations with instructions on how to counter this criticism, and more especially, how to impugn the integrity of the critics. Dated April 1, 1967, the memo is entitled: "COUNTERING CRITICISM OF THE WARREN REPORT" and is identified as CIA DOCUMENT NUMBER 1035-960. It was released under a Freedom of Information Act lawsuit in September 1976. The memo outlines the plan of attack to be utilized by the agency in an all-out effort to shore up the already sagging public trust in the conclusions of the Warren Report.

The CIA's "concern," as outlined in this 1967 memo, was that, "From the date of President Kennedy's assassination on, there has been speculation about the responsibility for his murder. Although this was stemmed for a time by the Warren Commission report [which appeared at the end of September 1964], various writers have now had time to scan the Commission's published report and documents for new pretexts for questioning, and there has been a new wave of books and articles criticizing the Commission's findings. In most cases the critics have speculated as to the existence of some kind of conspiracy, and often they have implied that the Commission itself was involved..."

The stated purpose of the 1967 CIA memo was "... to provide material for countering and discrediting the claims of the conspiracy theorists..." The memo went on to outline several courses of action to be taken in order to counter this "concern." Agents were ordered to "... discuss the publicity problem with liaison and friendly elite contacts (especially politicians and editors), pointing out that the Warren Commission made as thorough an investigation as was humanly possible, that the charges of the critics are without serious foundation, and that further speculative discussion only plays into the hands of the opposition..." They were also told to "... employ *propaganda assets* to answer and refute the attacks of the critics" and that "... book reviews and *feature articles* are particularly appropriate for this purpose ..." The memo went on to state that "... our play should point out, as applicable, that the critics are (i) wedded to theories adopted before the evidence was in, (ii) politically interested, (iii) *financially interested,* (iv) hasty and inaccurate in their research, or (v) *infatuated with their own theories...*" (Emphasis added).

Notice that the memo instructs recipients of the memo to "provide material," utilize "editors," employ "propaganda assets," and use "feature articles" in countering the critics.

Notice also, that the attack is to be directed primarily toward the Warren Commission critic and his motive rather than toward his allegations. This agenda has become the most commonly used ploy with respect to critics of the official version of the assassination—always attack the messenger rather than his message—for to do otherwise might cause confrontation with the real issue—and perhaps truth.

If this approach sounds all too familiar, it should. It is the exact blueprint used to attack both past and present Warren Commission critics, including Jim Garrison, Oliver Stone and his movie JFK, and now me. This does not imply in any way that the CIA is the only force at work in attempting to counter and discredit critics of the Warren Report. However, it does indicate that their well-thought-out agenda is still being utilized to defend the much-maligned and heavily flawed official version of the assassination.

The Counter-Attack Begins

The FBI was the first to speak out against our book. On April 8, 1992, a few days after my initial appearances on national television, the *Dallas Morning News* published an interview with Oliver "Buck" Revell, then director of the Dallas-based FBI division. Revell, it tuns out, was well acquainted with the JFK assassination. At the time of the President's death he was still in the Marine Corps and had been assigned to the FBI as the Marine Corps liaison to the FBI to help in its investigation of accused assassin Lee Harvey Oswald. A year later, in November 1964, he became an agent for the bureau.

In the late 1970s, Revell was serving as assistant director of criminal investigations in Washington, D.C. In this capacity, he worked with ranking members of the House Select Committee on Assassinations and was later responsible for follow-up investigations based on the committee's findings of "probable conspiracy." Revell, who is considered a Hoover protégé, had been transferred to the Dallas office in June 1991. Prior to his coming to Dallas, he had worked directly under FBI Director William Sessions in Washington as the bureau's third in command. The timing of his transfer could be significant, for it came on the heels of publicity surrounding the filming in Dallas of Oliver Stone's blockbuster movie *JFK*.

In the wake of the attention generated by Stone's *JFK* and our book, Revell publicly claimed that "there is no evidence of any conspiracy" in the assassination. He told the *Dallas Morning News* that "...the documentation does not show that the doctor [Crenshaw] was involved in any way. I'm very dubious as to his [Crenshaw's] motivations and whether or not he has any factual information to add to the investigation. But we'll wait and see. Until the FBI can examine Dr. Crenshaw's theory as set out in his new book and national television appearances, the FBI will not interview him."

Notice that Revell, in an obvious attempt at further denigrating my story, labeled the book "Crenshaw's theory." Of course, had he read the book he would have known that it does no theorizing. In truth, it is the Warren Report that presents a theory—and not a very good one at that.

Revell, of course, followed the "plan," and in good ol' FBI fashion, chose to cast aspersions on me and my motives rather than look at what I am on record as saying. In typical fashion, Revell countered my story following the well established guideline: if you cannot answer the allegations, then make allegations; if you cannot refute the message, then attack the messenger. These are lessons well taught by Revell's old boss, J. Edgar Hoover, and Revell appears to have learned them well.

A Warren Commission Apologist Speaks Out

A few weeks later, on May 17, 1992, the *Dallas Morning News* published an interview with David W. Belin, a Des Moines, Iowa, attorney who had served as counsel for the Warren

Commission in 1964 and executive director to the Rockefeller Commission investigating the CIA in 1975. In the interview, when asked his opinion of me, Belin replied that he thought the press should "demand" of me, "...full financial disclosure. Because hundreds of thousands and millions of dollars have been made out of the assassination."

When Belin, was asked, "What's your financial interest?" he piously replied, "None. All of my royalties from my two books about the assassination have been turned over to charity. I have not made one dollar out of the assassination. I've made my financial disclosure. Let Dr. Crenshaw make his."

Belin, of course, was paid counsel for his work on both the Warren and Rockefeller Commissions.

The American Medical Association Joins the Attack

On May 19, 1992, a few weeks after the release of the original book, I received a major attack initiated by the most unlikely, and completely unexpected source: the prestigious, powerful, and very influential *Journal of the American Medical Association (JAMA)*, the official scientific publication of the American Medical Association (AMA). In a major news conference, carried nationwide, *JAMA* editor Dr. George Lundberg announced that the May 27, 1992 issue of *JAMA* would contain two articles dealing with the medical aspects of the assassination of President John F. Kennedy.

Both articles were written by Dennis L. Breo. The first, entitled "JFK's Death—The Plain Truth from the MDs Who Did the Autopsy," drew on interviews with two of President Kennedy's autopsy pathologists, Dr. James J. Humes and Dr. J. Thornton Boswell. The second article, "JFK's Death—Dallas MDs Recall Their Memories," was said to be based on interviews with four of the Dallas doctors who participated in the treatment of President Kennedy at Parkland Hospital just minutes after he was shot. Both of these articles contained attacks on me and my book.

Apparently Drs. Perry, Carrico, Jenkins and Baxter chose to participate in an article which distorted the facts of this case. However, a record concerning the wounds of President Kennedy had already been created—a record began just after doctors saw the body, a record sworn to under oath. This record describes a large wound at the rear of President Kennedy's head, the same wound which I wrote about in *JFK: Conspiracy of Silence*. This record also describes a small wound in the front of the throat, just as I saw and described. One of the doctors (Perry) called this an entrance wound within two hours of seeing it, and another (Baxter) admitted in 1992 that it could have been an entrance wound. This record further describes cerebellar tissue extruding from the head wound, just as I described it in my book.

And what of the autopsy photographs? Those of the back of President Kennedy's head show no wound where they (and I) saw a large wound. My detractors say these photos are compatible with their observations. I say the autopsy photographs cannot be reconciled with what I saw at Parkland. Those of President Kennedy's throat show a defect more than twice as long as the tracheotomy incision I remember, and more than twice the length these doctors had earlier estimated. They say the photograph is "very compatible" with what they saw at Parkland on November 22.

This record, standing in stark contrast to the statements the four doctors are quoted as having made in the May 1992 *JAMA* article, will not go away. It's a pity that Dr. Lundberg, Dennis Breo and *JAMA* chose to ignore that record.

Without ever having talked with me, *JAMA* editor Dr. George Lundberg, prominently positioned behind the official seal of the American Medical Association, told the *New York Times* that my book was "a sad fabrication based on unsubstantiated allegations." In contrast, he proclaimed the information in the *JAMA* article to be "scientifically sound," furnishing "the definitive history of what happened," and proving "irrefutable proof that President Kennedy was killed by two bullets that struck him from above and behind."

A Local Newspaper Ads Their Denouncement

Another attack against me and this book came one month after the appearance of the *JAMA* articles. Apparently drawing encouragement from the denouncements of the FBI, Belin, and *JAMA,* the June 28, 1992 edition of the *Dallas Morning News* carried a stinging editorial attack by freelance journalist Larry Sutherland. This latest attack accused me of "peddling lies," denounced me for making "asinine comments," questioned my credibility, and endorsed the allegation of a former colleague that my motives for writing the book had been my "desire for personal recognition and monetary gain."

Without exception, each of the allegations and accusations made against me and this book are demonstrably untrue.

Last Word

I believe that powerful forces assassinated President Kennedy in 1963 and that influential bodies have lied to the American people about the circumstances of—and responsibility for—that murder. Something is terribly wrong in this country when these forces continue to orchestrate, 30 years after the fact, a concerted effort to perpetuate this lie. It is not un-American to demand answers as to why, and by whom.

My book was not written as a historical treatise but as the recollection of a major event in my life, one that affected me, the history of our nation, and the world. I was there thirty years ago. I saw the hole in the back of President Kennedy's head, as did Drs. Perry, Clark, Baxter, and others. And that is what serves as a threat to the cover-up. My book got too close to them—too close to the truth—and there was a reaction, a recoiling by the conspiracy, like fire in a snake pit. These attacks appear to have been another example of unjustified and defamatory remarks intended to enhance the highly controversial "official" version of John F. Kennedy's assassination, thereby perpetuating the "conspiracy of silence."

CHAPTER 7

On the Trial of the Character Assassins

BY D. BRADLEY KIZZIA

Good name in man and woman, dear my lord,
Is the immediate jewel of their souls;
Who steals my purse steals trash; 'tis something, nothing;
'Twas mine, 'tis his, and has been slave to thousands;
But he that filches from me my good name
Robs me of that which not enriches him,
And makes me poor indeed.

Othello (1602-4) act 3, sc. 3, 1.155

On May 19, 1992, the American Medical Association hosted a press conference in New York City to promote two related articles in *JAMA*'s May 27th edition concerning the assassination of President Kennedy. At the press conference, *JAMA*'s then editor, George Lundberg alleged that Dr. Crenshaw's book was a "sad fabrication based upon unsubstantiated allegations." Mr. Dennis Breo, a *JAMA* writer, was identified as the author of the articles, which erroneously suggested that Dr. Crenshaw's observations, as contained in his book, should not be relied upon because Dr. Crenshaw may not have even been in Parkland Hospital's Trauma Room One at the time that emergency treatment was provided to President Kennedy. The press conference received massive media attention, and the *JAMA* articles were widely distributed. References to the press conference and the *JAMA* articles were even made on the network news and on the front pages of major newspapers across the country.

On May 20, 1992, the day after the *JAMA* press conference, the *New York Times* published an article written by Lawrence Altman, M.D., describing *JAMA*'s "research [as] less than thorough," and pointing out that testimony to the Warren Commission clearly indicated that Dr. Crenshaw had been in Trauma Room One and participated in the efforts to save President Kennedy. Dr. Crenshaw thereafter requested that *JAMA* publish a retraction and apology. This request was denied, but Dr. Crenshaw was encouraged to submit his own piece for publication in *JAMA,* which he did. Dr. Crenshaw's rebuttal piece, which was entitled "Let's Set the Record Straight: Dr. Charles Crenshaw Replies," was refused publication by *JAMA* as allegedly being too long (even though it was barely one half the length of Mr. Breo's articles in the May 27, 1992 issue of *JAMA*), but Dr. Crenshaw was then encouraged by *JAMA* to submit a 500-word letter to the editor. Although believing that a mere 500-word letter would be insufficient to rectify the damage done to his reputation, Dr. Crenshaw nevertheless did submit a 500-word letter to the editor of *JAMA*; but again, *JAMA* did not publish it. In April, 1993, almost a year after the publication of the *JAMA* articles that attacked Dr. Crenshaw and the original version of this book, *JFK: Conspiracy of Silence,* after no apology, retraction, or even correction or clarification having been published by *JAMA*, litigation was instituted.

The Suit

A defamation suit was filed on behalf of Dr. Crenshaw and Mr. Shaw against the American Medical Association, d/b/a *Journal of the American Medical Association*, George Lundberg, M. D., Dennis Breo, and others, in the 18th District Court of Cleburne, Johnson County, Texas (Shaw's county of residence), in Cause No. 73-93. This was a case about the abuse of media power, the violation of journalistic ethics, and the harm perpetrated against outspoken individuals in an effort to silence them.

Following the release of the movie *JFK* in the late fall of 1991,

Warren Commission apologists like David Belin (the self-proclaimed most knowledgeable person in the world about the JFK assassination) embarked upon a crusade, which included a nationwide campaign to attack the movie *JFK* and those allegedly associated with the movie, including critics of the Warren Report like Dr. Crenshaw and Mr. Shaw. Such campaign made frequent use of the media, including appearances on television and publication of written pieces in the print media across the country. Despite the fact (and perhaps due to the fact) that polls unanimously indicated that the overwhelming majority of Americans disagree with the Warren Report, the usual tactic of such Warren Commission supporters has been to personally attack such Warren Report critics, besmirching their reputations and integrity and calling them liars and profiteers.

Contemporaneously with the campaign to attack those associated with the movie *JFK* and other Warren Report critics, George Lundberg, who was then editor-in-chief of *JAMA*, embarked upon an effort to utilize the pages of *JAMA* to respond to the movie "JFK" and, in his words, "to set the record straight," under the guise of "objective," "scientific," "peer-reviewed," medical research. (In truth, the resulting defamatory *JAMA* articles were none of these things.) Indeed, Lundberg himself certainly was not objective or detached, since he was a personal friend of some of his interviewees and had a personal agenda. (Lundberg was even pictured and praised in the same *JAMA* articles.) It was the intent of Lundberg, *JAMA*, and Breo (their writer) to utilize the seemingly credible and legitimate forum of *JAMA*, as well as the media and public relations apparatus of the AMA, to try to win back public opinion, silence the critics of the Warren Report, and terminate further discussion of the JFK assassination conspiracy controversy.

At the May 19, 1992, press conference in New York City, Lundberg even stood behind a podium or lectern that contained the official AMA seal, logo or emblem, so that photographs and videos taken of Lundberg during the press conference would show the AMA seal, logo or emblem. The result was to give the false impression that Lundberg's statements were made on behalf of the AMA or at least with the endorsement of the AMA, when in truth, none of what Lundberg, Breo, or *JAMA* said or published at the press conference or in the defamatory *JAMA* articles were the official position of the AMA, nor were such statements endorsed by the AMA.

The defamatory *JAMA* articles that were authored by Breo, edited by Lundberg, and published in *JAMA* on May 27, 1992, were masterfully conceived, slickly written, and cleverly worded to give the superficial impression of being based on scientific research. In truth, the articles were deceptive and, in fact, were not objective or well researched; they were not even scientific or subjected to outside peer review. Lundberg was clearly not objective, and Breo was obviously not knowledgeable about the evidence related to the JFK assassination (probably by design). Indeed, no expert on the JFK assassination at all reviewed the defamatory *JAMA* articles before publication. The articles did, however, successfully accomplish the purpose of creating false impressions regarding Dr. Crenshaw and his book.

The false accusations made by *JAMA*, Lundberg, and Breo concerning Dr. Crenshaw and the book were also all made without any attempt by them to even interview or talk with either Dr. Crenshaw or Mr. Shaw, which resulted in the one-sided, biased, and inaccurate stories that occurred. (Of course, if they had bothered to interview Dr. Crenshaw and Mr. Shaw, they would also have been referred to the Warren Commission testimony regarding Dr. Crenshaw's presence in Trauma Room One and of the witnesses with knowledge about the LBJ phone call, which would have deprived them of their ability to later claim lack of knowledge of such information, i.e. plausible deniability.)

The fact that they had failed to even try to interview Dr. Crenshaw was pointed out in an article written by Dr. Lawrence K. Altman, which was published in the *New York Times* on Wednesday, May 20, 1992, the day after the *JAMA* press conference. Dr. Altman's article also pointed out additional errors in the statements concerning Dr. Crenshaw. Dr. Altman wrote: " …the full [Warren] report makes several references to Dr. Crenshaw. In two, Dr. Charles R. Baxter and Dr. Robert McClelland, two of the Dallas doctors interviewed by Mr. Breo, told the Warren

Commission that Dr. Crenshaw was in the emergency room." Indeed, Dr. McClelland had previously told Breo the same thing, yet Breo and *JAMA* failed to mention that, but instead published the false statements to the contrary.

On May 26, 1992, the *New York Times* published a second article by Dr. Altman, in which he pointed out additional errors in *JAMA*'s accusations concerning Dr. Crenshaw. Dr. Altman wrote: "The merit of the book aside, it turns out that the journal's research was less than thorough. It did not try to interview Dr. Crenshaw. Although the Dallas doctors [allegedly] told the journal they never saw Dr. Crenshaw in the Kennedy trauma room, two actually had told the Warren Commission that he was a member of the team...Dr. Crenshaw was also on the team that tried to resuscitate Lee Harvey Oswald after the assassin was shot, and one of Dr. Crenshaw's most astonishing assertions is that he answered a call from the new President Lyndon B. Johnson, who asked about Oswald's condition....In the journal interviews, Dr. Charles Baxter, the emergency room chief, denied that such a call was received by any doctor. But the denial came from a surgeon who could not have known about the call because he was not present during Oswald's surgery, Dr. Crenshaw said. Indeed, another doctor has confirmed such a call, although the details and who made it are not clear. The doctor... said he had long remembered reports of two White House telephone calls to the operating room."

Both of Dr. Altman's articles that were published in the *New York Times* were made available and/or received by *JAMA*, Lundberg, and Breo *before* the May 27, 1992 official publication date of the *JAMA* edition that contained the defamatory articles written by Breo. Breo, on Lundberg's orders, even researched the criticisms leveled by Dr. Altman and confirmed that they were justified, yet no effort whatsoever was made by *JAMA* to retract or correct the errors before or after publication. Additionally, *JAMA* received complaints via telephone calls and letters from members of the American Medical Association and other knowledgeable readers again citing the false and defamatory statements made about Dr. Crenshaw in the *JAMA* articles, yet the false statements were never retracted or corrected by *JAMA*.

Instead, in reply to a letter to *JAMA* that criticized *JAMA* and Breo for falsely suggesting that Dr. Crenshaw was not even present in Parkland's Trauma Room One when President Kennedy was treated, Breo quoted from the defamatory remarks that he had made at the May 19, 1992 press conference: "For years the American public has been hearing from *people who were not in Trauma Room One in Dallas* and were not in the autopsy room at Bethesda [Md], and yet, who have claimed to know what must have happened during the medical care of President Kennedy. What we *now* have are the reports of the physicians *who were on the scene*...We now have the facts about these critical events in the words of *the only people who know these facts*—the very facts that the conspiracy theorists have chosen to ignore." (Emphasis supplied.) These defamatory remarks were republished by *JAMA* on October 7, 1992, long after Lundberg, its editor, and Breo, its writer, were fully aware of the evidence that Dr. Crenshaw was indeed on the scene and in Trauma Room One when President Kennedy was taken to Parkland on November 22, 1963.

The defamatory *JAMA* articles were published and distributed to hundreds of thousands of Dr. Crenshaw's peers in the AMA, and through the media and otherwise, to millions of readers, listeners, and viewers. Dr. Crenshaw attempted to respond to the defamatory attacks upon him by holding a press conference in June, 1992, in Washington, D.C., but the press conference was not well attended by the media and received little or no coverage. *JAMA* published nothing about Dr. Crenshaw's response. Dr. Crenshaw's book dropped off the best seller list.

The Discovery

During the course of the litigation, depositions were taken of Dr. Lundberg, Mr. Breo, his immediate editor, and other representatives of *JAMA* and the AMA. These depositions, as well as documents that *JAMA* was obligated to produce in connection with those depositions, provided significant evidence to support the suit against the *JAMA* defendants. The deposition testimony and documents also revealed troubling information about *JAMA*'s coverage of the JFK assassination topic.

Dr. Lundberg, *JAMA*'s editor, has acknowledged that he is no expert on the JFK assassination. He has stated: "I wasn't in Dallas or Bethesda those days. I am really not much of an expert on this at all. My role in this is that of a journalist along with Mr. Dennis Breo of my *JAMA* staff. I have essentially no primary source of information, nor do I plan any." Thus, when Dr. Lundberg decided to use the pages of *JAMA* to respond to the movie *JFK*, he called upon his friend, Dr. James Humes, one of the autopsists at Bethesda Naval Hospital on the evening of November 22, 1963.

On December 26, 1991, Dr. Lundberg wrote: "Dear Jim, Have you seen the movie "JFK?" Three hours and fifteen minutes of truth mixed with non-truth mixed with alleged truth. For the younger person, not knowledgeable about 1963—very difficult to tell the difference. Please either write the truth now for *JAMA* or let Dennis Breo (and me?) interview you (and Bosworth [sic]) soon to set the record straight—at least about the autopsy. O.k.? Best wishes, George." Thus, Dr. Lundberg's own letter indicates that there was an agenda prior to publication of the *JAMA* articles in May, 1992—"To Set the Record Straight." (Lundberg apparently misspelled Dr. Boswell's name as "Bosworth.")

In a news release publicizing Breo's JFK articles, the AMA publicity department claimed that Humes and Boswell agreed to talk to *JAMA* "their first-ever public discussion of the case—because the interview was to appear in a peer-reviewed, scientific journal." This declaration was, at best, misleading. First of all, both Humes and Boswell had previously testified to the Warren Commission and before the House Select Committee on Assassinations (the latter investigation resulted in a report very critical of Humes and Boswell's autopsy and reached the conclusion that President Kennedy was probably assassinated through a conspiracy). Also, the "interview" with Drs. Humes and Boswell was not published in *JAMA*, nor released at the May 19th press conference in New York City as claimed in the press release. Rather, Mr. Breo's articles based in part upon such interviews were published in *JAMA*, copies of which were disseminated at the press conference.

Furthermore, the press release suggested that the articles were "peer-reviewed" and "scientific." This was not the case. First, according to *JAMA*, the articles were written by Dennis Breo, who is not a medical doctor, nor a scientist by any means. In his sworn deposition testimony, Mr. Breo claimed that the articles that he wrote on the JFK assassination "were a work of journalism," not scientific articles, and therefore were not submitted for outside peer review. Indeed, Mr. Breo described himself as "illiterate about the peer review process," and stated that there is a different process for articles submitted by *JAMA* writers like himself.

Curiously, Mr. Breo, like Dr. Lundberg, was no expert on the subject of the JFK assassination. He testified under oath that he could not recall reading any books on the JFK assassination prior to 1992: "…it was not a burning interest of mine," he stated.

Indeed, Mr. Breo apparently did not even know much about Dr. Crenshaw or his book before writing the articles that attacked both. Excerpts from Mr. Breo's sworn deposition testimony include the following:

"Q. Is it true, Mr. Breo, that you believe that face-to-face interviews are preferable because they're more effective?

A. Normally, yes, I found that to be the case.

Q. And you normally do face-to-face interviews; is that right?

A. Yes.

Q. Isn't it true, Mr. Breo, that prior to writing that article you had not sat down and talked to Dr. Crenshaw?

A. That's correct.

Q. You did not interview him; is that right?

A. I did not.

Q. Just yes or no, sir. Did you read the 26 volumes of testimony to see if Dr. Crenshaw was mentioned in there prior to writing the articles?

A. No.

Q. Do you know whether any of the other AMA employees or representatives who were involved in the press conference had read Dr.

Crenshaw's book prior to the press conference?

A. Those involved in the press conference?

Q. Yes, sir.

A. I don't know. My belief they had not."

The editor of *JAMA*, Dr. Lundberg, was also apparently lacking in knowledge about Dr. Crenshaw and his book before making his derogatory statements at the May 19, 1992, press conference. The following are excerpts from Dr. Lundberg's sworn deposition testimony:

"Q. Did you try to find out anything about Dr. Crenshaw before you made your remarks at the press conference in New York City on May 19th, 1992?

A. I did not.

Q. Did you know that Mr. Breo had not—not only had not interviewed Dr. Crenshaw, had not even tried to interview Dr. Crenshaw before you—before he wrote his articles that were published in *JAMA* on May 27th, 1992?

A. Yes. I knew that.

Q. Can you state here today under oath that you know for a fact that you had received the copy of the book [*JFK: Conspiracy of Silence*] . . . before the press conference on May 19th, 1992?

A. I've testified that I do not remember what date I received it, so I cannot testify for a fact as to when I received it since I don't recall.

Q. As far as you know, had any employee or representative of the AMA or *JAMA* done any research to find out about Dr. Crenshaw and his background, credentials, and accomplishments?

A. I don't know.

Q. When did you first learn that Mr. Breo did not intend to or had not tried to interview Dr. Crenshaw?

A. I suppose in April—My best recollection is April, 1992.

Q. How was it brought to your attention that he did not try to interview Dr. Crenshaw or that he did not intend to try to interview Dr. Crenshaw?

A. I believe he told me.

Q. What did he tell you?

A. That he was not going to interview Dr. Crenshaw.

Q. Do you know whether or not Mr. Breo did any research into Dr. Crenshaw's involvement on the Parkland trauma team on November 22nd, 1963?

A. I do not know.

Q. Did you yourself do any research?

A. "I did not."

In view of the lack of expertise and scholarly research within *JAMA* concerning the JFK assassination in general, and Dr. Crenshaw and his book in particular, one wonders why the Breo articles were not submitted to outside experts for review before publication, particularly publication in a journal that was described as "peer reviewed" and "scientific." However, when asked about this, Mr. Breo's immediate editor, Richard M. Glass, M. D., stated in his sworn deposition as follows:

"Q. Was there any consideration given to submitting Mr. Breo's articles to some outside review?

A. No. That just wouldn't have been the process for journalism articles."

Perhaps the truth was just not that important to *JAMA*. The following are additional excerpts from the sworn deposition testimony of Dr. Lundberg:

Q. Was there an intent on your part, or as editor of *JAMA* on *JAMA*'s part, to create the impression through the second article that Dr. Crenshaw was not on the trauma team that tried to save President Kennedy's life?

A. No.

Q. Was it important to you as editor of *JAMA* to try to avoid creating that impression?

A. No.

Q. Did you do anything to try to verify what Dr. Altman said about the testimony of physicians to the Warren Commission concerning Dr. Crenshaw's involvement on the trauma team?

A. Yes.

Q. What did you do to verify that?

A. I asked Mr. Breo to check into whether somewhere in one of those volumes of the Warren Commission whether that was there.

Q. You didn't do it yourself?

A. I did not.

Q. Did Mr. Breo report back to you?

A. He did.

Q. And what did he tell you?

A. He said that there were some mentions of Crenshaw's name in some of the volumes at the Warren Commission.

Q. Did you give any consideration to publishing a clarification on that point?

A. No.

Q. Why not?

A. We don't publish clarifications.

Q. Did you give any consideration to publishing a correction on that point?

A. Yes.

Q. Was that around the time of your having read Dr. Altman's article in May 1992?

A. Yes.

Q. Why did you ask Mr. Breo to go check to see if Dr. Crenshaw was mentioned in testimony before the Warren Commission?

A. To see if he was.

Q. Why did you want to know?

A. To see whether there had been such testimony and whether Dr. Altman's statement was correct.

Q. It turned out that there had been that testimony?

A. According to what Mr. Breo told me.

Q. Which in your mind verified what Dr. Altman had said?

A. Yes.

Q. So what, if anything, did you do with this information you received from Mr. Breo to verify that point made by Dr. Altman?

A. I reviewed what Mr. Breo had written in his article and determined that it was factually correct as stated and did not warrant a correction or a retraction."

Although Mr. Breo stated in the second part of the JFK articles that "some suspect that Crenshaw was not even in the trauma room," when asked about that under oath, Mr. Breo could not identify any individuals who told him that they suspected that.

"Q. Who were you referring to as supposedly suspecting that Dr. Crenshaw was not in the trauma room?

A. That's just a literary reference. Nobody in particular."

But Mr. Breo did knowingly omit from the article mention of information that demonstrated Dr. Crenshaw's involvement.

"Q. You did not mention the fact that Dr. McClelland told you that he and Dr. Crenshaw had walked into Parkland's emergency room together in your article, did you?

A. I did not."

Of course, what Dr. McClelland told Mr. Breo was consistent with his testimony to the Warren Commission. Dr. Charles Baxter, another physician interviewed by Mr. Breo, had testified similarly to the Warren Commission verifying Dr. Crenshaw's presence.

Although Mr. Breo wrote in his articles that he interviewed these doctors "in the wake of a new book written by one of their former Parkland Hospital colleagues, Charles Crenshaw, M. D.," he denied under oath during his deposition testimony that one of the purposes in writing the *JAMA* articles was to respond to Dr. Crenshaw's book.

Mr. Breo's editor, Dr. Glass, however, acknowledged the opposite during his deposition:

"Q. Was one of the intents or purposes of part two of the articles that were published in *JAMA* on May 27th, 1992, that was written by Dennis Breo to respond to Dr. Crenshaw's book?

A. One of the intentions was to have the Dallas physicians who were there respond to the book."

Although during the May 19, 1992, press conference in New York City, Dr. Lundberg stood behind a podium upon which a large American Medical Association seal or emblem had been placed, so that it would be displayed in videotaping and photographs of the press conference, Dr. Lundberg acknowledged in his sworn deposition testimony that his statements and those of Mr. Breo, at the press conference and in the *JAMA* articles, were not the official position of, nor endorsed by, the AMA.

The Settlement

By the Fall of 1994, the litigation had been on going for a year and a half. Many pretrial battles had been fought, including time consuming procedural and discovery disputes. Dr. Crenshaw and Mr. Shaw had each undergone multiple days of deposition questioning. In October of 1994, the parties to the litigation attended a court-ordered mediation. Mediation in the Texas state court practice is an informal, non-binding gathering of the parties, their attorneys, and a court-appointed mediator with the intended purpose of trying to reach an amicable settlement. In this case, the mediation lasted a full day, but the *JAMA* defendants ultimately agreed to pay Dr. Crenshaw and Gary Shaw a sum of money, plus reimburse a substantial portion of their court costs, plus publish a rebuttal article (to be written by Dr. Crenshaw and Mr. Shaw) in *JAMA*. While the amount of the settlement money would not come close to full compensation for the damage caused to their reputations, both Dr. Crenshaw and Mr. Shaw placed considerable value on the publication of the rebuttal article, a remedy that no court or jury had the power to order.

Ultimately, in the May 24/31, 1995 edition of *JAMA*, a limited and edited version of Dr. Crenshaw's rebuttal article was finally published. Of course, this was more than three years after the original articles were published that lead to the defamation suit; and *JAMA* refused to publish the well-documented rebuttal article originally submitted by Dr. Crenshaw. Instead, *JAMA* insisted upon severely limiting the length and censoring the content of the piece. Also, no apology or retraction was published. Rather, *JAMA* aggravated the situation and emphasized its irresponsibility by publishing a new smear piece about Dr. Crenshaw, Mr. Shaw, their book, and the case. The medical oath of "do no harm" apparently did not apply to *JAMA*'s brand of medical journalism, at least at that time.

The Aftermath

Thanks to the public outcry created by the movie *JFK* and Dr. Crenshaw's book, federal legislation created the Assassinations Record Review Board and assigned it the task of disclosing suppressed government evidence on the JFK assassination. In 1998, the ARRB required the release of thousands of secret documents related to the investigation by the House Select Committee on Assassinations twenty years earlier. Much of this new evidence supports the observations made by Dr. Crenshaw regarding the location of President Kennedy's wounds.

It is also of note that in 1998, Dr. Lundberg was fired as editor-in-chief of *JAMA*, allegedly due to a series of controversial publications. He was preceded in leaving *JAMA* by his writer, Breo, who was discharged not long after the Crenshaw litigation was settled. Also, the Chicago Headline Club determined in 1999 that its award for exemplary journalism probably should not have been given to Breo in 1992 for the articles in *JAMA* on the JFK assassination because fairly clear-cut "evidence now available proves that the journalist who wrote the award-winning story purposefully did not report it fairly at the time."

CHAPTER 8

The Medical Case for Conspiracy

BY GARY L. AGUILAR, MD AND CYRIL WECHT, MD, JD

Introduction

With respect to the JFK assassination, George D. Lundberg, MD, a former military pathologist, and a defrocked, former high priest of "peer-reviewed" medical/scientific journalism, is a most unlikely hero. But the former editor of the *Journal of the American Medical Association* is a hero nonetheless, at least to skeptics of the Warren Commission. For despite the fact he is fiercely anticonspiracy on the question of who shot JFK, he can fairly be credited with almost single-handedly blazing a trail to some astounding new pro-conspiracy medical/autopsy evidence.

It was because of him, for example, that a lot of new, and disturbing, information surfaced about JFK's Navy autopsy surgeons, who Lundberg had showcased in *JAMA* in the early 1990s with a fawning, naïve enthusiasm. Although the autopsists were, by all accounts, competent, they had botched the Autopsy of the Century, making appalling and inexplicable errors all along the way. But this, as longtime students of the case know, is "old news."

What is new is the discovery, from documents and interviews released in the wake of their appearance in *JAMA*, that their failures may have had less to do with their own inadequacies than they had to do with outside interference in their work. Not, it should be emphasized, that they were the heroes the editor had made them out to be in *JAMA*. Quite the contrary. New evidence led to the discovery, since published in the mainstream media, that they had made false sworn statements about Kennedy's postmortem, and that they had signed false affidavits about autopsy photographs. Moreover, despite Lundberg's inspiring portrait of them as courageous and principled professionals, in the mid-1990s legal threats were required to prevent them from stonewalling government investigators.

Such unbecoming conduct by respected, well-trained, "professor" pathologists is a baffling footnote to the tragedy in Dallas. In light of recent revelations, however, there may be reason to think of their failures in a new way, in a way that is sympathetic to the autopsists. The fumbling in JFK's morgue, and the dissembling about it afterward, may have been a consequence of two factors. First, despite their good general qualifications, their capabilities were no match for JFK's complex injuries. Second, they apparently weren't given a free hand to properly do even the work they were capable of doing. In other words, had these able men been given a free hand, it is likely JFK's autopsy would have been vastly better than it was. Some have blamed the Kennedy family for intruding. Recent disclosures, however, have shifted the focus from the family to the military, the very group Lundberg sought to defend in *JAMA*. But the role of the military in JFK's postmortem is not the end of the revelations.

Uncovered also is substantial new evidence that some of JFK's autopsy photographs have vanished, a suggestion persuasively argued by Henry Hunt in his 1985 book, *Reasonable Doubt.*[1] The government, moreover, falsely reported that it had validated JFK's autopsy photographs in two seperate ways: The first consisted of endorsements of the photos from witnesses who, it turns out, never did endorse the images, but instead refuted them. The second supposed corroboration consisted of a report that scientific tests had matched the pictures to the camera used in JFK's morgue; declassified documents, however, prove that the pictures did *not* match the camera, and now that camera has disappeared, as have the tests that proved it did not match the photos. In effect, the government had covered up key evidence that pointed to Oswald's innocence while it had falsely reported that the secret evidence it withheld supported Oswald's guilt.

The significance of recent disclosures is difficult to overstate. Before, there had been little controversy about Kennedy's wounds, except, most notably, for the daring theory of author David Lifton—that JFK's body was intercepted en route to the morgue so that his wounds could be altered to excise evidence of a second gunman. Lifton's theory flew in the face of expert opinion. Two groups of medical experts, the so-called "Clark Panel" and the House Select Committee's forensic panel, examined the evidence and concluded that JFK's autopsy evidence was fully consistent with a lone assassin.

Both groups, however, believed that they had reached their conclusions after having seen all the physical evidence—including JFK's clothes, X-rays, and autopsy photographs—and after having reviewed all the pertinent documents and related evidence. It turns out that they had not seen it all; important evidence was withheld from them. Likewise, the experts believed that the autopsy photographs had been authenticated. Not only were they never authenticated, they failed an authentication test conducted by the Select Committee in 1978. This fact, which posed no national security threat, was nevertheless not only withheld from the public, but also from the Committee's own forensic consultants whose business it was to know such facts in deriving an informed assessment.

None of these discoveries, it should be emphasized, got coverage in *JAMA*, the magazine Lundberg once edited. (He was unceremoniously sacked by the American Medical Association in the aftermath of another, unrelated editorial faux pas in 1999.[2]) What Lundberg published instead was a series of poorly-researched, "journalism" articles in 1992 and 1993 about JFK's medical/autopsy evidence. Word of the shoddiness of the work, even by journalism standards (to say nothing of scientific standards), came quickly. The day before the official publication date (May 27, 1992), and before AMA members had received their copies of the issue, Lawrence Altman, MD, the *New York Times* medical correspondent, wrote that *JAMA*'s JFK "research was less than thorough."[3]

Despite that early, prescient slap, the initial media coverage was largely favorable, and Lundberg was widely quoted and featured in television and print interviews touting the articles. But as responsible journalists began to look a little more closely, the favor faded. Six months after the last article appeared, *JAMA* was awarded a stinging rebuke in the widely-respected *Columbia Journalism Review*.[4] This was no negligible embarrassment for the former military pathologist-turned editor who had once described himself as neither a doctor nor a pathologist, but as a journalist.[5] Following that was the legal humiliation discussed by J. Bradley Kizzia in the previous chapter. Then came a damning expose in the *Chicago Reader*, in which a respected journalism organization—the Chicago Headline Club—sought to retract a prize it had awarded *JAMA* for the JFK articles. "New information has come to light," a respected member wrote, "about grave flaws and unethical practices in the reporting and editing process that produced (*JAMA*'s) winning entry."[6]

PART I: Lundberg Shines the Light

The flaws of *JAMA*'s work aside, Lundberg's expedition into the Kennedy death led to a treasure trove of discoveries. The path was an indirect one, however. The JFK articles heightened public awareness of the still-mysterious medical autopsy evidence. A panel of government historians that had waded into the mysteries of the murder—the Assassinations Records Review Board (ARRB)—took special notice of this aspect of the murder. Established by congress in reaction to the public's outrage at learning, from Oliver Stone, that millions of documents were still held in secret thirty years after Kennedy's death, the ARRB set out to put all possible JFK evidence into the public record. (At last count, more than four-and-a-half-million pages of suppressed documents have been unsealed, and in its Final Report, the Board strongly rebuked the government for unnecessary secrecy.)

Aroused by the JFK articles, students of the case petitioned for a closer examination of the physician-witnesses featured in *JAMA*, and for scrutiny of the evidence they had explored. Taking up the challenge, the Board zealously mined what has turned out to be a rich lode that, had it not been for Lundberg, might have never have been excavated. Following leads from *JAMA*, the gems dug up by the Review Board are nothing short of amazing, and they continue to dazzle long after Lundberg's careless foray has been all but forgotten. But rather than enriching the public minority that remains loyal to the Warren Commission, as Lundberg had expressly intended, the nuggets have instead been a treasure to the skeptical majority.

Defending JFK's Military Autopsy

The story began on the day, 26 December, 1991, George Lundberg set out to right a grievous wrong. Writing on American Medical Association letterhead to James H. Humes, MD, JFK's chief autopsy pathologist, Lundberg asked him, in light of the movie *JFK,* to set the record straight about the JFK autopsy. What apparently most annoyed Lundberg was Oliver Stone's dark depiction of military meddling during Kennedy's autopsy in his then new film. During a public appearance in Chicago in 1993, Lundberg carped, "The movie *JFK* I consider primarily skillful fiction, very skillful filmed fiction, very nicely done. But I consider it a grave insult to the military physicians involved as well as pathologists in general, maybe medicine and a whole lot of innocent people as well."[7]

The depth of his feelings are perhaps best explained by the fact that before he became an editor, Lundberg had been a military pathologist himself. By the time Stone's film premiered, Lundberg, by his own admission, had had a personal friendship with Kennedy's chief pathologist, James Humes, MD, that had spanned 35 years.[8] "I know Jim Humes," Lundberg announced during a debate on the JFK case in 1993. "He is a friend of mine. I would trust him with my life."[9] Stone had not been kind to Lundberg's friend, nor to military physicians, nor to pathologists like Lundberg.

In the autopsy scene in *JFK*, Stone portrayed JFK's pathologists— James H. Humes, MD, J. Thornton Boswell, MD, and Pierre Finck, MD—as stumbling along under severe pressure by military superiors who were present in the morgue but who were not part of the autopsy team. In *JAMA*, the pathologists vigorously defended the quality of their work, repeatedly denying that there had been any interference during the autopsy.[10] But declassified files and other evidence appear to vindicate Stone's "filmed fiction."

JFK's Courageous Pathologists

One of the most peculiar and telling performances in the whole affair must surely be that of JFK's pathologists. Portrayed by Lundberg as capable, courageous and forthright, after *JAMA*'s JFK articles appeared, they suddenly exhibited quite different traits. They declined Lundberg's invitation to appear before the press at the flashy news conference the enthusiastic editor had orchestrated in New York City to introduce and promote "their" story—"The Truth about JFK's autopsy."[11] Then, in defiance of the customs of scientific discourse, they stonewalled every question put to them in letters by colleagues that *JAMA*'s editors had selected and published.[12] Finally, despite their bold declarations in *JAMA* that they had nothing to hide, when the civilian historians of the ARRB invited them to appear voluntarily to answer questions (including, they might have feared, about their prior contradictory statements), they refused.

But having cut its teeth by forcing seasoned stonewallers—FBI and CIA agents—to comply with the will of the people, the ARRB made quick work of Humes, Boswell and Finck. Under threat of subpoena, the fearless pathologists finally showed up.

Despite the abundance of new information, one fact should be emphasized at the outset. Even without the new disclosures, the medical/autopsy evidence for Oswald's innocence is hardly meager. Nor, alas, is it entirely unambiguous. Although a case can be made either way, the new evidence greatly strengthens the position of skeptics. It also reinforces, ironically, some pro-conspiracy evidence that appeared in *JAMA*, evidence that entirely escaped the grasp of both the sacked doctor-turned-editor, and the author of the series, Dennis Breo, who was also sacked by the American Medical Association.

Exactly what the new discoveries are, and what they tell us about who did, and who didn't, kill Kennedy, is the subject of this section.

JFK's Autopsy: A Botched Affair

By all accounts, John Kennedy got a lousy autopsy. Although the government determined that "the resources available for (JFK's) autopsy were extensive,"[13] they were woefully underutilized. "Where bungled autopsies are concerned, President Kennedy's is the exemplar," is how the chairman of the 1978 House Select Committee's (HSCA) forensic panel, former New York Coroner Michael Baden, put it.[14] The HSCA's criticisms included the fact that JFK's wounds were not properly dissected, nor were they properly described relative to standard anatomic landmarks. The pathologists did not examine JFK's clothes. The angles of the bullet tracks through the body were not measured relative to the body axis. The brain was not properly examined. Original autopsy notes were destroyed. Proper autopsy photographs were not taken, etc.[15] This last complaint, however, may be unfair. For as we will see, it is likely that key images may have been taken after all, only to then vanish after the autopsy.

The greatest problem was that JFK's postmortem called for an experienced, hands-on, forensic pathologist, but the military failed to provide one. What the military did provide was Navy Commander James H. Humes. He was then the senior operating pathologist at Bethesda Naval Hospital and, overall, a competent general pathologist who was entrusted with teaching resident physician pathologists. So while in the grand scheme of things Humes was a good pathologist, he was clearly over his head when the President was wheeled into the morgue. His first assistant, Navy Commander J. Thornton Boswell, was in Humes' league— certainly a competent generalist, but not up to this particular task.

Army Colonel Pierre Finck, MD, a consultant from the Air Force Institute of Pathology, was belatedly brought in. Though a properly accredited forensic specialist, the colonel was out of his league and out of his element. Describing his predicament as a lower-ranking Army officer in a Navy morgue, Finck admitted, "They were admirals, and when you are a lieutenant colonel in the U.S. Army you just follow orders."[16] The famed New York City coroner Milton Helpern, MD, has laid out the problem particularly well: "Colonel Finck's position throughout the entire proceeding was extremely uncomfortable. If it had not been for him, the autopsy would not have been handled as well as it was; but he was in the role of the poor bastard Army child foisted into the Navy family reunion. He was the only one of the three doctors with any experience with bullet wounds; but you have to remember that his experience was limited primarily to 'reviewing' files, pictures, and records of finished cases. There's a world of difference between standing at the autopsy table and trying to decide whether a hole in the body is a wound of entrance or a wound of exit, and in reviewing another man's work at some later date in the relaxed, academic atmosphere of a private office …."[17]

While Finck would certainly have been able to insure that the basics would be covered, Humes and Boswell unwisely elected to start the exam before Finck arrived. By the time Finck got there, 30 minutes into the proceedings, the fatal skull wound had already been pulled apart and JFK's brain had been removed. After he arrived, Finck offered suggestions, took notes (that are now missing), and mostly watched while Humes and Boswell did the actual manual work. This led to additional, avoidable failings.

For example, even though Finck was the first to recognize that JFK had a wound in the back, he didn't perform the customary delicate probing and examination such a wound deserved. Instead, Humes performed that examination, by crudely sticking his finger into the wound. Some of the subtle forensic clues it might have yielded were probably lost, a casualty of Humes' lack of forensics training and Finck's outsider status.

The Question of Interference
JFK's postmortem wasn't helped by the fact the pathologists probably felt under the gun to finish quickly. On the 17th floor of the hospital sat the mortified and exhausted Kennedy family entourage. More than once there were calls down to the morgue to inquire about the progress of the

examination and how much more time would be required. Might the military have buckled to Kennedy family pressure?

There was at least one good reason to suppose it had. Although the Air Force Institute of Pathology was by far the best place for a murder autopsy, and although the Institute was recommended to the Kennedy family, Jackie picked the less expert Naval hospital at Bethesda instead. Her reason? Not because she could control the Navy, but merely because Jack had been a lieutenant in the Navy. This is not to say Bethesda was a bad hospital; it wasn't. It was an active teaching hospital with an active autopsy service in 1963. But its cases came overwhelmingly from deaths due to natural causes, not murder. So the pathology staff had little experience with the types of injuries JFK sustained, and there was no "on-campus" forensic pathologist handy when they needed one.

Historian William Manchester,[18] author Gus Russo,[19] and John Lattimer, MD, a urologist who has published articles and a book about the Kennedy case,[20] have all argued that Kennedy family interference goes a long way towards explaining the failings of JFK's autopsy. However, the weight of the evidence, including some new evidence, suggests that the Kennedy family cannot be faulted for the most important failings of JFK's post mortem. (Not even the discredited[21][22][23][24][25][26][27][28][29] Warren Commission loyalist Gerald Posner believes they can.[30]) It is more likely that the military deserves *that* distinction.

For example, one cannot rule out the possibility that the Kennedy family tried to prevent an examination of JFK's Addison's disease-ravaged adrenal glands, then a dark family secret. But in 1993 in *JAMA*, Finck recalled that, "The Kennedy family did not want us to examine the abdominal cavity, but the abdominal cavity was examined."[31][32] And indeed it was. Kennedy was completely disemboweled.[33] So while there's no indisputable proof, perhaps the family *did* request that JFK's abdominal cavity, which houses the adrenals, be left alone, especially since JFK suffered no abdominal injuries. If Finck was right, so much for the military's cutting corners to kowtow to the Kennedys' need for speed. The doctors were not entirely insensitive to family wishes, however. They kept mum about JFK's atrophied adrenal glands, even 30 years later, in *JAMA*. But by then Kennedy's Addison's disease was an open secret, having been already discussed by Lattimer in his 1980 book.[34]

Though they might have been unsuccessful in keeping the military out of JFK's belly, it is not unreasonable to wonder if the family might have otherwise interfered. The simple answer is that they probably didn't, at least not in any way that influenced the outcome. Under oath to the ARRB, Humes admitted that JFK's personal physician, Burkley, seemed keen to move things along, but "as far as telling me what to do or how to do it, absolutely, irrevocably, no." By way of explanation, Humes made the obvious point that, since Burkley was not a pathologist, "he wouldn't presume to do such a thing."[35] Boswell told the ARRB that they were "not at all" in any rush or under any compulsion to hurry.[36] "It was always an extension of the autopsy," that was encouraged, "rather than further restrictions."[37] Similarly, after an interview with the Commanding officer of the Naval Medical Center, the HSCA reported that, "[Admiral Calvin B.] Galloway said that he was present throughout the autopsy," and that, "no orders were being sent in *from outside the autopsy room* either by phone or by person."[38] (emphasis added) In a sworn affidavit executed for the HSCA on November 28, 1978, JFK's personal physician, Admiral George Burkley, claimed, "I directed the autopsy surgeon to do a complete autopsy and take the time necessary for completion."[39]

The family didn't, for example, select the sub par autopsists; military authorities did. Realizing how over their heads they were, JFK's pathologists told Lattimer that they (wisely) requested to have non-military forensic consultants called in. Permission was denied.[40] The Autopsy of the Century was thus left in the hands of backbenchers. Given the "can do" mentality so prevalent in the military, this shortcut isn't surprising. But it is one the family didn't take. Had the government but asked, it is impossible to imagine that any expert forensic pathologist in the entire country would have refused his duty during this time of national tragedy, or that the family would have objected.

The HSCA explored the question of the family's role in considerable detail in 1978, concluding that, other than (reasonably) requesting the exam be done as expeditiously as possible, the Kennedys did *not* interfere in the autopsy.[41] Moreover, in an important legal matter, RFK left blank the space marked "restrictions" in the permit he signed for his brother's autopsy.

While a compelling case for family interference is difficult to sustain, a case can be made that there was at least *some* interference in JFK's autopsy. The most glaring errors—the selection of inexperienced pathologists and the exclusion of available, experienced ones, the failure to dissect JFK's back wound, and the failure to obtain his clothing—had nothing to do with camouflaging JFK's secret disease, or even with significantly speeding the examination. (Dissecting the back wound would have taken not much more than one hour. JFK was in the morgue more than eight.) Nor is it at all likely the Kennedys would have imposed those specific restrictions, in the off chance they had even thought of them. Instead, these peculiar decisions are more likely to have come from the military.

Military Meddling In JFK's Autopsy?

Why does suspicion for meddling fall on the military? Because it would have taken someone high in the military to deny the pathologists' sensible request for the civilian experts they so badly needed. Finck, who was not a practicing forensic pathologist, simply wasn't the sort of expert the situation called for. Though certified in forensic pathology, the House Select Committee determined that Finck had not done a hands-on forensic autopsy, or *any* autopsy, in two years.[42] But refusing Humes's call for expert assistance is not the only reason to wonder about military meddling.

For example, it is impossible to imagine that, unless ordered to do so, JFK's pathologists would have otherwise destroyed original autopsy notes and signed false declarations, which, as we will see, they did. (Would civilians have done such things?) There is also the disturbing testimony of Pierre Finck during the controversial 1968 trial of Clay

Shaw in New Orleans. It was this testimony, and not Oliver Stone's movie, that persuaded many that JFK's autopsy was not as unfettered as had been reported in *JAMA*.

"Who Is In Charge Here?"

Under oath in 1969 at the trial of Clay Shaw, Finck testified that during the autopsy, Humes, the ranking pathologist, had asked, "Who is in charge here?" Finck said that an Army General, whose name Finck said he could not recall, answered, "I am." Finck was then asked, "Was this Army General a qualified pathologist?" "No," said Finck. "Was he a doctor?" Finck answered, "No, not to my knowledge."[43] Finck's astounding claim that a non-physician was calling the shots was rebutted in *JAMA* in a manner that both typified the slovenly nature of the journal's work and only added to suspicions.

Humes had indignantly insisted in *JAMA* that, "There was no interference with our autopsy … Nobody tried to interfere." [44] Apparently rebutting Finck's testimony, Humes recounted an episode that was eerily similar to the one Finck had sworn to. Humes said that that before the autopsy he accosted an unknown man with a camera on the loading dock outside the morgue. Humes says he asked of the group that had assembled on the dock, "Who's in charge here?" "The answer," *JAMA* reassured, "was only 2 feet away, as a man in full military dress (who 'was some general representing the military section of the District of Columbia') answered, 'I am. Who wants to know?' "[45]

The two incidents could not have been the same one. The one Humes described occurred on the loading dock outside the morgue, *before* the autopsy had started, and so *before* Finck had arrived. Finck testified that Humes had asked "Who is in charge here?" *during* the autopsy. The obvious discrepancies between these episodes were not appreciated by *JAMA*. Nor, even, were they grasped by the HSCA's forensic consultants, to whom Humes had treated to the same irrelevant, if not purposely deceptive, story when its chairman, Michael Baden, gently inquired about Humes' asking who was in charge.[46] The controversy was *always* who controlled the autopsy, not the loading dock.

This odd coincidence has contributed to other suspicions about Humes' trustworthiness on the question of interference during JFK's autopsy.

JFK's Incomplete Autopsy

Dated November 22, 1963, the Navy "Clinical Record Authorization for Post Mortem Examination, U.S. Naval Hospital, Bethesda, Md." gave Humes the following directive: "You are hereby authorized to perform a complete post mortem examination on the remains of John F. Kennedy ... This authority shall be limited only by the conditions expressly stated below."[47] No restrictions were indicated on the form, which had been signed by JFK's brother, Robert Kennedy, and the President's personal physician, George Burkley, who, as already discussed, swore in an affidavit that there were no restrictions placed on JFK's autopsy. It is likely that Jackie had also authorized a complete autopsy because her name was typed at the bottom of the form. The HSCA found that, though a complete autopsy had been authorized, JFK got an incomplete one instead.[48]

At least one of the reasons Humes did not perform one may have been revealed in a memorandum from, of all places, *CBS*. In November 1993, a once-confidential, internal memo written in 1967 by a *CBS* executive (Bob Richter) was published by a committee chaired by Representative John Conyers. The memo described a conversation that Humes had had in 1967 with a personal friend, another *CBS* executive, Jim Snyder. In the memo Richter described Snyder's conversation with the pathologist, saying, "Humes also said he had orders from someone he refused to disclose—other than stating it was not Robert Kennedy—to not do a complete autopsy."[49] [This accords with Admiral Galloway's report that "no orders were being sent in from outside the autopsy room either by phone or by person."] So if not Robert Kennedy, who then, besides a higher-ranking officer than Humes, could have stalled the surgeon's scalpel? Though the memo was given to Rep. Conyers by an attorney, Roger Feinman, George Lundberg may nonetheless be responsible for it's reaching the public. For Feinman sent the memo to Conyers *after* he publicly debated Lundberg about JFK in Chicago in

April, 1993.

Besides Finck's report that an Army General claimed he was in charge during Kennedy's autopsy, and Humes confidential admission that someone outside the family limited the exam, Finck and Humes also gave additional, persuasive reasons to suspect there was high-level meddling.

Rudimentary Examinations Left Undone

During the Shaw trial, Finck testified that he was ordered *not* to dissect JFK's back wound by a superior in the morgue whose name, like the "in-charge" general, just wouldn't come to mind.[50] Defending his failure to perform this key exam, Finck testified, "Because we were told to examine the head and the chest cavity, and that [the dissection of the neck wound] doesn't include the removal of the organs of the neck."[51][52] Finck's version was corroborated by Lattimer who, after an interview with Humes, reported that, "[Commander Humes's and Boswell's] request for permission to dissect out this bullet hole, which led into the upper back and possibly into the neck, was denied."[53] No further information was provided to answer the obvious next question, "By whom?" The CBS memo suggests it wasn't RFK.

And then there is the fascinating 1965 memo Finck sent to his superior, General Joe Blumberg, the man who ordered Finck to report to JFK's autopsy team.[54] (It was Blumberg who had made Finck available to the autopsy team in the first place.) Conveniently absent in *JAMA*'s glowing account is Finck informing Blumberg that, "I was denied the opportunity to examine the clothing of Kennedy. One officer who outranked me told me that my request was only of academic interest."[55][56] It is impossible to imagine that any physician would have ever denied a forensic expert's request to examine JFK's clothes on the grounds they were "only of academic interest."

Both the dissection of Kennedy's back wound and the inspection of his clothes would have been aspects of the most rudimentary search for clues to the trajectory of the shots. Humes' being denied permission for these exams, as well as being directed to do an incomplete autopsy, suggests control of the autopsy did not rest with the physicians. Had Humes really been in charge, it is impossible to imagine that he, of all people, would have refused his own consultant's access to JFK's back wound. Nor Finck's access to JFK's clothes, especially since in *JAMA,* Humes lamented that, "If only we had seen the President's clothes, tracking the second bullet would have been a piece of cake, but we didn't have the clothes."[57] (Though outside the scope of this discussion, it would have been of considerable interest if the autopsists *had* examined JFK's clothes, because matching holes in JFK's shirt and coat were found well below where they appear in autopsy photographs of JFK's back.)

Ironically, the clothes were probably already in the morgue, or at least no further away than Air Force One. Secret Service agent William Greer, the driver of JFK's limousine who then accompanied the President's corpse on Air Force One, was present in the morgue during the entire autopsy. He testified that at Parkland Hospital he took sole possession of JFK's clothes,[58] and he said that, "I had this, his clothing, I kept it in my hand at all times, all the time."[59]

Recapping, in New Orleans Finck testified an Army General said he was in charge of the autopsy, while Humes apparently confided that he was ordered to not do a complete autopsy by someone other than Robert Kennedy. Finck, Boswell and Humes claimed permission to dissect JFK's back wound was denied. And in his 1965 memo, Finck said he was denied JFK's clothes. Finck's statements during the Shaw trial, it should be emphasized, carry considerable weight given that Finck's reluctant, yet sworn, admissions were, in essence, an admission 'against the interest' of his employer, the military.

Non-scientific Priorities

Given *JAMA*'s legendary research capabilities, it is tempting to wonder whether, but for Lundberg's military ties and his closeness to Humes, some of these discoveries might have premiered in his journal Unfortunately, the direction of the articles leaves little doubt that Lundberg's personal history played a role in articles that honored his military colleagues by straightening the Oliver Stone-twisted record of

Kennedy's autopsy. Nowhere is that more obvious than when, as he and his writer were building a case against any outside interference during JFK's autopsy, *JAMA* quoted from Finck's memo to Blumberg. And while reporting Humes' lamentation, "If only we had seen the President's clothes…," *JAMA* carefully omitted any mention of Finck's complaining about a higher ranking officer denying him JFK's clothes.[60] While Lundberg's constricted gaze prevented his seeing the fascinating new vistas, it was, ironically, the broad shoulders he gave others to stand upon that have provided a glimpse at vistas the editor missed.

Most of the foregoing is "old news." That is, though largely unknown to the public, it was available in the record before *JAMA* and the ARRB entered the arena. But the trail of evidence for military meddling in JFK's autopsy did not go cold after the *JAMA* articles appeared.

New Evidence for Military Meddling

Recent disclosures suggest high-level, military complicity in the destruction of, and dissimulation about, primary autopsy evidence. In addition, the extant autopsy evidence itself is under a cloud since the release of non-sensitive, yet suppressed, HSCA interviews dating to the late 1970s, and since the ARRB released interviews it conducted in the 1990s.

On August 2, 1998, the *Associated Press* reported an important ARRB finding: "Under oath [before the ARRB], Dr. Humes, finally acknowledged under persistent questioning—in testimony that differs from what he told the Warren Commission—that he had destroyed both his notes taken at the autopsy and the first draft of the autopsy report."[61] The Review Board had finally extracted Humes' admission of something long suspected: he had burned *both* a preliminary draft of the autopsy report, which he had admitted before, *as well as* original autopsy notes prepared on the night of the autopsy, an admission that contradicted his Warren Commission testimony.

Besides his ARRB admission conflicting with his 1964 testimony, it also contradicted two affidavits he had signed shortly after the assassination, a fact even the ARRB did not acknowledge. On November 24, 1963 Humes "certified" over his signature that he had "destroyed by burning certain preliminary draft notes relating to" JFK's autopsy,"[62] but that otherwise, "all working papers associated with [JFK's autopsy] have remained in my personal custody at all times. Autopsy notes and the holograph draft of the final report were handed to Commanding Officer, U.S. Naval Medical School, at 1700, 24 November 1963."[63]

Thus Humes was admitting to destroying "draft notes" that were written up while he worked at home drafting his autopsy report. But this affidavit, the substance of which he repeated to the Warren Commission, does not mention the destruction of original autopsy notes from the night of the autopsy. (Such an act, of course, would have been medicolegally frowned upon had it occurred in a civilian autopsy of even the most undistinguished murder victim.) Humes' affidavit, however, was not precisely true. All the "working papers" and "autopsy notes" had *not* remained with him until he turned them over to his superior. He destroyed some of them, including notes he took himself on the night of the autopsy, and perhaps also those of his consultant, Finck.

Arlan Spector's Solution

Former Commission counsel Senator Arlan Specter believes he recently solved the mystery. The cover of his book, *Passion for Truth*, published in 2000, announced that the book presented "the first public disclosure of why JFK's autopsy surgeon burned his notes." Specter produced a long quote from Humes in which the pathologist appeared to be coming clean. He said he had destroyed the bloodstained autopsy notes so they would never become objects of morbid curiosity the way the doilies on President Lincoln's chair had become, stained as they were with the blood of John Wilkes Booth's treason.[64]

Alas, Specter's passion for truth exceeds his passion for fact-checking. Humes had previously told this story to *JAMA* for the infamous May 27, 1992 issue. Neither Specter nor his fact-checkers noticed it apparently. But the story was even more stale than that. Humes had slipped this same improbable story to the HSCA in 1978,[65] and to

Lattimer in 1980.[66] In fact, on page 196 of his book, *Kennedy and Lincoln*, Lattimer reproduced a photograph of Lincoln's chair, adorned the stained doily, and captioned with Humes' anecdote.

Humes' touching tale, however, doesn't ring true. Boswell's "face sheet" autopsy notes, which Humes did *not* destroy, also bear the President's bloodstains. That fact prompted an amusing exchange when ARRB counsel Jeremy Gunn asked Humes, "Do you see any inconsistency at all between destroying some handwritten notes that contained blood on them but preserving other handwritten notes that also had blood on them?" Lamely, Humes answered, "Well, only that the others (that he destroyed) were of my own making. I didn't—wouldn't have the habit of destroying something someone else prepared." [67] Notes Finck prepared on the night of the autopsy happen also to be missing. So unless someone else in the military destroyed Finck's notes, Humes, who according to the records took sole possession of all the notes, probably made an exception to his customary habit that night.

Missing Autopsy Photographs

Photographing autopsies is as routine a practice today as it was when JFK's autopsy was photographed in 1963. Such images are especially important in murder cases to show the location and appearance of the wounds, and to document features of the wounds that provide trial evidence about how the murder happened. Given that the alleged assassin, Oswald, was then still alive, it is likely the images were taken with the understanding of the legal role they might someday play.

Betraying its unfamiliarity with the controversies swirling around Kennedy's death, *JAMA* sought to "dispel the myth that no [autopsy] photos were allowed."[68] That anyone has ever seriously agued that no autopsy photos were allowed is a far greater myth than that cameras were banned from JFK's morgue. All students of the case—both pro- and anticonspiracy—know photographs were taken. The controversy is not about *whether* they were taken. It is about whether the actual autopsy pictures—including bootleg copies first published in author David

Lifton's 1980 book, *Best Evidence*[69]—are accurate reflections of JFK's injuries.

To challenge the images, skeptics have cited such credible witnesses as, for just one example, Parkland cardiology professor Fuad Bashour, MD. When shown an autopsy photograph revealing that the backside area of the skull and scalp was completely intact behind JFK's right ear (Figure 1B), critics Robert Groden and Harrison Livingstone reported that Bashour exclaimed, "Why do they cover it up?...This is not the way it was!"[70] Bashour insisted that there was a significant skull wound in the backside of JFK's head while the photographs show no damage at all in this area. And as we will see, besides Bashour, myriad other witnesses—from the surgeons and photographers at the autopsy to credible witnesses both at Parkland and at the morgue—have also have also identified problems with the inventory of extant images. ("Fox" photo 3. Note: this image is virtually identical with the so-called "Ida Dox drawing," a drawing published by the HSCA to exactly reproduce the autopsy photograph showing the "pristine" backside of JFK's head dring the autopsy. See Figure 1.)

Whereas in *JAMA* Humes praised the senior autopsy photographer, John Stringer, as "one of the best medical photographers in the world,"[71] not a single acceptable image of the President's fatal skull wound is to be found anywhere in the official inventory. And yet Humes and Finck testified that they took such images. ARRB-declassified documents hint at a possible explanation: evidence destruction. All three of JFK's pathologists, both autopsy photographers, a White House photographer, and a National Photographic Center employee have testified that photographs taken at JFK's autopsy are missing.

PART II: JFK's Wounds—A Primer

With the President's shoddy autopsy as a backdrop, we will now move to a broader examination of the nature and implication of JFK's injuries, informed with much new evidence. A certain ambiguity will inevitably remain unfortunately, because Kennedy never had the expert post mortem he and the country deserved. Nevertheless, our under-standing of Kennedy's wounds has greatly advanced since *JAMA* brought this fascinating subject to the fore.

To best explain JFK's medical/autopsy evidence, we will begin with a brief review of the President's wounds. Based on the autopsy findings, the Warren Commission concluded that JFK was wounded by two, and only two, bullets fired from above and behind while he rode in the back-seat of a limousine through the streets of Dallas.

The first bullet is said to have struck the President in the upper back, passing then above his right lung to exit just below his Adam's apple. Following that, the Commission held that the same shell continued onward, inflicting all five wounds sustained by Governor John Connally, who was riding in the seat directly in front of JFK. This accomplished bullet, Warren Commission Exhibit # 399, has been derisively referred to as the "magic bullet." For, despite its having smashed two bones while passing completely through two bodies, and its having left a trail of frag-ments along the way, it was recovered virtually undamaged.

The second, fatal bullet has two "official" paths. The first is a low path. Summarizing the autopsy findings, the Warren Commission reported that, "The fatal missile entered the skull above and to the right of the external occipital protuberance. A portion of the projectile tra-versed the cranial cavity in a posterior-anterior direction ... A portion of the projectile made its exit through the parietal bone on the right carrying with it portions of cerebrum, skull and scalp." This path, thus, is from the bottom rear of the skull to the right side of the skull, near the top.

The second path, which was much higher, was determined by a panel of government-selected experts—the "Clark Panel"—after a review of JFK's autopsy photographs and X-rays in 1968. (Figures 1A and 1B) In 1978, a team of forensic experts working for the House Select Committee on Assassinations (HSCA) endorsed the Clark Panel's find-ings. The "new" entrance wound was located about 10-cm above the location first identified by the autopsists. Given that the rear of the skull only measures perhaps 12-cm, top-to-bottom, it is difficult to understand how "even" a general pathologist would have made such an error, to say nothing of two of them making it, as well as a third, forensics-trained specialist. Nevertheless, this is the current official position—the fatal bullet struck the top of JFK's skull, a fact three examining pathologists missed.

JFK's Pathologists Dispute the Experts

The HSCA's forensic consultants encouraged JFK's autopsists to come around to the Clark Panel's conclusion that the autopsy photographs and X-rays proved the wound was higher; they wouldn't budge, not even when confronted with the photographs.[72] Gazing at the autopsy photographs, both Drs. James Humes and J. Thornton Boswell scoffed at the notion the high spot on the back of JFK's otherwise unblemished scalp was a bullet hole. "I can assure you," Humes defiantly insisted, "that as we reflected the scalp to get to this point, there was no defect corresponding to this in the skull at any point. I don't know what that is. It could be to me clotted blood. I don't, I just don't know what it is, but it certainly was not a wound of entrance." (Figure 1B)[73] But after continued pestering, the HSCA managed to get Humes to make a second appearance before the committee, this time in front of klieg lights and rolling cameras.

Suddenly, Humes appeared to agree the wound was high, if with artfully chosen words. The HSCA reported that during his second interview, Dr. Humes agreed that the wound was high, not low.[74] Behind the scenes the HSCA used Humes' apparent turnabout to lean on Boswell and Finck. The ARRB declassified suppressed letters showing that the HSCA had asked Boswell and Finck to reconsider their placement of the skull wound in light of Humes' change of heart. They refused.

Leaving a divided opinion in the record, the HSCA wrote, "Finck believed strongly that the observations of the autopsy pathologists were more valid than individuals [meaning the Clark Panel and HSCA's forensic consultants] who might subsequently examine photographs."[75] But despite Humes' equivocation during his second HSCA interview, it appears that he had never really changed his mind. In 1992 Humes told *JAMA* the wound was low, and in 1997 he swore to the ARRB (as did Finck and Boswell), that he had never wavered from his view that JFK's skull wound was low.

To recap: the official version of Kennedy's murder has it that he was hit by only two bullets, one passing from his back to exit his throat, and one fatally striking him in the head. For thirty-five years the autopsists have remained firm, and unanimous, that the bullet hit JFK's skull at the bottom. Yet the photographs, though ambiguous, suggest it hit much higher. Warren loyalists are forced to disbelieve JFK's surgeons and to accept the interpretations of the Clark Panel and the HSCA. Skeptics have a difficult time swallowing the notion that JFK's 'professor pathologists'—they were active in teaching resident physicians—could have been so colossally wrong about the presence of an entrance wound, or at least *some* wound, low in Kennedy's skull.

Experimental "Duplication" of JFK's Skull Injuries

If the pathologists are right about the presence of a bullet hole low in Kennedy's rear skull, then Oswald didn't do it. Any bullet striking JFK at the base of his skull from Oswald's supposed perch would probably have created a "blow-out" exit wound in JFK's face. This is not mere speculation.

The Warren Commission published photographs of a human skull test-fired to simulate JFK's assassination. Dr. Alfred Olivier, the expert who performed the simulation, explained a photograph of his "duplication" to the Commission: "This particular skull blew out the right side in a manner very similar to the wounds of the President ... We found that this bullet could do exactly—could make the type of wound that the President received."[76] The images show a bullet entrance just above the EOP (the midline knob at the very base of the rear of the skull), with the exit wound involving virtually the entire right side of the skull, including a good portion of the right forehead, the entire right eye socket and part of the cheekbone.[77] (Figure 2)

No damage was reported to JFK's face in the autopsy report or testimonies. Nor was it depicted in the Warren Commission's autopsy diagrams (Figure 3). [Nor is it visible in the autopsy photographs (Figure

4).] These discrepancies should have been obvious even in 1964, when the Warren Commission reviewed Olivier's incompatible experimental "duplication." Yet none of the Commissioners or staff members took any notice of the contradictions.

What about the higher entrance location selected by the Clark Panel and the HSCA? Would a higher shot replicate JFK's wounds? While the match is better, it is by no means good. To test the higher entrance site favored by the HSCA, urologist John Lattimer test-fired human skulls, striking them from the rear at the higher location, in parietal bone rather than occipital bone. In his book, *Kennedy and Lincoln*, Lattimer reproduced a photograph of his results.[78] Claiming the wounds shown are "very similar to those of the President," the image shows a skull with extensive portions of both the right and left frontal and anterior parietal bones blown out, but no damage to the posterior parietal, temporal, or occipital bones, except for cracks. (Figure 5)

By contrast, the autopsy report, Warren Commission diagrams and witness testimony disclose no damage to the frontal or anterior parietal bones; instead, the damage was in the *posterior* parietal, temporal and occipital regions.[79] Had JFK taken the shot Lattimer's skull took, it likely would have blown off the entire top of his forehead just above the eyebrows, leaving undamaged the very area described by the autopsists and witnesses as destroyed. Lattimer's experiments on devitalized skulls, of course, don't prove exactly how a shot would affect a living head. They do, however, reveal a greater similarity to Olivier's results than they do to the wounds described by JFK's pathologists and credible witnesses (including experienced neurosurgeons and other physicians).

Unfortunately, though the autopsy surgeons reported the bullet entered "just above" the external occipital protuberance, they didn't say precisely how far above. The discrepancy, however, cannot be dismissed as verbal imprecision. The autopsists prepared skull diagrams for the Warren Commission (Figure 3) and later labeled a skull for the HSCA (Vol. 7:114-115) depicting in both cases the skull entrance wound as having been within 1-cm of the external occipital protuberance.[80] Even after repeated challenges by the forensic pathologists of the HSCA,

Humes reaffirmed the accuracy of the low spots the autopsists had marked on the human skull.[81] Both he and Boxwell also stressed that the wound was in occipital bone.[82] The 10-cm higher site, by contrast, is not in occipital bone, but rather in the so-called "parietal" bone. So if in fact the pathologists erred, they mistook not only the site of entrance but also the bone of entrance.

To summarize: Two fundamental considerations are central to the Commission's theory of the murder. First, Oswald fired from above and behind the upright-seated President. Whether JFK was hit in the back at Zapruder frame 224, as claimed by Lattimer (in *JAMA*, 10/7/92), who argued an exiting bullet explains the flapping of Governor Connally's jacket lapel that is visible in that frame,[83] or at approximately 231-234, as others believe, including Governor Connally himself,[84] the Commission's theory requires that JFK's back wound to be higher than the exit throat wound. Second, although the Commission itself did not recognize this fact, JFK's rear skull wound could not have been as low on JFK's skull as repeatedly described by his autopsists.

For if Oswald had indeed hit JFK at the base of the head from his supposed perch, the bullet would not have left the gaping rearward wound so many witnesses described. Nor, even, would it have blown out through the right side of JFK's skull. But instead, as the Warren Commission was shown, it would have blasted through JFK's face (Figure 2), or perhaps even lower, through his neck. The autopsy photographs, however, prove that the blowout exit wound was behind the hairline, yet toward the right-front side of JFK's skull. Since these images seem to prove that the original autopsy findings were wrong, and that even the earliest witnesses were wrong, they have naturally drawn considerable attention.

Skull Wound: Witnesses vs. Autopsy Photographs

JFK's most important, and most disputed, wound is his fatal skull wound. The dispute involves not only whether a bullet hit it high or low, but also whether more than one bullet hit JFK's head, and whether the autopsy photographs are accurate representations of Kennedy's skull injuries. The issues are intertwined.

The photographs show what could be explained by a single shot to the head: a small bullet hole at the top rear of his head and a gaping wound in the skull in front of JFK's right ear. If witness accounts had varied significantly, it would be reasonable to ignore them in favor of the "hard" photographic evidence. But they do not vary. Witnesses overwhelmingly described a gaping wound in the right rear of JFK's scalp and skull, an area that appears entirely undamaged in the autopsy photographs. (Figures 1A and 1B) These "pro-conspiracy" accounts of a rearward, gaping skull wound have encouraged skeptics that Kennedy was shot at least once from the front, the rearward skull damage marking that bullet's exit.

JFK's brain photographs and the autopsy report reveal no significant damage to the cerebellum, the small lobe of the brain found in the bottom, rear portion of the skull, or to the rear of the brain. Besides showing no cerebellum damage, JFK's autopsy photographs show that the portion of JFK's skull and scalp behind the right ear—in the region overlying the cerebellum—is fully intact. The only visible blemish is what appears to be a small wound, possibly a bullet wound, near the top rear of the skull in the area of JFK's cowlick.

The blow-out exit wound is on the right side of JFK's head. It involves the right side and right top portion of the head, including a small defect at the edge of JFK's forehead. (Figure 4) This forward damage implies damage to the bones in the area, the so-called anterior parietal, anterior temporal, and frontal bones. (Figure 6) On the basis of the photographs and the X-rays, the HSCA concluded that in fact there *was* frontal bone damage, because the bullet had exited through the frontal bone.[85] The autopsy photographs, however, have come under suspicion in the wake of ARRB findings. Witnesses claim autopsy photographs are missing, that they don't show the wounds the way they were, and that a different brain than JFK's appears in the official autopsy photographs.[86]

The wounds we see in the autopsy pictures, it should be emphasized, *could be* explained by a shot from Oswald's alleged perch, above and behind JFK. But this is only true if the autopsy report's claim that the bullet entered JFK's skull near the bottom, near the "external occipital protuberance," is wrong. If, instead, the bullet entered near the top of JFK's skull, then blasted out the right front, blowing out part of the frontal bone with it, the wounds might fit with a shot from Oswald's supposed position.

The autopsy X-rays, which have come under a cloud from work done by David Mantik, MD, Ph.D.,[87] do in fact "prove" a significant portion of JFK's right frontal bone was blasted away. Frontal bone loss is visible in both "projections"—that is, in X-rays taken from front-to-back, the "anteroposterior" or "AP" projection, and two images taken from the side, the "lateral." The lateral films, however, don't show posterior parietal and occipital bone to be missing where it appears to be missing in the AP X-rays. And so while there are inconsistencies between the AP and lateral X-rays, at least the lateral X-rays back up the autopsy photographs that show no damage to the rear of JFK's head, but only to the front, along the right side and the top.

With the compelling "hard" evidence of at least partially corroborating autopsy photographs and X-rays, one might expect the conflicts would be easily resolved. But they linger. And they linger not only because of the conflicts between the lateral and AP X-rays, which are significant, but also because there is overwhelming, contrary evidence from credible witnesses that can't be easily explained or disregarded. Those witnesses corroborate what is seen in the AP X-ray, but not the lateral: missing bone in the rear of JFK's skull.

The autopsy report, for example, contradicts *both* the photographs and X-rays. It says the bullet entered the rear of JFK's skull through the bottom of his skull, well below where any obvious wound appears in the autopsy photographs, and it mentions no loss of, or damage to, frontal bone. Instead, the report describes what the pathologists depicted in the Rydberg diagram for the Warren Commission (Figure 3): a continuous bony defect involving the right parietal, temporal and occipital bones, that is, in the right rear of JFK's skull, just where so many witnesses, including the Dallas doctors, said it was!

Thus the autopsy pathologists, who labored over the body for several hours, apparently agree with the Parkland doctors about where JFK's skull damage was. But neither agrees with the autopsy photographs and X-rays. Even ignoring that peculiarity, had Oswald truly inflicted the skull wound—with a rearward-entering bullet exploding out of the right front of JFK's skull—one might have expected that some witness—*any* witness—would have reported seeing this. But no one did, at least not when his memory was fresh.

Dallas Doctors and JFK's Skull Wound

To illustrate the conflict between the photographs and the witnesses, we will begin by citing the same treating physicians who were showcased in *JAMA*: Parkland Hospital's anesthesiology professor Marion, "Pepper," Jenkins, MD, and surgeons Malcolm Perry, MD, Charles Baxter, MD, Charles Carrico, MD and Robert McClelland, MD. JFK's unsuccessful, 30-minute resuscitation afforded these men ample opportunity to see JFK's skull damage. (In recounting witness statements, preference is accorded a given witness's earliest account, for it is widely recognized that later statements are subject to degradation from memory loss or outside influences.)

Marion Thomas Jenkins, MD:

On the day of the assassination, in clinical notes published by the Warren Commission, Pepper Jenkins wrote that there was, *"a great laceration on the right side of the head (temporal and occipital) [sic], causing a great defect in the skull ... even to the extent that the cerebellum had protruded from the wound."*[88] Before the Warren Commission, Jenkins testified, "Part of the brain was herniated; *I really think part of the cerebellum*, as I recognized it, was herniated from the wound...."[89] Jenkins added that he believed that the cerebellum-exuding wound was a wound of exit, saying, "...the wound with the exploded area of the scalp, as I interpreted it being exploded, I would interpret it being a wound of exit ...."[90] (emphasis added throughout) *

Charles Baxter, MD:

In longhand notes prepared on 11/22/63, and published in the Warren Report (p. 523), Charles Baxter wrote, "...the right temporal and *occipital* bones were missing and the brain was lying on the table...." Under oath to the Warren Commission, Baxter said, "...literally the right side of his head had been blown off. With this and the observation that the *cerebellum was present* ... ."[91] (emphasis added)

Charles James Carrico, MD:

Writing in longhand on the day of the assassination, Carrico, wrote, "(the skull) wound had avulsed the calvarium and shredded brain tissue present with profuse oozing ... attempts to control slow oozing from *cerebral and cerebellar tissue* via packs instituted...."[92] He described JFK's skull wound to the Warren Commission as a "*defect in the posterior skull, the occipital region.*"[93] (emphasis added)

Malcolm Perry, MD:

In a note written at Parkland Hospital and dated 11-22-63, Perry described the head wound as, "A large wound of the *right posterior cranium*...."[94] (emphasis added) Describing Kennedy's appearance to the Warren Commission, Perry stated, "... there was a large avulsive wound on the right posterior cranium ... ,"[95] and, "... I noted a large avulsive wound of the right parietal occipital area, in which both scalp and portions of skull were absent...."[96]

---

* The brain is composed of two major portions: the large right and left "cerebral" lobes (cerebrum), and the much smaller cerebellum. The cerebellum is a separate lobe of the brain that is confined to the bottom rear portion of the brain. It has a distinctive surface appearance that makes it easy to tell from the far larger cerebrum. (Figure 7)

Robert McClelland, MD:

Testifying before the Warren Commission, McClelland said, "... I could very closely examine the head wound, and I noted that the *right posterior portion* of the skull had been extremely blasted ...so that the parietal bone was protruded up through the scalp and seemed to be fractured almost along its right *posterior half,* as well as some of the *occipital bone being fractured in its lateral half,* and ... you could actually look down into the skull cavity itself and see that probably a third or so, at least, of the brain tissue, *posterior cerebral tissue and some of the cerebellar* tissue had been blasted out....."[97] (emphasis added) [*JAMA* reported that McClelland had said, "by looking at the head wound, as I did ... the wound I observed did appear consistent with a shot from the front."[98]]

Inconsistent Accounts

Although there is little reason to distrust the earliest accounts of *JAMA*'s sources, the most recent claims of at least three of them must be considered suspect. In government interviews in the late 70s, Drs. Jenkins, Carrico and Perry were still singing the same old songs they had sung in the 60s. But in the wake of Crenshaw's 1991 book, in which he implied that they had been part of a 'conspiracy of silence,' they abruptly changed melodies. They even went so far as to sing a sour note about a widely respected Parkland professor and colleague, Robert McClelland, for not changing his tune the way they had. The examples are illuminating.

In 1978, HSCA counsel D. Andy Purdy, JD interviewed Pepper Jenkins. "Regarding the head wound," Purdy reported, "Dr. Jenkins said that only one segment of bone was blown out—it was a segment of occipital or temporal bone. He noted that a portion of the cerebellum (lower rear brain) *[sic]* was hanging out from a hole in the right—rear of the head."[99] The following year, the *American Medical News* quoted Jenkins to say that Kennedy "had part of his head blown away and part of his cerebellum was hanging out."[100]

Never acknowledging that Jenkins had repeatedly used the terms "cerebellum" and "occipital," author Gerald Posner reported that Jenkins had told him, "The description of the cerebellum was my fault ... When I read my report over I realized there could not be any cerebellum. The autopsy photo, with the rear of the head intact and a protrusion in the parietal region, is the way I remember it. I never did say occipital."[101] (He had, of course.) When informed that his colleague, Bob McClelland, MD, had said, "I saw a piece of cerebellum fall out on the stretcher." Jenkins responded, "Bob is an excellent surgeon. He knows anatomy. I hate to say Bob is mistaken, but that is clearly not right ... ."[102]

Similarly, after an HSCA interview in 1978, Purdy reported that Charles Carrico had said, "[The skull wound] was a fairly large wound in the right side of the head, in the parietal, occipital area. [sic] One could see blood and brains, both cerebellum/and cerebrum fragments in that wound." [sic][103] Like Jenkins, Carrico's memory seemed to undergo a transformation when confronted by Posner. "We saw a large hole on the right side of his head," Carrico is reported to have said. "I don't believe we saw any occipital bone. It was not there. [The location of the skull defect] was parietal bone... ."[104]

The HSCA also interviewed Malcolm Perry in 1978, reporting that, "Dr. Perry...believed the head wound was located on the 'occipital parietal' [sic] region of the skull and that the right posterior aspect of the skull was missing... ,"[105] and that, "I looked at the head wound briefly by leaning over the table and noticed that the parietal occipital head wound was largely avulsive and there was visible brain tissue in the macard [sic] and some cerebellum seen... ."[106]

But then, when interviewed in 1992 by Posner, Perry apparently said, "I did not see any cerebellum."[107] When informed by Posner that McClelland had claimed, "I saw cerebellum fall out on the stretcher," Perry apparently responded, "I am astonished that Bob would say that ... It shows such poor judgment, and usually he has such good judgment." In 1998, after JFK Review Board counsel T. Jeremy Gunn quoted Perry's own Warren Commission description of JFK's "right posterior cranium" injury,[108] Perry quickly retreated, lamely lamenting that,

"I made only a cursory examination of the head … I didn't look at it. I was in some kind of a hurry."[109]

Prior to the moment these witnesses were challenged by *JAMA* and Posner, they had repeatedly given consistent "pro-conspiracy" descriptions of JFK's skull wound. That is, they had described a gaping rearward skull wound consistent with a shot from the front. But readers who relied solely upon *JAMA* and Posner for their information would never have learned of it. (It is difficult to square Posner's failing to explore the early accounts and testimonies of his interviewees with the advice he gave his readers: "Testimony closer to the event must be given greater weight than changes or additions made years later, when the witness's own memory is often muddied or influenced by television programs, films, books, and discussions with others."[110])

Additional Corroboration from Parkland

Though perhaps differing slightly in emphasis, it is clear that what was initially being described is not the blowout wound visible in the photograph in front of JFK's right ear, but instead one behind it. A diagram approved by McClelland—and first published in the 1967 book, *Six Seconds in Dallas*—graphically depicts the damage.[111] Parkland's Paul Peters also endorsed McClelland's image in a letter to author Harrison Livingstone (Figure 8) And there was additional corroboration from other Parkland witnesses:

Kemp Clark, MD was Professor and Director of Neurological Surgery at Parkland Hospital in 1963. In an undated note apparently written contemporaneously at Parkland and published by the Warren Commission, he described the President's skull wound as: "...*in the occipital region* of the skull …There was a large wound in the right *occipitoparietal region* … Both cerebral and *cerebellar tissue* were extruding from the wound."[112] In a hand-written hospital note dated 11-22-63, Dr. Clark wrote, "a large 3 x3 cm remnant of cerebral tissue present … there was a smaller amount of *cerebellar tissue* present also...There was a large wound beginning in the right *occiput extending into the parietal* region ... Much of the skull appeared gone at the brief examination...."[113] (emphasis added throughout.)

Robert Grossman, MD was an assistant professor of neurosurgery at Parkland Hospital in 1963. Grossman was not interviewed by the Warren Commission. His observations were first reported in a *Boston Globe* article: "... [Grossman] observed two separate wounds, a large defect in the parietal area 'above the right ear, and a second wound, about one-and-a-quarter [sic] inches in diameter,' *located squarely in the 'occiput.'* "[114] (emphasis added) (Grossman gave a similar account to the ARRB. (Figure 9)

Ronald Coy Jones, MD was a surgery resident at Parkland Hospital in 1963. He told the Warren Commission, "(JFK) had a large wound in the right *posterior side* of the head...There was large defect in the *back side of the head* ... (there) appeared to be an *exit wound in the posterior portion of the skull.*"[115] (emphasis added)

Gene Aiken, MD was an anesthesiologist at Parkland Hospital in 1963. He told the Warren Commisison, "The back of the right *occipitalparietal portion of his head* was shattered with brain substance extruding ... I assume *the right occipitalparietal region was the exit*, so to speak, that he had probably been hit on the other side of the head, or at least tangentially in the back of the head...."[116] (emphasis added)

Paul Peters, MD was a surgery resident at Parkland Hospital. In 1964 he testified that, "I noticed that there was a large defect in the *occiput*...It seemed to me that in the right *occipitalparietal area* that there was a large defect."[117] (emphasis added) Peters, moreover, validated the "McClelland" diagram (Figure 8) in a letter to authors Robert Groden and Harrison Livingstone.

Pat Hutton, RN, was an attending registered nurse at Parkland Hospital in 1963. In a contemporaneous memo published by the Warren Commission, Hutton wrote that, "Mr. Kennedy was bleeding profusely from a wound in the *back of his head*, and was lying there unresponsive ... (there was a) massive opening in the *back of the head*."[118] (emphasis added)

JFK Evidence and *JAMA*

Having reviewed the contemporaneous accounts, it is worth considering how *JAMA* handled JFK's medical/autopsy witnesses and evidence. *JAMA*'s approach suggested its objectives were not entirely scientific. Crowing that they were resolving all the important controversies about JFK's autopsy in the first article in the May 27, 1992 issue, Breo/Lundberg clobbered Oliver Stone's popular movie on every page. Pummeling the dissident doctor in Dallas by citing his Parkland colleagues' refutations, they bashed Crenshaw and his then best-selling book, *JFK: Conspiracy of Silence*, on every page of the second article.

Perhaps because the articles were considered "mere" journalism, to his discredit Lundberg elected to forgo *JAMA's* customary fact-checking. With Stone and Crenshaw in their crosshairs, Breo and Lundberg may have seen little reason to check up on bona fide witnesses who were passing them precisely the kind of ammunition they were looking for.

The unfortunate results were immediately apparent. In the first sentence of his first article, Breo commenced fire: "There are two and only two physicians who know exactly what happened—and didn't happen—during their autopsy of President John F. Kennedy on the night on November 22, 1963 ... ."[119] The two, Humes and Boswell, were *not* the "only two." Nor were either even the best qualified of Kennedy's three pathologists. Breo forgot to mention, or to feature, Pierre Finck, MD, the only forensics-trained autopsist who participated. (Singed by criticism for this omission, Breo subsequently flew to Switzerland and interviewed Finck.[120])

In the third sentence, Breo struck again. "It [*JAMA*'s interview] is the only time that Humes and Boswell have publicly discussed their famous case...." Breo missed the mark again. As noted in Josiah Thompson's book, *Six Seconds in Dallas,* it turns out that Boswell had given Thompson an interview way back on January 11, 1967.[121] Humes had given an interview to Dan Rather in June, 1967 for a CBS special that was broadcast on June 25th to 28th.[122] Humes, Boswell (and Finck) had been publicly interviewed by the HSCA, Humes even appearing on television during a second, solo interview.[123] Boswell had given an interview to the *Baltimore Sun*[124] and to the *New York Times,*[125] and Humes had given an interview to author David Lifton.[126] Though not important in terms of our understanding of the facts of the case, these sloppy errors reflect the unfamiliarity and laziness of *JAMA*'s author and reviewers concerning the facts in the case, and they typify the rest of the work.

The first article consisted of little more than JFK's pathologists validating their original work and findings, something, as we will see, they'd previously done at the behest of the U.S. Justice Department. The *HSCA*'s scathing criticisms, including its (perhaps wrong) conclusion that the pathologists had mislocated JFK's fatal skull wound by a whopping 100-mm, were ignored. The authors were apparently so unfamiliar with the evidence that they failed to even mention the colossal error that, by then, had already long been an important controversy. This particular "mistake" was a central finding of the Clark Panel and HSCA probes, and it had even been an important theme of several books on the murder.[127] Why, after all, should even Warren loyalists, to say nothing of skeptics, have been expected to trust the self-aggrandizing assertions of men who (government experts had concluded) mistook the top of JFK's head for the bottom? Such a simple oversight would have been easily avoided had the *JAMA* but retained a consultant with even a rudimentary grasp of the case.

Breo paid greater attention to JFK's wounds in the second article, the one that featured the Parkland doctors. A comment attributed to Charles Carrico pretty much summed up *JAMA*'s exploration: "Nothing we observed contradicts the autopsy finding that the bullets were fired from above and behind by a high-velocity rifle."[128] Of course the autopsy-contradicting statements these same men had made from the day of the assassination did precisely that. Unfortunately, the information *JAMA* reported from the Dallas doctors was as scientifically unhelpful to an understanding of Kennedy's injuries as it was harmful to the American Medical Association's legal and financial position vis-à-vis Charles Crenshaw. (The Parkland doctors apparently only elaborated upon the specifics of JFK's injuries to Posner. See below.)

A Costly Mistake

Broadly hinting that Crenshaw was a fraud who had never witnessed the events described in his book, *JAMA* wrote: "Since it is hard to prove a negative, no one can say with certainty what some suspect—that Crenshaw was *not even in* the trauma room; none of the four [Jenkins, Baxter, Carrico and Perry] recalls ever seeing him at the scene,"[129] and, "...Most of those who know the facts express disgust at Crenshaw's actions and question if he was involved in the care of the President at all...".[130] (emphasis added) This was a damning charge, and *JAMA* was not the only source reporting that Parkland physicians were skeptical about Crenshaw's participation. Gerald Posner wrote that Parkland's Ronald Jones had told him, "I don't remember (Crenshaw) in there (JFK's trauma room) at any time," and Charles Baxter, MD allegedly chimed in, "Neither do I!"[131]

Besides suggesting he was a non-witness, Crenshaw's colleagues also employed extraordinarily harsh language in *JAMA* to ridicule several claims in *JFK: Conspiracy of Silence:* that Crenshaw had been in the forefront of the resuscitation effort; that JFK's throat wound had been tampered with after he left Parkland; and that perhaps the autopsy photographs had been falsified. His book was dismissed as "bogus stuff" and "pathetic," and *JAMA* attributed to Dr. Baxter the opinion that Crenshaw's only wrote the book out of "a desire for personal recognition and monetary gain."[132]

JAMA was right, at least about one of the charges. But it was one that Crenshaw had acknowledged in the *New York Times* the moment Breo's articles were publicized: Crenshaw's book *had* exaggerated his role. The *Times* reported: "Dr. Crenshaw ... admitted in an interview that the role he played in Kennedy's case was minor ... Dr. Crenshaw said that he relied on his co-authors ... for the facts of the assassination and that they took 'poetic license' in describing his role ... 'I am sorry that image came through,' Dr. Crenshaw said, but 'it's the way they edited it' after he last saw the material."[133] The other assertions of Breo's interviewees, however, were less well founded.

For example, though in 1992 Dr. Baxter was the first to suggest that Crenshaw was not in JFK's trauma room, in 1964, when his memory was fresh, Warren Commission counsel Arlan Specter asked Baxter under oath, "Can you identify any other doctors who were there at that time?" Baxter answered, "There was Crenshaw, Peters, and Kemp Clark, Dr Bashour finally came ... ."[134] The January 1964 issue of the *Texas State Journal of Medicine* reported that, "Dr. Jenkins recalls that the following physicians were members of the resuscitation team: Drs. Jenkins and Akin...Drs. Gerry Gustafson, Dale Coln, and Charles Crenshaw...."[135] Besides also being named as a participant by the *UPI*'s Bryce Miller in a story on 11/29/63, Warren Commission testimony from five witnesses placed Crenshaw at the scene,[136] including the testimony of another *JAMA*-featured witness, Robert McClelland, MD. Thus, although *JAMA* implied that its interviewees had proved Crenshaw never saw JFK, three of *JAMA*'s own sources had said Crenshaw was present in 1964.

Had Breo, or a responsible editor, merely bothered to check the published index to the Warren Commission's hearings, he would have found Crenshaw's name listed as appearing in volume VI, on pages 31–32, 40, 60, 80–81, and 141. A quick peek at the referenced pages would have proved Crenshaw's participation. It would also have proved the unreliability of Crenshaw's detractors, and one hopes it would have saved the AMA a morally and financially costly libel suit. Besides putting the AMA into a legal swamp, some of the Dallas doctors also tried to rewrite history.

Parkland Doctors vs. Crenshaw

For example, to refute Crenshaw's claim that JFK had a large rearward skull defect—which supported Crenshaw's frontal-entry-rearward-exit trajectory—Posner reported Baxter had said: "... I never even saw the back of (JFK's) head. The wound was on the right side, not the back."[137] (Posner neglected to ask Baxter why he was so sure JFK's skull wound was *not* in a location he *never even saw*.) It is worth recalling from the testimonies cited above that in 1964 Drs. Jenkins, Aiken, Jones and McClelland said that they thought the wound in the back of JFK's skull was an exit wound. Tipped off by skeptics to the fickle memories of the Dallas doctors, the ARRB challenged them.

On August 27, 1998, Review Board counsel, T. Jeremy Gunn, MD, Ph.D., conducted sworn interviews with Drs. Baxter, Jones, McClelland, Perry, and Peters. At the outset of the group interview, Gunn reviewed their descriptions of JFK's skull wound to the Warren Commission. Gunn remarked, "In my very lay sense—and I am not a doctor—there seems to be a fair degree of coherence among the testimony that you offered about the (rearward) location of the (skull) wound."[138] Confronted with so many near identical descriptions, including his own, Baxter quickly backpedaled: "None of us at that time, I don't think, were in any position to view the head injury. And, in fact, I never saw anything above the scalpline, forehead line that I could comment on."[139] *JAMA* had heard much the same thing, reporting: "Dr. Jenkins doubts if any of the Parkland physicians even had a good look at the President's head."[140]

Of course, the "temporal and occipital" skull bones Baxter mentioned on the day of the assassination are far behind the scalp line and it is difficult to imagine he would have specified them originally if he'd not at least gotten a reasonable glimpse. They are structures found on the back and side of the skull, as is the cerebellum that he, Carrico, Perry, McClelland, Clark, and Jenkins described seeing. Moreover, Paul Peters said that it was Jenkins who, while sitting at the President's head, advised the other Dallas doctors to take a closer look at JFK's skull damage before pressing forward with efforts to save his life.[141] But

Baxter's comments raise an interesting question: Did they really get a good look at JFK's wounds at Parkland?

Parkland Witnesses and JFK's Skull Wound

Because the autopsy photographs show no wound in the rear of JFK's skull, an explanation has been sought for how it was that so many Parkland physicians, including neurosurgeons, said they saw such a wound. The *Boston Globe* raised the issue, reporting that, "some [Parkland] doctors doubted the extent to which a wound to the rear of the head would have been visible since the President was lying supine with the back of his head on a hospital cart."

The *Globe* immediately refuted that speculation: "But others, like [Dr. Richard] Dulaney and [neurosurgeon Dr. Robert] Grossman, said the head at some point was lifted up, thereby exposing the rear wound."[142] Similarly, author David Lifton reported that Parkland emergency nurse Audrey Bell, who couldn't see JFK's head wound though she was standing on the right side, asked Dr. Perry, "'Where was the wound?' Perry pointed to the back of the President's head and moved the head slightly in order to show her the wound."[143] During sworn interviews with the JFK Review Board in 1998, Dr. Paul Peters reported, "[anesthesiologist Dr. Marion T.] Jenkins said, 'Boys, before you think about opening the chest, you'd better step up here and look at this brain.' And so at that point I did step around Dr. Baxter and looked in the President's head...."[144] (Figure 8) The ARRB's Gunn interviewed neurosurgeon Robert Grossman, MD on March 21, 1997, reporting, "[Grossman] and Kemp Clark [Chairman of Neurosurgery at Parkland] [sic] together lifted President Kennedy's head so as to be able to observe the damage to the President's head."[145]

Thus it seems reasonable to suppose that not only did they have plenty of time to get a good look at Kennedy's skull injuries, the Dallas doctors took responsible and appropriate steps to examine the skull wound before pronouncing the President dead. However, their early descriptions don't square well with the autopsy photographs.

Were Dallas Doctors Wrong About Autopsy Photographs?

In all, over 20 witnesses from Parkland Hospital gave accounts that closely mirrored the witnesses cited above. (Table 1) Besides conflicting with the autopsy photographs, there were other problems with the descriptions of the Parkland witnesses. It is common knowledge that bullets tend to leave a small wound at the point of entrance in a skull and—after tumbling through bone, brain, bone again, then blasting out through the scalp—a larger wound at the point of exit. The reports from Parkland encouraged skeptics who were convinced JFK had been hit twice in the head, from both the front and the rear.[146] Even if not an exit wound, a gaping rearward wound of any sort seemed the unlikely outcome of a single shot that had done what the Warren Commission said it had: enter from behind and blast out thorough the right side of the skull.

The HSCA clearly understood the implications of the conflict between the witnesses and the autopsy photographs. After investigating, the HSCA dealt a severe blow to the skeptics. It wrote, "Critics of the Warren Commission's medical evidence findings have found [sic] on the observations recorded by the Parkland Hospital doctors. They believe it is unlikely that trained medical personnel could be so consistently in error regarding the nature of the wound, even though their recollections were not based on careful examinations of the wounds...."[147] Drawing upon "Staff interviews with persons present at the autopsy," the HSCA countered that, "In disagreement with the observations of the Parkland doctors are the 26 people present at the autopsy. *All of those interviewed* who attended the autopsy corroborated the general location of the wounds as depicted in the photographs; *none had differing accounts*...it appears more probable that the observations of the Parkland doctors are incorrect."[148](emphasis added)

The HSCA's finding was devastating to skeptics who believed that Parkland witnesses proved a different wound, a different bullet trajectory, and, most importantly, perhaps even a different gunman than Oswald. *JAMA* tried to put the mistake in perspective, explaining that Parkland witnesses were more concerned with saving JFK's life in an emergency situation than accurately observing his wounds.[149] The refuting autopsy witnesses, some of whom were physicians, were clearly in a better position than witnesses in Dallas. They calmly watched as the pathologists explored JFK's wounds over a period of several hours. But the proof—the autopsy witnesses' interviews—did not appear anywhere in the 12 volumes the HSCA published. Nor were they in any way accessible to the public. Had it not been for the ARRB's interest in this area, for which credit may be due to the attention drawn to the topic by *JAMA*, these non-sensitive interviews might have remained state secrets until the required declassification date, sometime in 2028.

Suppressed Evidence Supports Dallas Doctors

ARRB-released documents have revealed for the first time that the HSCA misrepresented the statements of its own Bethesda autopsy witnesses on the location of JFK's skull defect. The HSCA also misrepresented the Warren Commission statements of the autopsy witnesses as well, that is, assuming the HSCA author was aware of them. It was not true, as the HSCA had reported, that it had 26 autopsy witnesses refuting the Dallas doctors. The HSCA had interviewed perhaps 13 autopsy witnesses. None of them had disagreed with the descriptions given by the Dallas doctors. On the contrary, whereas over 20 witnesses at Parkland described JFK's skull defect as rearward, as many autopsy witnesses said the same thing, whether in public Warren Commission documents and interviews, or in the suppressed HSCA interviews. In fact, not a single one of the autopsy witnesses did what the HSCA said they all had done—corroborate the right-front skull wound that appears in the photographs. (Table 2)

For example, in his Warren Commission testimony Secret Service Agent Clinton J. Hill, said, "When I arrived the autopsy had been completed and ... I observed ... (a) *wound on the right rear portion of the skull*."[150] This is the same wound he described as perhaps the first person to ever really see JFK's skull wound up close. Describing his scampering aboard JFK's limo the moment the shots rang out, Hill, in a Warren Commission-published memo, said, "As I lay over the top of the back seat [of the President's limousine] I noticed a *portion of the*

President's head on the right rear side was missing...."[151] Though unacknowledged by the HSCA, Hill's recollections, as well as other, similar descriptions by witnesses who were at the autopsy, had been available in the Warren Commission volumes since 1964. But what of the HSCA's suppressed autopsy witnesses?

Jan Gail Rudnicki, a lab assistant on the night of the autopsy, was interviewed on 5/2/78 by the HSCA. Though no transcript survives, the interviewer, HSCA counsel Mark Flanagan, JD, reported Rudnicki told him, the *"back-right quadrant of the head was missing."*[152] Philip C. Wehle, Commanding officer of the military District of Washington, D. C., was interviewed by HSCA Counsel D. Andy Purdy, JD on 8-19-77. Purdy's recently released memo, released with no transcript, states, "[Wehle] noted that the wound was in the *back of the head* so he would not see it because the President was lying face up ... ."[153] Several of the autopsy witnesses, including two FBI agents, prepared diagrams for the HSCA that depicted JFK's skull defect as rearward. (Figure 10)These interviews and diagrams were all suppressed.

We searched for the author of the HSCA's inaccurate summary, and the identity of the person who decided to keep the interviews and diagrams from the public. Author Aguilar wrote HSCA Counsel Mark Flanagan, JD, who had conducted a number of the interviews, but he never wrote back. HSCA Counsel D. Andy Purdy, JD, who conducted many of the interviews, and the former HSCA chief counsel, Robert Blakey, now a Notre Dame University law professor, both denied any knowledge of who had written the inaccurate passage. Purdy did allow, however, that he was "not happy" with the passage.

As previously noted, the public was not the only group that was kept in the dark about the HSCA's autopsy witnesses. So too were the HSCA's own expert forensic consultants. In 1994, author Aguilar showed both the head of the HSCA's forensic panel, Michael Baden, MD, and one of the panelists, co-author Wecht, the suppressed autopsy interviews and diagrams. Neither had ever seen them before, despite the fact it was their responsibility to assess this evidence for the HSCA.

Since their analysis assumed the photographs accurately represented

JFK's wounds, had the forensic panel known that the Dallas and morgue witnesses had *both* contradicted the images, their task would have become even more difficult than it already was. It's no mystery why. For not only would they have had to explain (at least to themselves) how over 40 witnesses from two different locations got it wrong, they would also have had to explain how the witnesses nevertheless all agreed on the same wrong location. A simple and convincing explanation does not easily leap to mind. Nevertheless, had this knowledge not been withheld from the HSCA's forensics consultants, it might have led the HSCA investigators toward evidence only finally unearthed by the ARRB nearly twenty years later: the possibility that autopsy photographs are missing, and perhaps even that some of those that remain have been somehow tampered with.

Unreliable Witnesses?

What about witness reliability? Though sometimes dismissed as unreliable, the reigning authority on eyewitness testimony, Elizabeth Loftus, claims witnesses are not *always* unreliable. In fact, there are circumstances in which their reliability is high.[154] In part, her evidence is based upon a 1971 *Harvard Law Review* study. Marshall, Marquis and Oskamp found that when test subjects were asked about "salient" details of a complex and novel film clip scene they were shown, their accuracy rate was high: 78% to 98%. Even when a detail was *not* considered salient, as judged by the witnesses themselves, they were still accurate 60% of the time.[155]

Loftus has identified the factors that tend to degrade witness accuracy, most of which are relevant to the Kennedy case by not applying to it. Principal among them are: poor lighting, short duration of event, or a long duration between the event and when a witness is asked questions about it, the unimportance of event to the witness, the perceived threat of violence during the event, witness stress or drug/alcohol influence, and the absence of specialized training on the witness's part. Absent these factors, Loftus's work shows that witnesses are very reliable.[156]

With respect to JFK's skull damage, which in the Marshall study would have been considered a "salient detail," none of Loftus's adverse circumstances were present that would explain how both the witnesses in Dallas and in the morgue might have erred. Both groups were working as highly trained experts in their usual capacity, and in their usual circumstances and setting. Moreover, both groups had more than ample time and opportunity to make accurate observations, many of which were recorded immediately. The odds are overwhelming that they were right. Yet the autopsy photographs apparently prove that virtually all the witnesses were wrong, and wrong in the same way. So even if one were to accept witness error as the explanation, one would then have to explain how the witnesses made the exact same mistake by agreeing JFK had a gaping skull wound in the back of his head.

PART III: New Evidence Suggesting Tampering with the Autopsy Photographs

The file of John F. Kennedy's autopsy photographs is central to the case against Oswald. It is also controversial and confusing. The government reported that the images were authentic. But suppressed files show that the government tried, and failed, to match the images to the camera that took them. It reported nothing to the public about the failure, claiming instead that the images had been authenticated. The conflicts with the witnesses and inability of the images to jump that authentication hurdle are not the only blots on the photographic record of JFK's autopsy.

• All three of JFK's pathologists, Bethesda pathologist-witness Robert Karnai, MD and both autopsy photographers, recalled that specific photographs were taken during the President's autopsy that do not now exist.

• Chief White House Photographer Robert Knudsen told the HSCA, in formerly suppressed interviews conducted in 1978, that right after the assassination he developed images that do not now exist. In 1997 former government photographer Joe O'Donnell told the ARRB that in 1963 his friend, Robert Knudsen, showed him a photograph of JFK's head that revealed a large hole in the backside of the skull. No such image can now be found in the official inventory.

• Naval Photographic Center employee Saundra Spencer told the ARRB that while developing JFK's autopsy photographs shortly after the assassination she, like Joseph O'Donnell, also saw an image revealing a hole in the back of JFK's skull. In addition, she asserted that the film on which current autopsy photographs appear is film that was *not* used in the lab that is supposed to have developed the films in 1963.

• Chief autopsy photographer John Stringer disavowed the extant autopsy photographs of JFK's brain. Though Stringer was the photographer of record, he swore to the ARRB that he did not take the current images. And like Saundra Spencer, he said that the current images were taken on film he is certain he did not use in 1963.

• Robert Grossman, MD, a neurosurgeon who attended JFK at Parkland hospital in Dallas, was shown an image of the back of JFK's head taken during the autopsy. As ARRB investigator Doug Horne put it in an ARRB memo, "When shown the Ida Dox drawing of the back of the head autopsy image found on page 104 of HSCA Volume 7 (Figure 1A), Dr. Grossman immediately opined, 'that's completely incorrect.'"[157] Dr. Grossman then drew on a diagram of a human skull a moderately large defect square in the occiput that coincided with his clear recollection of the size and location of a defect in JFK's skull. (Figures 9A and 9B)

• Upon being shown the autopsy photographs for the first time in 1997, the two FBI agents who witnessed the autopsy, Francis X. O'Neill and James Sibert, told the ARRB that the image showing the backside of JFK's skull intact had been, as agent O'Neill put it, "doctored." Both agents corroborated Dallas and morgue witnesses who said that there was a sizable defect in the rear of JFK's skull, a contention first put forward in 1977 when O'Neill drew a diagram of JFK's skull for the HSCA—a diagram the HSCA suppressed. (Figure 10)

Is JFK's Photographic Inventory Complete?

But as with so much else in the Kennedy case, the photographic record of the autopsy is conflicted. There is, in fact, some evidence that the photographic file *is* complete. But that evidence is U. S. Justice Department-orchestrated evidence, and it is suspect.

The proof that the file of autopsy photographs is complete consists almost entirely of an affidavit (really an inventory of the autopsy evidence) entitled "Report of Inspection" that bears the signatures of two of JFK's pathologists, Humes and Boswell, the attending autopsy radiologist, John Ebersole, and the autopsy photographer, John Stringer. It was signed on November 10, 1966, after they had, at the request of the Department of Justice, "examine(d), identif(ied) and inventor(ied) the autopsy photographs for the first time."[158] The final sentence of the affidavit states, "The X-rays and photographs described and listed above include all the X-rays and photographs taken by us during the autopsy, and we have no reason to believe that any other photographs or X-rays were made during the autopsy."[159] Newly released files reveal that this exercise was but the first in a series of maneuvers in which the Justice Department, through JFK's autopsy team, energetically sought to reestablish its case for a sole assassin.

Although the 11/10/66 affidavit attested to completeness of the inventory, it did not address the key question of whether the photographs and X-rays supported the Warren Commission's autopsy conclusions. Apparently realizing this oversight, the Justice Department moved again. It arranged for yet another examination of the same material two months later, on January 20, 1967, "for the purpose," the autopsy team said, "of determining whether they (the photographs and X-rays) are consistent with the autopsy report."[160] Humes and Boswell were brought back. And this time Pierre Finck was recalled from duty in Vietnam for the reexamination. Not unexpectedly, they signed a second affidavit that declared that, "The photographs and x-rays *[sic]* corroborate ... our autopsy report."[161]

These two affidavits—the first an inventory of the autopsy photographs, the second an assertion the images validated the original autopsy findings—apparently reflect the importance LBJ's Attorney General Ramsey Clark, and perhaps even the President, attached to getting additional corroboration for the Warren Commission's autopsy conclusions, even if only the self-affirmations from JFK's original pathologists. For on January 21, 1967, 10 weeks after the inventory was signed, and the day after the autopsy team had reconvened, Ramsey Clark called LBJ.

In the tape-recorded call, Clark reported, "Ah, we had the three pathologists that performed the autopsy on the evening of November 22nd come in. We had to bring Finck from Vietnam ... They went into archives last night [sic] ... Now, we're run into one problem last night [sic] that we didn't know of. That is, there may be a photo missing. Dr. Humes ... testified before the Warren Commission that this one photo [was] made of the highest portion of the right lung. The other two doctors don't recall if such a photo was made. They do recall discussing the desired ability of making such a photo. But there is no such photo in these exhibits."[162] Thus, 10 weeks after Humes and Boswell had signed off on the completeness of the photo inventory, Humes was apparently grousing about a missing autopsy photograph.

LBJ took the matter seriously. In the President's own, once-secret, memo he memorialized Clark's comments, quoting Clark saying that, "On the other matter, I [Ramsey Clark] think we have the three pathologists and the photographer signed up now on the autopsy review and their conclusion is that the autopsy photos and x-rays [sic] conclusively support the autopsy report rendered by them to the Warren Commission *though we were not able to tie down the question of the missing photo entirely* but we feel much better about it and we have three of the four sign an affidavit that says these are all the photos that they took and they do not believe anybody else took any others. *There is this unfortunate reference in the Warren Commission report by Dr. Hinn* [sic—certainly "Dr. Humes," who was accurately named by Clark himself] *to a picture that just does not exist as far as we know.*"[163] (emphasis added)

So although the two attestations declared that no autopsy photos were missing, and that the images support the original autopsy conclusions, Ramsey Clark's recorded call and LBJ's memo prove that even in 1967, no less than the chief autopsy surgeon, the President and the Attorney General had specifically mentioned at least one autopsy photograph that did not exist. But with the pathologists' signing off that the photo file was whole in 1966, there seemed little reason to carry on a dispute. New files, however, have revived the dispute. They have also revealed the exertions the Justice Department undertook to extinguish that dispute.

The upshot is that it now appears likely that Justice arranged for the principals to falsely affirm the integrity of the autopsy proof of Oswald's guilt. In fact, there is reason to doubt that the signers really believed no autopsy photographs were missing when they signed "their" affidavit.

Part of the explanation for their signing can be inferred from the comment LBJ attributed to Clark, "we have [had] three of the four sign an affidavit." In other words, the signatories didn't prepare the affidavit, "we" at the U.S. Justice Department did. And *we* gave it to them to sign. Justice—the agency under whose authority the FBI disproved conspiracy in 1964—was scarcely a disinterested party. And yet, perhaps predictably, released files show that Justice probably prepared this dubious, if reassuring, document, and that Justice was also active in other ways behind the scene.

The Justice Department's role was shown by another declassified memorandum that was signed by one Carl W. Belcher of the U.S. Justice Department. It reads, "On the afternoon of November 10, 1966, I took the original and one carbon copy of the document entitled 'Report of Inspection by Naval Medical Staff on November 1, 1966 at National Archives of X-Rays and Photographs of Autopsy of President John F. Kennedy' to the Naval Medical Center, Bethesda, MD, where it was read and signed by Captain Humes, Dr. Boswell, Captain Ebersole and Mr. John T. Stringer. Certain ink corrections were made in the document before they signed it ... ."[164] If the signatories had written the document themselves, the Justice Department's Carl Belcher would hardly have had to take it to them to correct and sign.

And sure enough, the signed "Report of Inspection" affidavit on file at the National Archives has the "certain ink corrections" Belcher referred to. It also bears the signatures of only the four men he referred to, listed in exactly the same order he wrote them in this memo. But files released by the ARRB reveal even more. It turns out that this signed affidavit was but one of two, nearly identical affidavits. In the other one, however, the unsigned one, the final sentence that reads, "The X-rays and photographs described and listed above include all the X-rays and photographs taken by us during the autopsy … " is missing.

As mentioned, the Justice Department's 11/10/66 "Report of Inspection" was apparently judged insufficient to quell all doubts about JFK's autopsy findings. Nor was the department's January 26, 1967 re-exam enough—the episode in which JFK's autopsy team confirmed that the "validated" inventory validated their original findings. There was still more to be done. One year later, on January 26, 1968, Boswell wrote the Justice Department to request an independent reexamination of JFK's autopsy evidence.[165] In response, Ramsey Clark convened a civilian panel to do just that: the so-called "Clark Panel," of which we have already spoken. But was the request for a second opinion Boswell's idea?

Though Boswell's signature is affixed to the request, behind him one again finds the Justice Department in motion. Under oath, Boswell told the ARRB, "I was asked by … one of the attorneys for the Justice Department that I write them a letter and request a civilian group be appointed by the Justice Department, I believe, or the President or somebody. And I did write a letter to him, Carl Eardley."[166]

Noted Warren skeptic Harold Weisberg saw the signs of Boswell's having been nudged way back in 1969. "I am suggesting that Boswell's letter was both inspired and prepared by the federal government," Weisberg wrote. "Strangely for a man with an office and a profession," Weisberg reasoned, "[the letter] is typed and signed but on no letterhead, with no return address and, even more intriguing, on government-size paper, which is a half-inch smaller than standard."[167] (It appears that after this episode Boswell became a favorite of the Justice Department.

In *JAMA*, Boswell admitted that, "the US Justice Department … summoned me to New Orleans to refute Finck's testimony, if necessary. It turned out it wasn't necessary."[168])

While Clark's call to LBJ is apparently the first official reference to a missing autopsy photograph, neither Clark's recorded call nor LBJ's memo are quite accurate. Before the Warren Commission, Humes did not describe just one missing image, but *at least* two: a photograph of the interior of JFK's chest, and at least one more showing the entrance wound in skull bone. But more importantly, although they signed off on the completeness of the photo file in 1966, a case can be made (see below) that at least three of the four signatories signed fully aware that the declaration was false.

In summary, the U. S. Justice Department, whose investigative arm, the FBI, had allegedly disproved conspiracy in the early 1960s, coordinated a process in the late 1960s that sought to validate the original autopsy findings that were central to Oswald's guilt. That process consisted of at least three parts: The first was obtaining the signatures of JFK's autopsy team on an affidavit that asserted (falsely, as we will see) that they believed no autopsy photographs were missing. The second consisted of arranging for JFK's autopsists to review the autopsy evidence again for the purpose of declaring that it supported their original autopsy findings. The third consisted of directing one of the pathologists to call for an independent examination of the X-ray and photographic evidence.

Word of a fourth possible aspect of the Justice Department's energetic campaign came belatedly from Drs. Finck and Boswell, in declassified files and in new testimony.

In a memo dated March 11, 1969, Pierre Finck meticulously recounted that on February 16, 1969, he had received a telephone call from "E. F. Wegmann, a defense attorney for Clay Shaw," who "defends the conclusions of the Warren Commission and wanted me to come to New Orleans to testify."[169] After advising his superiors of the request, and after (inexplicably) notifying the Deputy Assistant Attorney General, Carl Eardley, Finck's memo recounts that he then went to Eardley's office and reviewed numerous documents pertaining to JFK's autopsy. Finck then flew to New Orleans and met with Shaw's defense counsels prior to testifying. However, Finck's damaging testimony was scant reward for this elaborate choreography. Justice sent in Boswell to refute Finck.

Both in *JAMA* and under oath to the ARRB, Boswell explained the rest of the story. He said that the Justice Department was "really upset" when Pierre Finck testified that a general, and not the chief pathologist, Humes, was in charge of JFK's autopsy. "So," Boswell testified, "[Justice] put me on a plane that day to New Orleans." "They [the Justice Department] ... talked to me and tried to get me to agree that [Finck] was very strange ...."[170] Then, Boswell explained, "They showed me the transcript of Pierre [Finck's] testimony for the past couple of days, and I spent all night reviewing that testimony."[171] The Justice Department's purpose, Boswell recalled, was to prepare him "to refute Finck's testimony."[172]

Ultimately, however, Boswell was never called to the stand. Nevertheless it is worth asking, as ARRB's counsel Gunn astutely put it to Boswell, "What was the United States Department of Justice doing in relationship to a case between the district attorney of New Orleans and a resident of New Orleans?"[173] And it is also interesting that the Justice Department worried so much about Finck that it prepared to undermine the better-credentialed, Army forensics specialist by sending in a Navy generalist, albeit someone who had already proved himself to be a willing Justice Department front during the creation of the Clark Panel. (Boswell's helpfulness was noted by the Justice Department. When Martin Luther King was shot, Boswell testified that he got yet another call from Carl Eardley. "J," Eardley pled, "we got a problem down in Memphis ... Would you go down there and supervise the autopsy?"[174])

Missing Photograph(s) of the Chest

Ramsey Clark's lament about the missing image "of the highest portion of the right lung" is clearly a reference to a picture that was taken of the interior of JFK's chest. In order to document the path of the nonfatal bullet through a bruised area at the top of JFK's lung cavity, Humes had told the Warren Commission, "Kodachrome photographs were made … in the interior of the President's chest." No such images are known to exist. Despite his signing off that the file of photographs was complete in 1966, Humes nevertheless continued to remember that he had taken these images. In 1978, the HSCA reported, "[Humes] specifically recall[ed photographs]...were taken of the President's chest...[these photographs] do not exist."[175] Under oath before the HSCA's forensic consultants, Humes said, "I distinctly recall going to great lengths trying to get the interior-upper portion of the right thorax illuminated … and what happened to that film I don't know."[176] Eighteen years later Humes said the same to the ARRB: "We took one of the interior of the right side of the thorax … and I never saw it. It never—whether it was underexposed or over-exposed or what happened to it, I don't know."[177] Humes was not the only person who had signed off on the completeness of the inventory who remembered taking these pictures.

Although Ramsey Clark reports Boswell was not certain about that image, a declassified 1977 HSCA interview with Boswell tells a different story. The HSCA reported that Boswell "thought they photographed 'the exposed thoracic cavity and lung,' but doesn't remember ever seeing those photographs."[178] In 1996, he told the same story. ARRB general counsel T. Jeremy Gunn asked Boswell, "Are there any other photographs that you remember having been taken during the time of the autopsy that you don't see here?" Boswell answered, "The only one that I have a faint memory of was the anterior of the right thorax. I don't see it, and haven't [*sic*] when we tried to find it on previous occasions, because that was very important because it did show the extra-pleural blood clot and was very important to our positioning that wound."[179]

Similarly, the chief autopsy photographer, John Stringer, told both the HSCA and the ARRB that chest photographs were missing.

The HSCA reported, "Stringer remembers taking at least two exposures of the body cavity."[180] He swore to the ARRB that, "There were some views that we—that were taken that were missing … I remember [photographing] some things inside the body that weren't there."[181] There is a particular irony to Stringer's account. During Ramsey Clark's call to LBJ, he stated that there was a way to track down the question of the missing image—by asking the autopsy photographer. "The only other witness that would have any judgment at all," Clark said, "would be the corpsman, naval corpsman, that took the photos. We have to talk to him." Either Stringer wasn't helpful or Clark never followed up. For there are no records that Stringer was ever asked about missing autopsy photographs before the HSCA in the late 1970s.

Nevertheless, Stringer later did say more about the general question of missing autopsy photographs. He took specific exception to the fact that the record reflects that he submitted 11 duplex film holders of undeveloped film to authorities, which should have yielded 22 images. And yet only 16 duplex images exist in the current inventory. (To the authors' knowledge, the last signatory, radiologist John Ebersole, who died in September 1993,[182] was never asked about the autopsy photographs.)

The taking of interior body photographs was also recalled by another autopsy participant, albeit one who had not signed the 11/1/66 affidavit. The HSCA reported that assistant autopsy photographer Floyd Reibe "thought he took about six pictures—'I think it was three [duplex] film packs'—of internal portions of the body."[183] Reibe also gave the HSCA new evidence pertaining to missing autopsy photographs. "Riebe said he took photographs (using) a Canon 35-mm single lens reflex and a Speedgraph [sic] lens 4 x 5."[184] There is no 35-mm film in the current inventory. Reibe repeated his claim about 35-mm film under oath to the ARRB, asserting that he'd taken six or seven 35-mm photographs with a Canon camera.[185] So besides the missing chest images Stringer, and possibly Reibe, took with the large format camera, there may also be 35-mm images missing.

Two questions naturally come to mind: First, does it make sense that the autopsy team would have really wanted to, or needed to, photograph the interior of JFK's chest? Second, why would witnesses who have repeatedly said autopsy photographs are missing have signed an affidavit saying the opposite?

On their reasons for taking the images, it must be recalled that the autopsy report described both a bruise of the tissues overlying, and outside of, the top of the lung ("parietal pleura"), as well as a bruise involving the tip of the right lung itself. Those bruises could not have been caused by the tracheostomy performed by the Dallas doctors. So they had to somehow be explained by JFK's bullet wounds. They took biopsy slides of the bruised lung tissue to document damage to that organ. But photographs were the best way to document, both medically and legally, the location of the "extra-pleural blood clot" at the top of JFK's chest cavity.

On why they signed a false affidavit, it is unlikely an indisputable explanation will ever be found to account for the actions of all the signatories. Nevertheless, the autopsy photographers gave the ARRB an illuminating explanation for having signed a similar, false affidavit. The ARRB located an affidavit dated 11/22/63—ARRB Exhibit #78—that specified the number of photographs that were taken on the night of the autopsy and surrendered by the photographers to the custody of Secret Service Agent Roy H. Kellerman. Exhibit # 78 was signed by both autopsy photographers.[186]

ARRB counsel Gunn asked Stringer: "Do you see the phrase, next to last sentence, of the document—that I'll read it to you: 'To my personal knowledge, this is the total amount of film exposed on this occasion.' Do you see that?"

> Stringer: "Yes."
> Gunn: "Is it your understanding that that statement is
>   incorrect?"
> Stringer: "Well, yes …."

Gunn: "When you signed this document, Exhibit 78, were you intending to either agree or disagree with the conclusion reached in the second to last—next to last sentence?"

Stringer: "I told him that I disagreed with him, but they said, 'Sign it.'"

Gunn: "And who is 'they' who said, 'Sign it.'?

Stringer: "Captain Stover." [Stringer's superior, the Commanding Officer of U.S. Naval Medical School.][187]

Although Gunn did not ask Stringer whether he further resisted in any way, later in this same interview Stringer made a concession that as a man under orders, "You don't object to things."

Guinn responded, "Some people do."

"Yeah, they do." Stringer observed, "But they don't last long."[188]

Similarly, the assistant autopsy photographer, Floyd Riebe, testified that this same affidavit, which also bore his signature, "would be incorrect, yes,"[189] for it did not list the 35-mm images he said he had taken. Reibe justified his signing in much the way Stringer had. ARRB counsel Gunn asked him: "If this statement had been given to you to sign to authenticate rather than [Captain] Stover, would you have signed this statement?"

Riebe: "If I was ordered to, yes ... We was shown this and told to sign it and that was it."[190]

Jeremy Gunn did not further explore this matter with Riebe. And, alas, though he had the opportunity to ask Drs. Humes and Boswell why they had signed off on the completeness of the inventory, he unfortunately never did. This, despite the fact the ARRB believed that Humes' prior testimony about missing autopsy notes had not been entirely truthful.

Missing Photographs of the Skull

The other, now missing, photographs Humes referred to in his Warren Commission testimony are at least as interesting as the missing chest photographs: images showing the entrance wound in the skull bone. As Humes described them to the Warren Commission, these photographs had been taken in such a way as to visually document the fatal bullet's direction. He said, "This [skull] wound then had the characteristics of wound of entrance from this direction through the two tables of the skull … and incidentally photographs illustrating this ["coning" or "beveling"] phenomenon [that show the bullet's direction] from both the external surface of the skull and from the internal surface were prepared."[191]

In 1978, Humes' claim was independently corroborated by Pierre Finck, MD. While testifying before the HSCA, he referred to some old notes he had brought along on the JFK case to help him. In these notes, which Finck apparently wrote near the time of the autopsy and submitted to the HSCA, he had written: "I help the Navy photographer to take photographs of the occipital wound (external and internal aspects) [sic]."[192] The purpose of such photographs, of course, was to show a forensically important feature of a bullet entrance wound: "beveling," or "coning." As with a B-B hitting a pane of glass, when a bullet goes through bone a small hole is usually left on the outside, and a larger, "beveled," crater is left on the inside. This "beveling phenomenon" is used by pathologists as a useful, if not infallible, aid in determining the direction of the bullet.

Since proving the cause of death with images of the fatal wound would have been the central purpose to photographing the autopsy, capturing the "beveling" in JFK's skull bone would have been a routine, elemental kind of documentation. Suitable images would only have been taken of bone, and not "soft tissue" such as scalp. For soft tissue will not demonstrate beveling, just as a bullet "wound" through a carpet will not show the "beveling" one would see in a "wound" through a pane of glass.

Before the HSCA in 1977, Finck described how he had directed the taking of images to specifically demonstrate how the beveling in the bone proved the bullet had entered low in JFK's skull, through the occipital bone. His testimony, originally suppressed and only released by the ARRB 15 years after the fact, shows him under siege before the HSCA's forensic consultants who were convinced the bullet had entered much higher than the occipital bone. Under oath Finck insisted he directed the taking of photographs of the low wound, photographs that have vanished.

In the following exchange, Finck was being shown the autopsy photographs before the forensics panel and asked to comment on them:

> HSCA Counsel D. Andy Purdy: "We have here a black and white blow up of that same spot [on the rear of JFK's scalp which he claimed was the location of the bullet's entrance]. You previously mentioned that your attempt here was to photograph the crater, I think was the word that you used."
>
> Finck: "In the bone, not in the scalp, because to determine the direction of the projectile the bone is a very good source of information so I emphasize the photographs of the crater seen from the inside the skull. What you are showing me is soft tissue wound [sic] in the scalp."

A few moments later, the following exchange occurred:

> Charles Petty, MD: "If I understand you correctly, Dr. Finck, you wanted particularly to have a photograph made of the external aspect of the skull from the back to show that there was no cratering to the outside of the skull."
>
> Finck: "Absolutely."

Petty: "Did you ever see such a photograph?"

Finck: "I don't think so and I brought with me memorandum referring to the examination of photographs in 1967... and as I can recall I never saw pictures of the outer aspect of the wound of entry in the back of the head and inner aspect in the skull in order to show a crater although I was there asking [the photographer to take] these photographs. I don't remember seeing those photographs."

Petty: "All right. Let me ask you one other question. In order to expose that area where the wound was present in the bone, did you have to or did someone have to dissect the scalp off of the bone in order to show this?"

Finck: "Yes."

Petty: "Was this a difficult dissection and did it go very low into the head so as to expose the external aspect of the posterior cranial fascia [*sic*—meant "fossa"]?"

Finck: "I don't remember the difficulty involved in separating the scalp from the skull but this was done in order to have a clear view of the outside and inside to show the crater from the inside ... the skull had to be separated from it in order to show in the back of the head the wound in the bone."[193]

There are no photographs showing JFK's scalp being reflected from the skull so as to demonstrate the skull wound, or anything else for that matter. The HSCA had no reason to publicly suppress this specific Finck interview except, perhaps, that it impugned the integrity of the very autopsy photographs that had supposedly been authenticated. Yet on this point, Finck was not alone. Both autopsy photographers also recalled that the scalp had been reflected for autopsy photographs. Testifying for the ARRB, Riebe was asked, "Do you recall whether any pictures were taken from angles very close to the inside of the cranium?" "Yes, I think Mr. Stringer did that when the body was on its side."[194] Stringer was asked, "Did you take any photographs of the head after scalp had been pulled down or reflected?" "Yes," Stringer answered.[195]

FBI Agents Suggest Photographs Tampered With

The ARRB interviewed the two FBI agents who were present during JFK's autopsy, Special Agents Francis X. O'Neill and James Sibert. Both had previously prepared diagrams of JFK's skull for the HSCA that had been originally suppressed and only finally declassified by the ARRB. The diagrams depicted a rearward defect in JFK's skull. (Figure 10) Interviewed by the ARRB and shown the autopsy images for the first time, both agents provided what is perhaps the most direct indictment of the extant autopsy images of JFK's skull.

ARRB Counsel Gunn asked agent O'Neill: "I'd like to ask you whether that photograph (Figure 1B) resembles what you saw from the back of the head at the time of the autopsy?"

O'Neill: "This looks like it's been doctored in some way[196]... I specifically do not recall those—I mean, being that clean or that fixed up. To me, it looks like these pictures have been ... It would appear to me that there was a—more of a massive wound...."[197]

Similarly, Gunn asked agent Sibert, "Mr. Sibert, does that photograph [of the back of JFK's head] correspond to your recollection of the back of President Kennedy's head?"

Sibert: "Well, I don't have a recollection of it being that intact, as compared with these other pictures. I don't remember seeing anything that was like this photo (126) ... I don't recall anything like this at all during the autopsy. There was much—well, the wound was more pronounced. And it looks like it could have been reconstructed or something, as compared with what my recollection was...."[198]

Have Autopsy Photogrpahs Disappeared?

With so many reports of images having been taken that do not now exist, the question naturally arises: Did anyone ever see autopsy images that have since disappeared? The answer, apparently, is yes.

In another previously suppressed HSCA interview, former White House photographer, Robert Knudsen, who has since died, reported that he developed some negatives from JFK's autopsy, which he examined while he processed them on November 23, 1963. During the HSCA's investigation, he was shown the complete photographic inventory. Repeatedly resisting pressure to back down, Knudsen insisted that in 1963 he saw at least one image not in the inventory he was shown in 1978: "I feel certain that there was the one [photograph] with the two probes [passed through JFK's chest]."[199]

Knudsen said he saw an image with metal probes passed completely through JFK's body from the back to the throat. Describing the path of the probes under oath, he said, "the point in the back (where the probe entered) was a little bit lower than the point in the front … So the probe was going diagonally from top to bottom, front to back…."[200] (The HSCA's forensics panel was not advised of the existence of this interview.) Robert Karnei, MD, a pathologist who attended the President's autopsy, gave the HSCA a similar account. The HSCA reported that, " [Karnei] recalls them putting the probe in and taking pictures [the body was on the side at the time] [sic]."[201] Oswald is supposed to have fired from above and behind JFK, who was sitting bolt upright when he took the nonfatal bullet. If the back wound was indeed the point of entrance, and the throat the exit, Oswald would have had to have fired from a much lower perch than the sixth floor of the School Depository for the back wound to have been lower than the throat wound.

There are two witnesses who said they saw photographs of JFK's head in 1963 that have since disappeared:

The first was a photographer with the United States Information Agency, Joseph O'Donnell. He was frequently detailed to the White House during the Kennedy era. Interviewed by ARRB Counsel T. Jeremy Gunn in 1997, O'Donnell claimed that within a month of the assassination he was shown JFK's autopsy photographs on two separate occasions by his personal friend, Robert Knudsen.

Gunn reported that on the first viewing O'Donnell "remembers a photograph of a gaping wound in the back of the head which was big enough to put a fist through, in which the image clearly showed a total absence of hair and bone, and a cavity which was the result of a lot of interior matter missing from inside the cranium."[202] On the second occasion, Gunn reported that Knudsen showed him a photograph, "in which the back of the head now looked completely intact. [O'Donnell] said that the appearance of the hair in the 'intact back of the head' photographs was wet, clean, and freshly combed. His interpretation of the differences in the photographs of the President's head was to attribute the differences to the restorative world of the embalmers."[203] [Knudsen, however, said nothing about such an image during his HSCA testimony.]

Saundra Kay Spencer, a photographic technician who developed and printed JFK autopsy images at the Naval Photographic Center (NPC) in November 1963, told the ARRB that she saw an image that revealed a hole one to two inches in diameter in the backside of JFK's skull. She located the spot on a diagram of a human skull, marking a defect that is considerably larger than, and well below, the small spot interpreted by the HSCA as a wound of entrance.[204] (Figure 11)

Moreover, she said that the images she developed looked nothing like those in the current inventory, but instead showed JFK's wounds all "cleaned up": "...none of the heavy damage that shows in these [National Archives] photographs were visible in the photographs that we did."[205] Moreover, the paper on which the current photographs are printed is not the paper that was used by her lab in 1963, a point on which she expressed confidence because she had kept in her personal possession, and produced for the ARRB, some of the paper that was used at the NPC at the time she printed JFK's autopsy images.[206]

The significant witness evidence that the ARRB compiled undermining the HSCA's autopsy conclusions is not the only reason the ARRB found to mistrust the HSCA on the autopsy evidence. It also found that the Select Committee had not been entirely honest when it reported that it had authenticated JFK's autopsy photographs.

Authenticated Autopsy Photographs?

Bolstering its case that the autopsy evidence was consistent with Oswald's guilt, the HSCA announced that it had authenticated the autopsy photographs. However, the HSCA admitted that its authentication was not quite complete: "Because the Department of Defense was unable to locate the camera and lens that were used to take these [autopsy] photographs, the [photographic] panel was unable to engage in an analysis similar to the one undertaken with the Oswald backyard pictures that was designed to determine whether a particular camera in issue had been used to take the photographs that were the subject of inquiry."[207]

In effect, the HSCA was saying that it was unhappy the original camera was unavailable to totally close the loop. Nevertheless, it expressed satisfaction the loop had been closed enough for confidence in the images because it had found features in the extant images that showed a kind of internal consistency one would find only in authentic images. Those consistencies essentially comprise virtually the entire HSCA case for "authentication." But there was an important part of the story the HSCA didn't tell.

Luckily, the JFK Review Board's Doug Horne did tell it, after he excavated that part of the story from suppressed HSCA files. It is a rather different story than the one implied by the HSCA's comment, "Because the Department of Defense was unable to locate the camera and lens that were used to take these [autopsy] photographs." Regarding that sentence, Horne wrote, "By late 1997, enough related documents had been located and assembled by the authors to bring into serious doubt the accuracy of the HSCA's [statement]."[208] It was not precisely true the Department of Defense had been unable to locate the camera used to take JFK's autopsy photographs.

Apparently, the DoD *had* found the camera. The DoD wrote the HSCA that "the only [camera] in use at the National Naval Medical Center in 1963"[209] had been sent to the HSCA for study. The HSCA, however, wasn't pleased with the DoD's camera. In a letter asking the Secretary of Defense to look for another one, HSCA Chief Counsel

Robert Blakey explained the problem: "[O]ur photographic experts have determined that this camera, or at least the particular lens and shutter attached to it, could not have been used to take [JFK's] autopsy pictures."[210] Whereas the HSCA had publicly claimed the original autopsy camera could not be found, the suppressed record suggests that camera *was* found, and that it was tested. And it also found that it couldn't be matched to Kennedy's images. The HSCA staff elected not to share any of this information with the public nor its panel of forensic consultants.

Horne reported that Kodak, which did work for the Review Board, found no evidence the current autopsy images had been falsified. And as Horne emphasized in his memo, the HSCA's misstatement, as misleading as it is, may not be as sinister as it seems at first blush. The type of camera used was a "view" camera. It had a flat, square back that houses the double-sided film packs, and an attached bellows. Attached to the front of the bellows are an interchangeable lens and a shutter mechanism, which may be switched out for different tasks. The lens and shutter used in 1963 may have been replaced by the time the DoD fetched the camera for the HSCA in 1977. And so a different lens or shutter *might* explain why the camera didn't match JFK's photographs. But unfortunately, there is no certainty that a different lens and shutter *do* explain the mismatch. Horne searched through the files for the tests the HSCA conducted that proved a mismatch, but could find none. He also searched for the camera, and reported it has vanished.

So while Horne was unable to confirm an innocent explanation for the mismatch, he was unable to exclude the obvious, sinister explanation: photo tampering. The Kodak finding that the extant images reveal no tampering proves that the extant images themselves have no internal inconsistencies that would prove tampering. It cannot, however, prove that no images are missing, which, evidence suggests, may well be the case. Nor can it disprove another possibility: that the current inventory is an entirely separate set of internally consistent images, but a different one than the one that may have originally existed.

The theory of some kind of photographic "doctoring," therefore, is not mere lunacy; it has significant support in the record. In fact, the word "doctored" was precisely the word the FBI agent who was at the autopsy used when he was shown JFK's autopsy photographs by the JFK Review Board.

Making Sense of the Mysteries

The stark differences between JFK's autopsy photographs and witness accounts make it reasonable to ask whether they can be reconciled without positing either an elaborate falsification of the extant images, or that myriad witnesses independently mistook a wound toward the front of JFK's skull for one in the back. There is some evidence that might provide such relief. But before offering speculation, some assumptions have to be made.

The autopsy team could have had little other purpose in taking autopsy photographs than to record the number and nature of JFK's wounds. Certain "diagnostic" pictures would have been wanted not only for the scientific record, but also to establish a factual, legal record for the anticipated trial of the then-living Oswald. Given those assumptions, there are baffling problems with the current inventory of autopsy pictures. Baffling, that is, if one also assumes that all the images that were taken on the night of the autopsy have survived to the present.

Perhaps the most peculiar aspect of the images to those of us who have seen the originals at the National Archives is what they don't show. For example, there is an image of the left profile of JFK lying on the table. It shows his neck and the undamaged side of his head, the camera positioned parallel to the plane of JFK's head and body, as it lay face up on the morgue table. This image would provide a perfect contrast to a photo of Kennedy's injured side. But there is no similar image showing the injured side. The closest analogous image is one shot from above and below JFK (Figure 4), but it is shot from such a low position that the full extent of JFK's skull wound is simply not visible. And since it was taken from above, the skull and scalp behind JFK's right ear are obscured by his ear. Would the autopsy team not have thought to take a picture of the injured side of JFK that shows the injuries in relation to his entire head and neck, that is, a picture taken with the same perspective as one taken of his uninjured side?

Similarly, there is really only a single photograph of JFK's skull wound. It is shot at such close proximity to JFK's skull that, as no less than Boswell put it himself when he was shown the image by the ARRB, "I'm sorry. I cannot orient this at all."[211] (Figure 12) It is virtually impossible to know which side is up, to know which bones are in the image, what part of the skull is being photographed, etc. Is frontal bone or occipital bone visible in this image? Not even Kennedy's pathologists know for sure. JFK's brain is absent in this key image, and the hollow interior of the skull is poorly illuminated. Would not a single, additional image have been taken of JFK's fatal wound, one taken from a slightly greater distance to allow an appreciation of the full extent of the damage, and its relation to JFK's cranial structures, such as his ear? Moreover, though they reported that photographs were taken before the autopsy commenced, there are no photographs taken of JFK's fatal skull wound before the brain was removed. Would trained surgeons not have appreciated what is obvious even to laymen—the importance of taking more than a single view of the fatal wound?

Then there are the statements of Humes, Finck and Stringer. They said they reflected JFK's scalp to photograph the precise location in the skull where the bullet entered. As discussed, Finck said he took pictures from both the inside and outside of the skull so that the diagnostic features of the bullet's passing would be visible in the photograph. Quite independently, Humes backed him up. Such an image would have been nothing more than rudimentary documentation. And it is only makes sense that the team would have wanted a picture like that. Moreover, both Humes and Finck said that they'd taken such images—in the early 60s, when their memories were fresh, and before the images became conspicuous by their absence.

Finally, there are the missing images of the interior of the chest that Humes, Boswell, Stringer and Riebe recalled having taken. It is common sense that they took such images. The autopsy team said that a bruise was visible at the very top of the lung cavity after the lungs had been removed. Boswell testified that by the end of the autopsy they had "reached the conclusion that there had been a transit wound through the neck during the autopsy."[212] Though the tissue slide taken from the lung proved that the blood had reached that organ, the only good way they had to show the location of the hemorrhage in JFK's chest wall was to photograph it. Humes, Boswell, and Stringer said they took at least one such image. But now it, or they, can't be found.

So while one can make a good case for the disappearance of autopsy photographs, what about direct falsification of images? Such tampering offers a tempting solution to the contradictions between the witnesses who said Kennedy had a large hole in the backside of his head, and photographs that show an undamaged scalp. And it would explain why the pictures didn't match the autopsy camera. Perhaps falsification is the answer after all. But there is at least one other possibility, one that was suggested by Boswell on two occasions.

During his appearance before the HSCA, Boswell said that there was a laceration that tore down into the backside of JFK's scalp. "It tore right down to that point," he said, indicating a spot on the low backside of JFK's scalp.[213] (Figure 1B) Elaborating to the ARRB, he explained that, while a large segment of bone measuring 10-cm x 17-cm was missing when JFK's skull was first examined, "the scalp could be closed from side to side so that it didn't appear that there was any scalp actually—scalp missing [sic]."[214] The image showing the backside of JFK's scalp intact, Boswell explained, "is the scalp of President Kennedy pulled forward" in order to take the photograph of the bullet wound.[215] However, behind JFK's right ear, under the scalp flap, Boswell said skull bone was missing. The scalp, however, was torn, and the controversial photograph was taken with the torn scalp flap being pulled across the backside of JFK's skull in a way that obscured the fact a large segment of bone was missing from the rear of the skull. [Boswell repeated to the ARRB his claim, first made to the HSCA, that the "spot" visible toward the top of JFK's scalp in this image (Figures 1A and 1B) was not the entrance wound. The real entrance wound was much lower in the back of JFK's scalp.]

This "innocent" explanation has the advantage of obviating need for sustaining the difficult argument for direct tampering with selected autopsy pictures. It does not, however, speak to the issue of missing images. With the members of the autopsy team having repeatedly, and independently, and with good reason, testified that pictures they took are missing, and with photo technicians having testified that images they developed are gone, there is reason to suspect images have been removed. The case is strengthened by additional factors, too. Although the central purpose of taking the photographs was to document JFK's fatal skull wound, unless some images of it are missing, one is constrained to believe that a surgical team settled for what any layman would likely not have settled for: taking only the few "nondiagnostic" images we have of the wound that killed a President.

"Nondiagnostic" Autopsy Photographs

The "nondiagnostic" nature of JFK's autopsy photography is perhaps best illustrated by comparing the relevant photos with the diagrams of JFK's skull damage that were prepared by members of the autopsy team. The first diagram, the so-called "face sheet" diagram, is a view of JFK's skull from the top. With the help of his colleagues, Boswell drew this sketch by hand during the autopsy, accidentally splattering JFK's blood on the page. The most meaningful marks on the sheet are the notations, "10," with arrows pointing right-to-left, and "17," written over the word "missing," and with arrows adjacent to the "17" pointing front-to-back. (Figure 13) Boswell told the HSCA[216] and ARRB[217] that when he first examined JFK's skull, he measured the area of missing bone at 10cm by 17cm. In 1996, ARRB Counsel Jeremy Gunn asked him, "[W]ould it be fair to say that when you first examined the body prior to any arrival of fragments from Dallas, the skull was missing from approximately those dimensions of 10 by 17(-cm)?" Boswell answered, "Yes."[218]

Yet there isn't a photograph in the entire inventory that depicts the full panorama of Kennedy's skull wound with the perspective that would satisfy the eye about the orientation or dimensions depicted in Boswell's diagram. Moreover, the autopsy report puts JFK's skull defect at 13-cm. This smaller dimension looks more like the size depicted in the Rydberg diagram (Figure 3), an image that depicts the entire right side of JFK's skull so that one can get an idea about orientation and dimension. Unless the current inventory has been trimmed, it appears that the same men who knew the value of perspective when they prepared Rydberg, knew nothing at all about it when they were wielding a camera.

JFK's Skull Wound: 13-cm or 17-cm?

Given that the Rydberg diagram shows a skull wound that seems to fit the size noted in the autopsy report—13-cm, what about the "17" noted on the autopsy face sheet? Boswell explained that the Rydberg diagram, which was drawn months after the autopsy,[219] and only from memory, "does not depict any of the skull wounds."[220] Though the rear portion of Rydberg's "skull" appears to show only a small entrance hole in otherwise intact occipital bone, the diagram, Boswell said, was meant only to show the appearance of the scalp in the rear, not the defect in the skull bone. The real defect in Kennedy's skull was far larger, Boswell explained.

Why, then, is there a 4-cm discrepancy between his face sheet and the autopsy report? Boswell gave the HSCA,[221] the ARRB, and one of the authors (Aguilar, in a recorded call)[222] the same explanation: after a late-arriving fragment was replaced into the backside of JFK's skull defect, the remaining gap then measured "only" 13-cm, the number used in the autopsy report. Given that the larger number was taken down at the time of the autopsy it carries greater weight as evidence than even the autopsy report. Thus, although Rydberg shows a skull defect involving the rear of the skull, evidence from the night of the autopsy, informed with Boswell's commonsense explanation, suggests JFK's skull wound was far larger than it appears in the Rydberg diagram, and that it extended even further rearward than it appears in Rydberg. In 1996, Boswell amplified upon his original diagram by drawing JFK's skull defect onto a model of a human skull. Diagrams prepared by the ARRB based on Boswell's markings show, again, that Kennedy had a gaping skull defect from the middle of his occipital bone to his frontal bone. Most of the parietal bone on the right side was gone, as was a large segment of JFK's occipital bone. (Figure 14) The Clark Panel and HSCA believed that Kennedy's occipital bone was fully intact, save, perhaps, for bullet-caused cracks.

The theory of Oswald as the sole shooter requires that myriad witnesses were wrong about the gaping wound in the backside of JFK's skull, including nurses and neurosurgeons in Dallas, and the FBI agents and autopsy surgeons in the morgue. The autopsy photographs only compound the confusion, except if one takes seriously witness allegations that images have vanished. If one rejects that charge, the validity of the current photographic record must be accepted. But in order to do that, one must then accept that the pathologists were mindful enough to properly photograph numerous irrelevant features of the slain President, but paid scant attention to the central purpose of photographing the autopsy. That they took a photograph of the backside of JFK's head while pulling a flap of scalp across its injured contents to show that the scalp was uninjured, and then somehow forgot to let the flap fall away so as to capture the underlying mortal injury with just another click of the shutter.

Were Two Different JFK Brains Examined?

On November 10, 1998, headlines in the *Washington Post* reported: "Archive photos not of JFK's brain, concludes aide to review board; staff member contends 2 different specimens were examined." The report was the first public acknowledgement of an ARRB memo advancing the "two brain" hypothesis of former Naval officer and review board staffer, Douglas Horne. Carefully comparing accounts of the appearance of JFK's brain on the night of the autopsy with the photographs of what are said to be images of JFK's brain taken at a later, "supplemental," examination, Horne found significant discrepancies. Additional conflicts were found between credible accounts of when the supplemental examination was performed.

Witnesses described that a large portion of the right side of JFK's brain was absent on the night of the autopsy and that there was damage to the cerebellum. Yet, the brain photographed during the supplemental examination reveals only a disruption of the right cerebrum with no appreciable loss of tissue, and with no loss of cerebellum. Moreover, the brain examined during the supplemental examination weighed 1500 grams, which is the upper weight limit for a complete and undamaged brain.

FBI Agent O'Neill told the ARRB in 1997 that when JFK's brain was removed, "more than half of the brain was missing."[223] (The assistant autopsy photographer, Floyd Riebe, recalled things much the same way. When asked by ARRB counsel, "Did you see the brain removed from President Kennedy?" Riebe answered, "What little bit there was left, yes ... Well, it was less than half of a brain there."[224]) Moreover, in *JAMA*, Humes reported that, "Two thirds of the right cerebrum had been blown away."[225] Boswell recalled that one half of the right cerebrum was missing.[226] The Zapruder film shows a massive explosion of Kennedy's head, with such a shower of brain matter being ejected from the right side of the skull that no one would dispute these autopsy witnesses. Moreover, the chief of anesthesia at Parkland Hospital reported that Jackie Kennedy had handed him "a large chunk of her husband's brain tissues"[227] during the resuscitation effort.

The brain photographs, like the photographs of the backside of JFK's head, apparently prove that all the witnesses were as wrong about his brain as they had been about the President's head. Shown the photos in the National Archives, FBI Agent Francis O'Neill rejected them, claiming, correctly, "This looks almost like a complete brain."[228] (Figure 15) The brain images show that there was no significant loss of brain tissue, but only a disruption and displacement along the right side. The given brain weight supports the impression of the eye against the witnesses who said a lot of the brain was missing: the brain weight was measured at 1500 grams, a higher-than-average weight for a full and complete human brain.

The FBI agent was not the only witness to challenge the brain pictures. The photographer of record, John Stringer, rejected the authenticity of the extant brain photographs. Stringer claimed that he took images of sections of the brain, which are missing, and that the images in the current file were *not* taken with the type of camera, or the kind of film, he had used.

Finally, whereas several lines of evidence suggest an examination of JFK's brain was performed before the body was buried on 11/25/63—including Humes' comment in *JAMA* that he was told by JFK's personal physician (George Burkley) that the Kennedy family "wanted to inter the brain with the President's body,"[229] contemporaneous notes of pathologist Pierre Finck, MD show that he was not even contacted by chief pathologist James Humes, MD to examine the brain until November 29, 1963, four days after JFK's burial. Yet Boswell unhesitatingly swore that he and Humes had performed the examination of Kennedy's brain on the Monday following the assassination, November 25th.[230] The Chief Petty Officer in charge of the lab, Chester Boyers, "told the House Assassinations Committee in 1978 that he processed brain tissue"[231] on December 2, 1963, a time that supports Finck's recollection of the later examination of JFK's brain.

If Horne's analysis is right, this was likely the second brain examination, an exam of the 1500 gram brain seen in the autopsy photographs, but not of a brain whose right side can be seen being blasted about Dallas in the Zapruder film. Not of a brain that was missing the "large chunk" Mrs. Kenedy carried into Parkland Hospital.

Press Coverage of JFK's Autopsy Evidence

On August 2, 1998, the Associated Press quoted an ARRB finding: "Under oath, Dr. Humes, finally acknowledged under persistent questioning—in testimony that differs from what he told the Warren Commission—that he had destroyed both his notes taken at the autopsy and the first draft of the autopsy report."[232] While Humes had admitted that he had destroyed by burning in his fireplace the first draft of his autopsy report, for the first time he admitted under oath that he had *also* destroyed original notes from the autopsy. The explanation Humes gave—that he destroyed notes that were bloodstained to eliminate macabre nature of this evidence—is unconvincing. As already discussed, Humes did not destroy the notes of his assistant, Boswell, despite the fact they also bore JFK's bloodstains. There are, however, still other notes unaccounted for.

Mike Feinsilber of the *Associated Press* reported an ARRB discovery: "In an affidavit, Leonard D. Saslaw (Ph.D.), a biochemist who worked at the Armed Forces Institute of Pathology in Bethesda, Md., said that at lunch in the week following the assassination he overheard one of the autopsy doctors, Pierre Finck, 'complain that he had been unable to locate the handwritten notes that he had taken during the autopsy... Dr. Finck elaborated to his companions, with considerable irritation, that immediately after washing up following the autopsy, he looked for his notes, and could not find them anywhere.'" The ARRB added that, "Dr. Saslaw's main concern with what he heard Dr. Finck say is that as a scientist, he is well aware that any observations which are not written down contemporaneously, but reconstructed from memory after the fact, are not likely to be as accurate or complete as the original observations were."[233] Feinsilber also reported that, "Finck told the board he couldn't recall the lunchroom conversation."[234] Yet Finck testified to the HSCA and the ARRB that he had taken measurements and written notes but both his notes and measurements "were turned over to Dr. Humes." Those documents have vanished.[235]

SUMMARY

After one of the authors (Aguilar) made a presentation on JFK's medical/autopsy evidence at *The Nation* magazine on September 13, 1999, Victor Navasky, the publisher and editorial director, just shook his head. He expressed skepticism that the medical experts of the Clark Panel and HSCA experts, who both sided with the sole assassin explanation of JFK's injuries, would have gotten it wrong. Not all of them did. The HSCA's verdict was not unanimous. Cyril Wecht, one of the authors of this piece, and one of the HSCA's experts, issued a spirited dissent. Having been the first person to publicly report that key pieces of autopsy evidence were missing, including JFK's brain and several tissue slides, Wecht realized early on that the evidentiary basis for a confident conclusion was suspiciously incomplete. But Navasky's comment goes to the heart of the current status of the Kennedy case: other than the published articles cited above, there has been little public coverage, and even less analysis, of recent disclosures and discoveries.

These disclosures establish that Wecht's disturbing discovery wasn't the half of it. Besides the President's brain and tissue slides, the camera that took JFK's "best evidence" autopsy photographs has vanished, as have the HSCA tests that showed that the camera did not match the current pictures. Original autopsy notes were vaporized by JFK's chief pathologist, who followed that up by signing false affidavits about them, and then by giving the Warren Commission misleading testimony. Also, multiple lines of evidence suggest that crucial—"diagnostic"— autopsy photographs are also missing, if not falsified.

The prior experts Navasky deferred to never knew anything about any of this. Instead, they worked under the reasonable presumption that they had been given full access to all information. But they had not. A particularly telling and tragic episode exemplifies the blind spots that hobbled the analysis of the authorities whose opinions would normally be definitive, the experts that Navasky quite understandably abides. It involves the peculiar treatment paid Admiral George Burkley, the President's personal physician.

Although Dr. Burkley was intimately familiar with JFK's medical history, had participated in the failed efforts at Parkland Hospital, had traveled with the body to the morgue, and then had watched the entire autopsy and embalming procedures, communicating with the family all along the way, he was ignored by official investigators.

Burkley, however, harbored private doubts. During an oral history taken for the JFK Library on 10/17/67, Burkley was asked, "Do you agree with the Warren Report on the number of bullets that entered the President's body?" Burkley answered, "I would not care to be quoted on that."[236] Had Burkley accepted the Commission's verdict, he'd scarcely have given such an answer. Yet this remarkable response from the physician closest to all the autopsy-related events elicited no official interest. Ten years later, Burkley was still troubled.

In early 1977, Burkley's attorney, William F. Illig, contacted HSCA Counsel Richard A. Sprague. Sprague's needlessly suppressed memo recounts that Burkley wanted to get some information to the Select Committee. Namely, as Sprague put it, that "although he, Burkley, had signed the death certificate of President Kennedy in Dallas, he had never been interviewed and that he has information in the Kennedy assassination indicating that others besides Oswald must have participated."[237] Given Burkley's central vantage point, this was a hot investigative prospect if there ever was one. The staff of the HSCA wasn't interested. But it did more than just ignore the lead. It shielded its own forensic consultants from the existence of this contact, including Wecht.

However Burkley wasn't ignored completely. In January 1978, two HSCA counsels, D. Andy Purdy and Mark Flanagan, contacted Burkley. Their purpose was to extract an affidavit saying that that no one could have intercepted JFK's body before it got to the morgue, and that JFK's wounds had not been altered between Dallas and the postmortem.[238] Dutifully, Burkley wrote up an affidavit, declaring that, "[he, Burkley, had remained] in the ambulance with the President's body in the casket and also on the plane; the casket was neither opened or disturbed in any way." And that, "There was no difference in the nature of the wounds" seen in Dallas compared to those seen in the morgue.[239] Thus Burkely was pressed into service to help the HSCA refute the theory that JFK's body was intercepted so as to rearrange the wounds and erase evidence of another shooter. Questions about how Burkley knew that "others besides Oswald must have participated" merited none of Purdy or Flanagan's attention. Nor did the HSCA staff feel any need to pass this lead to their own forensic consultants, the fellows whose job it was to follow up such leads.

Burkley apparently remained a skeptic. Author Henry Hurt reported that, "In 1982 Dr. Burkley told the author in a telephone conversation that he believed that President Kennedy's assassination was the result of a conspiracy."[240] But when Hurt contacted Burkley to arrange a face-to-face interview—two months after they had exchanged agreeable letters, "The doctor responded with an abrupt refusal to discuss any aspect of the case." Burkley's change of heart in 1982, as frustrating as it is, is still less unfortunate than the fact the HSCA's physician experts were hampered by the HSCA staff having kept them ignorant of Burkley's petition. The experts were similarly kept ignorant of other key evidence.

The staff of the HSCA also shielded its own forensic experts, and the public, from the fact that the autopsy photographs had failed an authentication test. And, in order to demolish the pro-conspiracy Parkland witnesses, the HSCA staff falsely reported that 26 autopsy witnesses had refuted the doctors in Dallas by endorsing the autopsy photographs that show wounds supporting the Oswald theory. It was only after opening these suspiciously suppressed files that the experts and the public, long after it mattered, discovered the truth: the autopsy witnesses had *not* endorsed the autopsy photographs, they'd refuted them; and they had not, as the HSCA reported, refuted the Dallas doctors on JFK's injuries, but, instead, the autopsy witnesses had agreed with the Dallas doctors, both by verbal description and by diagram. (Figure 10)

The experts likely believed that the autopsists had spoken truthfully and withheld nothing of importance; that pertinent original autopsy material had not been destroyed and that they had seen it all, including every autopsy photograph that was ever taken; that Kennedy's skull damage was almost entirely confined to the right front and side of JFK's head, near where the bullet exited. We now know very differently: It is probable that none of these working assumptions is true.

As a result, it must now be asked whether the experts would have thought differently, or pursued their investigations any differently, if they had known what we now know. Would the experts have regarded the autopsy team any differently if they had realized that the same men who had told them autopsy photographs were missing had signed a false Justice Department affidavit saying the opposite? Would the experts have considered the pressure the Justice Department had exerted on the autopsy team to reaffirm the original conclusions relevant to the objectivity of the pathologists and the Justice Department? Would they have wondered why the Justice Department, which had no legal standing in Garrison's trial of Clay Shaw, nevertheless flew Finck down to New Orleans to testify, and then sent Boswell to refute Finck? Would they have wondered why Boswell was so cooperative with the Justice Department's extralegal clandestine arrangements?

Would the HSCA's forensic experts have investigated the HSCA's selective withholding of important medical/autopsy evidence—the inconvenient testimonies and diagrams obtained from witnesses who were present at the autopsy? And if they had known of these witnesses, would they have conducted some interviews of their own?

Would it have made a difference to the experts if they had been familiar with the evidence that more than one "JFK" brain was autopsied? That autopsy photographs are missing, including brain images the photographer reported have vanished? How would they have regarded the fact that despite questionable autopsy photographs showing the opposite, that it is likely that JFK had a sizable segment of the rear of his skull, including part of his occipital bone, blasted out? Would they have investigated why the HSCA reported it had authenticated the autopsy photographs that had in fact failed authentication tests? Would the fact that the original autopsy camera is missing, along with the tests that proved a mismatch between camera and autopsy pictures, have made any difference in their thinking?

Since the best scientific judgments cannot be rendered until all data has been analyzed, the best scientific judgments are not yet in on the JFK medical/autopsy evidence. So does the evidence merit a reexamination by a new panel of experts? The reader will have to decide for himself how much suppressed and contradictory evidence it takes to justify a reappraisal—or to justify a lack of confidence in prior appraisals. But today, for one of the HSCA experts, one of the authors, the medical/autopsy case for the sole assassin is not closed. There are just too many unanswered questions.

Had JFK's death been a simple matter of a sole deranged act by a disgruntled loner, how likely is it that so much inconvenient evidence would have been suppressed or ignored? This evidence includes signed false affidavits arranged by the Justice Department that just happen to endorse the Justice Department's preferred conclusions; key witnesses—like Burkley—being brushed aside; overwhelming witness testimony at odds with the "hard evidence," key portions of which are missing; and selectively suppressed and exculpatory medical and autopsy evidence that might have forced a new official theory of the President's death, had sanctioned experts but been allowed to see it?

The proven mishandling of evidence, and the discovery of so much suppressed contrary evidence, has increased the already heavy burden of proof on the proponents of the Oswald solution to the assassination. That, intriguingly, is what the record now shows. It is a record that *JAMA* could have begun to unravel, had its agenda been an honest investigative effort, rather than one of demolishing skeptics of the suspiciously inadequate Autopsy of the Century.

ENDNOTES

1 Henry Hurt. *Reasonable Doubt.* New York: *Henry Holt and Co.*, 1985, p. 37 and 53.

2 Gina Kolata. "A.M.A. Drops Journal Editor Over Sex Paper," *New York Times*, 1/16/99, p. A-1.

3 Lawrence K. Altman, MD. "28 Years After Dallas, A Doctor Tells His Story Amid Troubling Doubts," *New York Times*. 5/26/92.

4 Wayne Smith. "*JAMA* Knows Best—The medical journal called the JFK case closed—and the verdict went unchallenged," *Columbia Journalism Review*, Sept./Oct. 1993, p. 49. See also letter to the editor by author Aguilar in the Nov./Dec. 1993 *Columbia Journalism Review*, p. 6.

5 "I am a journalist," announced Lundberg during a debate on the JFK medical/autopsy evidence at "The Second Annual Midwest Symposium on Assassination Politics," in Chicago, Illinois on Saturday, April 3, 1993.

6 Quote from: Michael Miner. "Autopsy of a Lisagor," *Chicago Reader*, March 5, 1999, Section One, p. 4.

7 From transcript of presentation by George D. Lundberg, MD during a debate on the JFK medical/autopsy evidence at "The Second Annual Midwest Symposium on Assassination Politics," held at the State of Illinois Center in Chicago, Illinois on Saturday, April 3, 1993.

8 "I have known Dr. James Humes since 1957 … He is a friend of mine. I would trust him with my life." From transcript of statement by G. Lundberg delivered at the Midwest Symposium in Chicago, Illinois.

9 Recorded comments of George D. Lundberg during debate at Midwest Symposium, Chicago, Illinois.

10 Breo, Dennis. "JFK's death—the plain truth from the MDs who did the autopsy," *JAMA*, May 27, 1992 1992. V. 267:2804, ff.

11 News conference was held on May 19, 1992. See *New York Times*, 5/20/92.

12 See letters section in the October 7, 1992 issue of *JAMA*, "The injuries to JFK," including unanswered letter by author Aguilar: v. 268:1681–1685. See unanswered letter by author Wecht in the March 24/31, 1993 issue of *JAMA*, vol. 269:1507.

13 Select Committee on Assassinations of the U.S. House of Representatives (HSCA), Appendix to Hearings, Vol. VII, p. 194.

[14] Baden, Michael M. *Unnatural Death: Confessions of a Medical Examiner*. New York: Ivy Books, published by *Ballantine Books*, 1989, p. 5.

[15] Select Committee on Assassinations of the U.S. House of Representatives (HSCA), Appendix to Hearings, Vol. VII, p. 192—193.

[16] From transcript of testimony of Pierre Finck, MD during the trial of Clay Shaw in New Orleans, La. February 24–25, 1969, p. 55.

[17] Quote cited in: Josiah Thompson. *Six Seconds in Dallas*. New York: Bernard Geis Associates for Random House, 1967, p. 198.

[18] William Manchester. *The Death of a President*. New York: Harper & Row, 1967, p. 419. (Note: Manchester makes the flat statement quoted by Russo's in his book on page 324): "The Kennedy who was really in charge in the tower suite was the Attorney General." But the decisions Manchester attributes to RFK had nothing whatsoever to do with autopsy limitations.

[19] Gus Russo. *Live by the Sword*. Baltimore. Bancroft Press, 1998, p. 324–328. (Russo cites Livingstone's assertion, in *High Treason*, [1992, p. 182] that Robert Karnie, MD—a Bethesda pathologist who was in the morgue but not part of the surgical team—claimed the Kennedys were limiting the autopsy. However, the ARRB released an 8/29/77 memo from the HSCA's Andy Purdy, JD [ARRB MD # 61], in which, on page 3, Purdy writes: "Dr. Karnei doesn't ' … know if any limitations were placed on how the autopsy was to be done.' He said he didn't know who was running things.")

[20] John Lattimer. *Kennedy and Lincoln*. New York: Harcourt Brace Jovanovich, 1980, p. 195. ("He [Dr. Humes] was severely limited in what he was permitted to do by constraints imposed by the family.")

[21] While Posner's book, not unexpectedly, won praise in the *New York Times* (J. Ward, *NY Times Book Review*, 11/21/93), University of Wisconsin historian David Wrone, a legitimate JFK authority who Posner approvingly cited repeatedly in *Case Closed*, described Posner's book as "so theory driven, so rife with speculation, and so frequently unable to conform his text with the factual content in his sources that it stands as one of the stellar instances of irresponsible publishing on this subject." (In: *Journal of Southern History*. V.61(#1):186, 2/95). However, another historian, Thomas C. Reeves—whose credentials on the JFK case are so meager that he is nowhere cited in any book on the JFK subject (including *Case Closed*)—did write a favorable review in the *Journal of American History*, Vol. 81 (12/94): 1379–1380. Michael Parenti described Reeves' review as "more like a promotional piece than an evaluation of a historical *[sic]* investigation." (In: Parenti, M. *History as Mystery*. San Francisco: City Lights Books, 1999, p. 195.) Parenti provides an extensive review of the peculiar media flattery of Posner in his book, *History as Mystery*.

[22] Notre Dame Law professor, and former HSCA chief counsel, Robert Blakey, another legitimate authority Posner repeatedly cited in *Case Closed,* wrote: "Posner often distorts the evidence by selective citation and by striking omissions ... (he) picks and chooses his witnesses on the basis of their consistency with the thesis he wants to prove." (In: G. Robert Blakey's article "The Mafia and JFK's Murder—Thirty years later, the question remains: Did Oswald act alone?" *The Washington Post National Weekly Edition,* November 15–21, 1993, p. 23.)

[23] *Case Closed* cited in extenso, but selectively, the work of Failure Analysis Associates, Inc. (FaAA) of Menlo Park, California, which prepared evidence for both sides of an American Bar Association mock trial of Lee Harvey Oswald in 1992. On December 6, 1993, FaAA's CEO, Roger McCarthy, swore out an affidavit in which he declared that Posner had requested FaAA's prosecution material, but not the defense material; that Posner failed to disclose that FaAA had also prepared a defense, and that the jury that heard both sides "could not reach a verdict."[24] McCarthy's affidavit is available on the web at: <http://www.assassination-science.com/mccarthy.html>

[24] In testimony before the Congress, Posner reported that both Humes and Boswell had told him they'd changed their minds, and that the autopsy report was wrong about JFK's skull wound being low. Posner claimed they had admitted to him that they'd come around to the view the wound was high, and so consistent with a shot from Oswald's position. But as author Aguilar first reported in the *Federal Bar News and Journal* [Vol. 41(5):388, June, 1994], both Humes and Boswell, in recorded conversations (now available at the National Archives), denied having ever changed their minds that JFK's skull wound was low. (They repeated their assertion that they had never changed their minds JFK's skull wound was low under oath to the ARRB.) Boswell also told Aguilar, twice, that he'd never spoken with Posner. Aguilar gave the recordings, which suggested Posner had perjured himself, to the ARRB. Aguilar also sent the ARRB a copy of a letter calling Posner's testimony into question, a letter that had been published by a committee chaired by Rep. John Conyers. (See letter in: *Hearing before the Legislation and National Security Subcommittee of the Committee on Government Operations House of Representatives,* One Hundred Third Congress, First Session, November 17, 1993. Washington, D. C.: U.S. Government Printing Office, 1994. It appears on the final 5 pages of the report.) Subsequently, the ARRB asked Posner for his notes and records substantiating his claims regarding Humes and Boswell. As the ARRB reported on page 134 of the "Final Report of the ARRB," Posner declined to cooperate.

[25] Scott, Peter Dale. "Case Closed? Or Oswald Framed?" *The San Francisco Review of Books,* Nov./Dec., 11993, p.6. (This review is perhaps the most eloquent, concise, authoritative and damning of all the reviews of *Case Closed.*)

[26] Kwitny, Jonathan. "Bad News: Your Mother Killed JFK," *Los Angeles Times Book Review,* 11/7/93.

[27] Nichols, Mary Perot. "R.I.P., conspiracy theories?" Book review in: *Philadelphia Inquirer*, 8/29/93, p. K1 and K4.

[28] Costello, George. "The Kennedy Assassination: Case Still Open." *Federal Bar News & Journal.* V.41(3):233, March/April, 1994.

[29] Frank, Jeffrey A. "Who Shot JFK? The 30-Year Mystery," *Washington Post—Book World,* 10/31/93.

[30] Summarizing what appears to be his own view, Posner writes, "The House Select Committee concluded that Humes had the authority for a full autopsy but only performed a partial one." Posner, G. *Case Closed*, New York: Anchor Books/Doubleday edition, 1993, p. 303, n.

[31] Dennis Breo. "JFK's death, part III—Dr. Finck speaks out: 'two bullets, from the rear,'" *JAMA* Vol. 268(13):1752, October 7, 1992.

[32] Without citation, this episode was also cited by Gus Russo in: *Live by the Sword.* Baltimore. Bancroft Press, 1998, p. 325.

[33] Breo, Dennis. "JFK's death—the plain truth from the MDs who did the autopsy," *JAMA*, May 27, 1992, vol. 267:2794, ff.

[34] John Lattimer. *Kennedy and Lincoln.* New York: Harcourt Brace *Jovanovich,* 1980, p. 223–224.

[35] ARRB testimony James H. Humes, College Park, Maryland, p. 32–33.

[36] ARRB testimony J. Thornton Boswell, College Park Maryland, 2/26/96, p. 29.

[37] ARRB testimony J. Thornton Boswell, College Park Maryland, 2/26/96, p. 30.

[38] Interview of Admiral Calvin B. Galloway by HSCA counsel Mark Flanagan, 5/17/78. HSCA Record Number 180–10078–10460, Agency File # 009409.

[39] Sworn affidavit of Vice Admiral George G. Burkley. HSCA record # 180–10104–10271, Agency File # 013416, p. 3.

[40] Lattimer writes, "Commanders Humes and Boswell inquired as to whether or not any of their consultants from the medical examiner's office in Washington or Baltimore should be summoned, but this action was discouraged." In: John Lattimer. *Kennedy and Lincoln.* New York: Harcourt Brace Jovanovich, 1980, p. 155.

[41] HSCA volume 7, p. 14:

"(79) The Committee also investigated the possibility that the Kennedy family may have unduly influenced the pathologists once the autopsy began, possibly by transmitting messages by telephone into the autopsy room. Brig. Gen. Godfrey McHugh, then an Air Force military aide to the President, informed the committee that Attorney General Robert F. Kennedy and Kenneth O'Donnell, a presidential aide, frequently telephoned him during the autopsy from the 17th floor suite. McHugh said that on all occasions, Kennedy and O'Donnell asked only to speak with him. They inquired about the results, why the autopsy was consuming so much time, and the need for speed and efficiency, while still performing the required examinations. *McHugh said he forwarded this information to the pathologists, never stating or implying that the doctors should limit the autopsy in any manner, but merely reminding them to work as efficiently and quickly as possible.*" (emphasis added)

[42] Select Committee on Assassinations of the U.S. House of Representatives (HSCA), Appendix to Hearings, Vol. VII, p. 190.

[43] Testimony of Pierre Finck during the Clay Shaw trial in New Orleans. In: DiEugenio, James. *Destiny Betrayed*. New York: Sheridan Square Press, 1992, p. 291:

Finck: "I will remind you that I was not in charge of this autopsy, that I was called—
Q "You were a co-author of the report though, weren't you, Doctor?"
A "Wait. I was called as a consultant to look at these wounds; that doesn't mean I am running the show."
Q "Was Dr. Humes running the show?"
A "Well, I heard Dr. Humes stating that—he said, 'Who is in charge here?' and I heard an Army General, I don't remember his name stating, 'I am.' You must understand that in those circumstances, there were law enforcement officials, military people with various ranks, and you have to co-ordinate the operation according to directions."
Q "But you were one of the three qualified pathologists standing at that autopsy table, were you not, Doctor?"
A "Yes, I was."
Q "Was this Army General a qualified pathologist?"
A "No."
Q "Was he a doctor?"
A "No, not to my knowledge."
Q "Can you give me his name, Colonel?"
A "No, I can't. I don't remember."

[44] Breo, Dennis. "JFK's death—the plain truth from the MDs who did the autops,". *JAMA*, May 27, 1992, vol. 267:2794–2795.

[45] Breo, Dennis. "JFK's death—the plain truth from the MDs who did the autops,". *JAMA*, May 27, 1992, vol. 267:2796–2797.

[46] HSCA vol. 7:261.

[47] HSCA vol. 8:181.

[48] HSCA vol. 8:192.

[49] Memo reproduced in: *Hearing before the Legislation and National Security Subcommittee of the Committee on Government Operations House of Representatives,* One Hundred Third Congress, First Session, November 17, 1993. Washington, D. C.: U.S. Government Printing Office, 1994, p.233–234.

[50] Only the verbatim transcript reveals Finck's disgraceful evasiveness. He indirectly used the Kennedy family as only one of many stratagems to avoid answering why he had not dissected the track of the back wound Such a dissection would have been a rudimentary procedure in any murder case. It was especially important here, where that information would have been important evidence in the expected trial of the then living, alleged assassin, Oswald.

The uninterrupted transcript from the Shaw trial on the matter of the dissection of the neck wound reads:

Mr. Oser: "Colonel [Finck], did you feel that you had to take orders from this Army general (the one Finck claimed had answered Humes' question , "Who's in charge here?" with "I am.") that was there directing the autopsy?"

Finck: "No, because there were others, there were admirals."

Mr. Oser: "There were admirals?"

Dr. Finck: "Oh, yes, there were admirals, and when you are a lieutenant colonel in the Army you just follow orders, and at the end of the autopsy we were specifically told—as I recall it, it was by Admiral Kenney, the Surgeon (General) of he Navy—this is subject to verification—we were specifically told not to discuss the case."

Oser: "Did you have occasion to dissect the track of that particular bullet in the victim as it lay on the autopsy table?"

Dr. Finck: "I did not dissect the track in the neck."

Mr. Oser: "Why?"

Dr. Finck: "This leads us into the disclosure of medical records." (Note: not the fact that the family had opposed the dissection, which was not a portion of the medical records.)

Mr. Oser: "Your Honor, I would like an answer from the colonel and I wound ask the Court to direct."

The Court: "That is correct, you should answer, Doctor."

Dr. Finck: "We didn't remove the organs of the neck."

Mr. Oser: "Why not, doctor?'

Mr. Finck: "For the reason we were told to examine the head wounds and the—"

Mr. Oser: "Are you saying someone told you not to dissect the track?"

The Court: "Let him finish his answer."

Dr. Finck: "I was told that the family wanted an examination of the head, as I recall, the head and chest, but prosectors in this autopsy didn't remove the organs of the neck, to my recollection."

Mr. Oser: "You have said they did not. I want to know why didn't you as an autopsy pathologist attempt to ascertain the track through the body which you had on the autopsy table in trying to ascertain the cause or causes of death? Why?'

Dr. Finck: I had the cause of death."

Mr. Oser: "Why did you not trace the track of the wound?"

Dr. Finck: "As I recall I didn't remove these organs from the neck."

Mr. Oser: "I didn't hear you."

Dr. Finck: I examined the wounds but I didn't remove the organs of the neck."

Mr. Oser: "You said you didn't do this; I am asking you why you didn't do this as a pathologist?"

Dr. Finck: From what I recall I looked at the trachea, there was a tracheostomy wound the best I can remember, but I didn't dissect or remove these organs."

Mr. Oser: Your Honor, I would ask Your Honor to direct the witness to answer my question. I will ask you the question one more time: Why did you not dissect the track of the bullet wound that you have described today and you saw at the time of the autopsy at the time you examined the body? Why? I ask you to answer that question."

Dr. Finck: "As I recall I was told not to, but I don't remember by whom."

Mr. Oser: "You were told not to but you don't remember by whom?"

Dr. Finck: "Right."

Mr. Oser: 'Could it have been one of the Admirals or one of the Generals in the room?"

Dr. Finck: "I don't recall."

Mr. Oser: "Do you have any particular reason why you cannot recall at this time?"

Dr. Finck: "Because we were told to examine the head and the chest cavity, and that doesn't include the removal of the organs of the neck."

Mr. Oser; "You are one of the three autopsy specialists and pathologists at the time, and you saw what you described as an entrance wound in the neck area of the President of the United States who had just been assassinated, and you were only interested in the other wound but not interested in the track through his neck, is that what you are telling me?"

Dr. Finck: "I was interested in the track and I had observed the conditions of bruising between the point of entry in the back of the neck and the point of exit at the front of the neck, which is entirely compatible with the bullet path.

Mr. Oser: "But you were told not to go into the area of the neck, is that your testimony?"

Dr. Finck: "From what I recall, yes, but I don't remember by whom." (Pierre Finck's testimony at the New Orleans trial of Clay Shaw. Reproduced in: DiEugenio, J. *Destiny Betrayed*. New York, Sheridan Square Press. 1992, p. 301–302.)

One is tempted to wonder whether Finck's inability to recall who issued the order had anything to do with the fact that he was probably fully aware that the U.S. Justice Department had sent the second-in-command, J. Thornton Boswell, MD, to New Orleans to wait in the wings during Finck's testimony. See the text.

Could Finck not have known what Michael Baden, MD explained to the HSCA, "(We forensic pathologists) are very careful to dissect out the tracks of bullets to identify all of the injuries caused by the bullet; even if these would not change the final cause of death..."? (HSCA—V1:317)

[51] Testimony of Pierre Finck at the Shaw trial, p. 121–122.

[52] This incident was also explored in: Select Committee on Assassinations of the U.S. House of Representatives (HSCA), Appendix to Hearings, Vol. VII, p. 191–192.

[53] John Lattimer. *Kennedy and Lincoln*. New York: Harcourt Brace Jovanovich, 1980, p. 156.

[54] "Lt. Col. Pierre Finck ... was made available to (Humes) by Brigadier General Blumberg, the commanding officer of the Armed Forces Institute of Pathology— 'I (Blumberg) requested Colonel Finck to appear'." Select Committee on Assassinations of the U.S. House of Representatives (HSCA), Appendix to Hearings, Vol. VII, p. 182.

[55] In a February 1, 1965 memo, Finck wrote to his superior, General Joe Blumberg, "I was denied the opportunity to examine the clothing of Kennedy. One officer who out-ranked me told me that my request was only of academic interest. The same officer did not agree to state in the autopsy report that the autopsy was incomplete, as I had suggested to indicate."

Might Finck not have known the importance of this examination? It seems unlikely that he, the "Chief of the Wound Ballistics Pathology Branch and the Director of the Armed Forces Institute of Pathology" (HSCA testimony of Pierre Finck, 3/11/78, p. 70–71), would not have then known what is obvious even to laymen, and what Finck explained himself in 1965: "In some perforating wounds of the body (such as JFK's), the weapon produces fouling of the clothes at the site of the missile entrance. If the clothing is not available to the pathologist, he will be handicapped in identifying the entrance and exit wounds upon examination of the skin only." (Finck PA. "Ballistic and forensic pathologic aspects of missile wounds," *Military Medicine*. 1965; 130(5):554)

Might it be common that a forensic pathologist like Finck ignores the clothing in a gunshot autopsy? The HSCA's Baden claimed, "We forensic pathologists insist on seeing the clothing because we know from experience that the clothing tells us a great deal about bullet holes, about injuries, that may be obscured in the body." (HSCA-V1:319.)

Might the Kennedy family have objected? With the pathologists disemboweling the President, concerns about the fate of JFK's clothing would scarcely have merited attention. And there would have been no requirement that the clothes be produced before the completion of the autopsy, although that would of course have been preferred.

56 See also: Select Committee on Assassinations of the U.S. House of Representatives (HSCA), Appendix to Hearings, Vol. VII, p. 193–194.

57 Breo, Dennis. "JFK's death—the plain truth from the MDs who did the autopsy,". *JAMA*, May 27, 1992, vol. 267:2798.

58 Testimony of Secret Service agent William Robert Greer, Warren Commission vol. II:125.

59 Testimony of Secret Service agent William Robert Greer, Warren Commission vol. II:126.

60 Breo, DL. "JFK's death, part III—Dr Finck speaks out: 'two bullets, from the rear,'" *JAMA,* October 7, 1992; 268:1752.

61 Mike Feinsalber, "JFK Autopsy Files Are Incomplete," *Associated Press*, August 2, 1998, 11:48 a.m. EDT.

62 See "CERTIFICATE" signed by "J. J. Humes," 11/24/63, and cosigned by George Burkley, MD. Reproduced in: Weisberg, Harold, *Post Mortem.* Frederick, Maryland, 1975, p. 524.

63 See "CERTIFICATE" signed by "J. J. Humes," 11/24/63, and cosigned by George Burkley, MD,. Reproduced in: Weisberg, Harold, *Post Mortem.* Frederick, Maryland, 1975, p. 525

64 Arlen Specter. *Passion for Truth.* New York: William Morrow, 2000, p. 78–79.

65 HSCA, vol. 7:257–258.

66 See *JAMA*, as well as: John Lattimer. *Kennedy and Lincoln.* New York: *Harcourt Brace Jovanovich*,1980, p. 194–196.

67 ARRB interview with James H. Humes, MD.

68 Breo, Dennis. "JFK's death—the plain truth from the MDs who did the autopsy,". *JAMA*, May 27, 1992, vol. 267:2797.

69 First published in association with the Richard Gallen & Co, Inc., 1980. First *Carroll & Graf* edition published in New York in 1988.

[70] Groden R, Livingston, H. *High Treason*. Baltimore: Conservatory Press, 1989, p. 39. Or: New York: Berkeley Books, 1989, p. 45.

[71] Breo, Dennis. "JFK's death—the plain truth from the MDs who did the autopsy,". *JAMA*, May 27, 1992, vol. 267:2797

[72] HSCA 7:246–260.

[73] HSCA 7:254.

[74] HSCA 7:115. ("Dr. Humes agreed that the defect was in the 'cowlick' area and not [low] in the area of the brain tissue.")

[75] HSCA 7:115.

[76] Warren Commission, vol. 5, p. 89. Hereafter cited as, 5H89.

[77] Warren Commission Exhibit # 862.

[78] Lattimer, John. *Kennedy and Lincoln—Medical and Ballistic Comparisons of Their Assassinations*. New York: Harcourt, Brace, Jovanovich, 1980, p. 254.

[79] *Warren Report,* Washington, D.C.: U. S. Government Printing Office, 1964 , p.501 –502. Hereafter referred to as WR, p. 501–502.

[80] Warren Commission Exhibits #386 and #388, and HSCA Vol.7:114, 115.

[81] HSCA. Vol. 7:261.

[82] HSCA. V. 7:246.

[83] John K. Lattimer. "Additional Data on the Shooting of President Kennedy," *JAMA*, March 24/31, 1993, p. 1545. See also: Gerald Posner, *Case Closed.* New York: *Random House*, 1993, p. 330.

[84] WR, p. 106.

[85] HSCA. vol. 7:251–252.

[86] #1. Lardner, George. "Archive Photos not of JFK's Brain, Concludes Aide to Review Board; Staff Member Contends 2 different Specimens Were Examined," *Washington Post*, November 10, 1998, p. A-3.

#2. Feinsilber, Mike. "JFK Autopsy Files are Incomplete," *AP*, 8/2/98. In: *Washington Post*, 8/2/98.

[87] See Mantik's essays in *Assassination Science*, edited by James Fetzer and published by *Catfeet Press*, Chicago: 1998. See also. James Fetzer, ed., *Murder in Dealey Plaza*, Chicago: Catfeet Press 1998, p. 219–298.

[88] Warren Commission Exhibit #392.

[89] 6H48.

[90] 6H51.

[91] 6H41.

[92] Warren Commission Exhibit # 392. (17H4-5)

[93] 3H361.

[94] Warren Commission Exhibit # 392.

[95] 3H368.

[96] 3H372.

[97] 6H33-34

[98] *JAMA*. May 27, 1992, v. 267:2807.

[99] HSCA-V7:286-287.

[100] *American Medical News*, November 24, 1978.

[101] Posner, G. *Case Closed*. New York. Random House, 1993, p. 312.

[102] Posner, G. *Case Closed*. New York. Random House, 1993, p. 313.

[103] HSCA-V7:268

[104] Posner, G. *Case Closed*. New York. Random House, 1993, p. 311.

[105] HSCA-V7:292-293.

[106] HSCA-V7:302-interview with Purdy 1-11-78.

[107] Posner, G. *Case Closed*. New York. Random House, 1993, p.312.

[108] ARRB depositions of Parkland witnesses, p. 19.

[109] ARRB depositions of Parkland witnesses, p. 23.

[110] Posner G. *Case Closed*. New York: Random House, 1993, p. 235.

[111] Josiah Thompson. *Six Seconds in Dallas*. New York: Bernard Geis Associates for Random House, 1967, p. 107.

[112] Warren Commission Exhibit #392.

[113] Warren Commission Exhibit #392. (17H9-10)

[114] Ben Bradlee, "Dispute on JFK assassination evidence persists," *Boston Sunday Globe*, June 21, 1981, p. A-23.

[115] Warren Commission testimony: 6H53–56.

[116] Warren Commission testimony. 6H65–67.

[117] Warren Commission testimony. 6H71.

[118] See Price Exhibit, Warren Commission vol. 21, p. 216.

[119] Dennis L. Breo. "JFK's death—the plain truth from the MDs who did the autopsy," *JAMA*, May 27, 1992. V. 267:2794.

[120] Dennis L. Breo. "JFK's Death, part III—Dr. Finck speaks out: 'two bullets, from the rear,'" *JAMA*, October 7, 1992, Vol. 268: 1748–1754.

[121] Josiah Thompson. *Six Seconds in Dallas.* New York: *Bernard Geis Associates* for *Random House*, 1967, p. 110.

[122] The dates were noted in Harold Weisberg's book, *Post Mortem*, p. 39.

[123] The testimony Humes gave during his second interview (See HSCA, vol. #1) was televised.

[124] Richard Levine. "Pathologist Who Made Examination Defends Commission's Version," *Baltimore Sun*, 11/25/66, p. A-1.

[125] Peter Kihss. "Autopsy Surgeon Says Photos Support Warren Report on Wound in Neck," *New York Times*, 11/25/66, p. 30.

[126] Recorded interview with James Humes, MD. Recording played publicly by David Lifton during a debate on the medical/autopsy evidence conducted during "The Second Annual Midwest Symposium on Assassination Politics," held at the State of Illinois Center in Chicago, Illinois, Saturday, April 3, 1993.

127 Henry Hurt. *Reasonable Doubt.* New York: Henry Holt and Co., 1985, p. 53. Robert Groden, Harrison Livingstone. *High Treason.* New York: Berkley Books, 1990, p. 35, 230; David Lifton. *Best Evidence.* New York: Carroll & Graf, 1980, pp. 428–429, 501–502, 535–536, 549, 552.

128 Breo, D. "JFK's death, part II—Dallas MDs recall their memories," *JAMA,* May 27, 1992; v. 267(20):2805.

129 Breo. *JAMA.* 267:2804.

130 Breo. *JAMA.* 267:2805.

131 Posner G. *Case Closed.* New York. Random House. p. 314.

132 Breo, D. "JFK's death, part II—Dallas MDs recall their memories," *JAMA,* 1992; 267(20):2804, May 27, 1992.

133 Altman, Lawrence. "28 Years After Dallas, A Doctor Tells His Story Amid Troubling Doubts," *New York Times*, 5/26/92, p. C-3.

134 6H40.

135 *Texas State Journal of Medicine*, January 1964, p. 72.

136 Warren Commission volume 6 on pp. 32, 40, 60, 80 and 131.

137 Posner G. *Case Closed.* New York: Random House, 1993, p. 312.

138 Depositions of Charles Baxter, MD, Ronald Coy Jones, MD, Robert McClelland, MD, Malcolm O. Perry, MD, and Paul Peters, MD before the Assassinations Records Review Board, taken on August 27, 1998 at the offices of University of Texas, Southwest Medical Center, p. 20. (Hereafter referred to as ARRB depositions of Parkland witnesses.)

139 ARRB depositions of Parkland witnesses, p. 32.

140 *JAMA.* V. 267:2805.

141 ARRB depositions of Parkland witnesses, p. 30.

142 Bradlee, Ben. "Dispute on JFK assassination evidence persists," *Boston Globe,* 6/21/81, p. A-23.

143 Lifton, David. *Best Evidence.* New York: Carroll & Graf, 1988, p.704.

144 ARRB depositions of Parkland witnesses, p. 30.

[145] ARRB MD #185. ARRB interview with Dr. Robert G. Grossman, 3/21/97.

[146] A good discussion of this hypothesis appears in: Josiah Thompson. *Six Seconds in Dallas*. New York: Bernard Geis Assoc. for Random House, 1967.

[147] HSCA, vol. 7:37.

[148] HSCA, vol. 7:39.

[149] Breo, Dennis. "JFK Part II," *JAMA*. 5/27/92.

[150] Warren Commission Exhibit, CE#1024, V.18:744 (18H744).

[151] Warren Commission Exhibit # 1024.

[152] HSCA record # 180-10105-10397, agency file number # 014461, p.2.

[153] HSCA record # 10010042, agency file # 002086, p. 2

[154] Elizabeth F. Loftus. *Eyewitness Testimony*. Cambridge: Harvard University Press, 1996, p, 25–28.

[155] Loftus, Elizabeth F. *Eyewitness Testimony*. Cambridge, Harvard University Press, 1996, p. 25–26. "Items that were highest of all in salience ("salience" being determined by the witnesses themselves) received accuracy and completeness scores of 98. Those that were lowest in salience received scores below 70." Please note that an item judged not to be salient at all, i.e. "Salience category 0.00," was still accurately recounted 61% of the time. See also the study to which Loftus refers, Marshall, J, Marquis, KH, Oskamp, S. "Effects of kind of question and atmosphere of interrogation on accuracy and completeness of testimony," *Harvard Law Review*, Vol.84:1620–1643, 1971.

[156] Elizabeth Loftus, James M. Doyle. *Eyewitness Testomony: Civil and Criminal*, Second Edition. Charlottesville: The Michie Company, 1992.

[157] February 11, 1998. ARRB memorandum to Jeremy Gunn and Tom Samoluk by Doug Horne entitled "Wrapping Up ARRB Efforts to 'Clarify the Record' Re: The Medical Evidence in the Assassination of President John F. Kennedy."

[158] Quotes taken from an undated, untitled affidavit signed by James H. Humes, J. Thornton Boswell and Pierre Finck, and reproduced in: Weisberg, Harold. *Post Mortem*, p. 575. While this document describes an examination of the autopsy inventory performed on January 20, 1967, reference is made in this document to the fact that the first look the principals ever got of the autopsy photographs occurred on November 1, 1966, after a request by the Justice Department that they "examine, identify and inventory" the autopsy photographs.

159 "Report of Inspection by Naval Medical Staff on 11/1/66 at National Archives of X-rays and Photographs of President John F. Kennedy." Reproduced in: Weisberg, Harold, *Post Mortem*, p.573.

160 Quotes appear in an undated, untitled report signed by James H. Humes, J. Thornton Boswell and Pierre Finck, and reproduced in: Weisberg, Harold. *Post Mortem*, p. 575–576.

161 Weisberg, Harold. *Post Mortem*, p. 576.

162 Taped phone conversation between acting Attorney General Ramsey Clark and President Lyndon Johnson, 1/21/76, obtained from LBJ Presidential Library. Transcribed by Debra Conway, and available at: http://www.jfklancer.com/Clark.LBJ.html.

163 From a memo titled "President Johnson's Notes on Conversation with Acting Attorney General Ramsey Clark—January 26, 1967—6:29 P.M.," obtained from the Lyndon B. Johnson Library.

164 From: *Carl W. Belcher*, Chief, General Crimes Section, Criminal Division, US Dept. of Justice, 11/22/66
Agency: DOJCIVIL, Record # 182-10001-100021

165 Dr. Boswell's 1/26/68 letter to Ramsey Clark is reproduced in Harold Weisberg's book, *Post Mortem*, p. 574.

166 Deposition of J. Thornton Boswell by ARRB, 2/26/96, p. 10. (Note, Boswell also told this same story in the May 27, 1992 issue of *JAMA*. Op. cit.)

167 Harold Weisberg. *Post Mortem*. Frederick, Maryland: 1975, p. 139. (First printing was in 1969. See p. 574 for a copy of Boswell's letter.)

168 *JAMA*, May 27, 1992, v. 267:2802.

169 Memo by Pierre Finck to Director, Air Force Institute of Pathology, dated 3/11/69, regarding subject, "Shaw Trial, New Orleans."

170 ARRB testimony J. Thornton Boswell, College Park Maryland, 2/26/96, p. 211.

171 ARRB testimony J. Thornton Boswell, College Park Maryland, 2/26/96, p. 209."

172 Dennis Breo. "JFK's death—the plain t6ruth from the MDs who did the autopsy," *JAMA*, may 27, 1992, v. 267:2802.

173 ARRB testimony J. Thornton Boswell, College Park Maryland, 2/26/96, p, 210.

174 ARRB testimony J. Thornton Boswell, College Park Maryland, 2/26/96, p. 213.

175 HSCA record # 180-10093-10429), Agency file # 002070, p. 17.

176 HSCA vol. 7: 253.

177 ARRB testimony of James H. Humes, February 13, 1999, p. 97.

178 A. Purdy.memo. HSCA rec# 180-10093-10430. Agency file # 002071-p. 6

179 ARRB testimony of J. Thornton Boswell, MD, February 26, 1996, p. 176–177.

180 A. Purdy memo. HSCA rec. # 180-10093-10429. Agency file # 002070, p. 2.

181 ARRB Depostion of John T. Stringer, July 16, 1996, p. 133.

182 Obituary, *New York Times*, 9/25/93.

183 David Lifton, *Best Evidence*, p.638.

184 HSCA counsel, Mark Flanagan, JD, telephone interview with Floyd Albert Riebe, 4/30/78. In: HSCA Record Number: 180-10105-10400, Agency file number: 014464.

185 Testimony of Floyd Albert Riebe before the ARRB, May 7, 1997, p. 32–33.

186 ARRB exhibit "MD 78."

187 ARRB deposition of John T. Stringer, July 16, 1996, p. 136–137.

188 ARRB deposition of John T. Stringer, July 16, 1996, p. 155.

189 ARRB deposition of Floyd Albert Riebe, May 7, 1997, p. 54.

190 ARRB deposition of Floyd Albert Riebe, May 7, 1997, p. 53.

191 2H352. (The "phenomenon" Humes referred to is the so-called "beveling" phenomenon, which Humes correctly explained to the Warren Commission. See text for discussion, or Humes at 2H352.)

192 HSCA Rec. # 180-10081-10347; agency file # 006165, p. 8.

193 HSCA interview with Finck, p.90–91. Agency File 013617.

194 ARRB deposition of Floyd Albert Riebe, 5/12/97, p. 39.

195 ARRB deposition of John T. Stringer, 7/17/96, p. 71.

[196] FBI agent, Francis X. O'Neill. Sworn testimony before the ARRB, 9/12/97, p. 158.

[197] FBI agent, Francis X. O'Neill. Sworn testimony before the ARRB, 9/12/97, p. 161–162.

[198] FBI agent, James W. Sibert. Sworn testimony before the ARRB, 9/11/97, p. 128.

[199] HSCA Agency File # 014028, p. 38–39.

[200] HSCA Agency File # 014028, and HSCA Agency File # 002198, p. 34–35.

[201] HSCA Agency File Number 002198, page 5.

[202] ARRB interview of Joe O'Donnell, 2/28/97, p. 2.

[203] ARRB interview of Joe O'Donnell, 2/28/97, p. 2.

[204] ARRB MD #148.

[205] Deposition of Saundra Kay Spencer, 6/7/97, before the ARRB, p. 50.

[206] Deposition of Saundra Kay Spencer, 6/7/97, before the ARRB, p. 45.

[207] HSCA, Vol. 6:226, footnote #1.

[208] Memorandum for File, written by Doug Horne for the JFK Review Board, entitled, "Unanswered Questions Raised by the HSCA's Analysis and Conclusions Regarding the Camera Identified by the Navy and the department of Defense as the Camera Used at President' Kennedy's Autopsy, p. 2–4.

[209] This sentence is taken from a letter Sent by John G. Kester, Assistant to Secretary of Defense Brown for HSCA-related matters in response to the HSCA's request for the camera used at the autopsy. Cited in Memorandum for File, written by Doug Horne for the JFK Review Board, entitled, "Unanswered Questions Raised by the HSCA's Analysis and Conclusions Regarding the Camera Identified by the Navy and the department of Defense as the Camera Used at President' Kennedy's Autopsy, p. 4.

[210] IBID.

[211] ARRB testimony J. Thornton Boswell, College Park Maryland, 2/26/96, p. 167.

[212] ARRB testimony J. Thornton Boswell, College Park Maryland, 2/26/96, p 34.

[213] HSCA testimony of J. Thornton Boswell, HSCA vol. 7: 246.

[214] ARRB testimony J. Thornton Boswell, College Park Maryland, 2/26/96, p 60.

215 ARRB testimony J. Thornton Boswell, College Park Maryland, 2/26/96, p 160.

216 Testimony of Humes and Boswell. HSCA vol. 7, p. 253.

217 ARRB testimony J. Thornton Boswell, College Park Maryland, 2/26/96, p. 57–58.

218 ARRB testimony J. Thornton Boswell, College Park Maryland, 2/26/96, p. 71–72.

219 ARRB testimony J. Thornton Boswell, College Park Maryland, 2/26/96, p. 84.

220 ARRB testimony J. Thornton Boswell, College Park Maryland, 2/26/96, p. 84.

221 HSCA memo of conversation with J.T. Boswell, HSCA record #180-10093-10430-, agency file number 002071, p. 6.

222 A copy of my recorded call to Boswell is available at the National Archives, and is apparently available for public listening.

223 *Washington Post*, 11/10/98, p. A-3.

224 Deposition of Floyd Albert Riebe, 5/7/97, p. 43–44.

225 *JAMA*, May 27, 1992, v. 267:2798.

226 ARRB testimony J. Thornton Boswell, College Park Maryland, 2/26/96.

227 Dennis Breo. "JFK's death, part II—Dallas MDs recall their memories," *JAMA*, May 27, 1992, v. 267:2806.

228 *Washington Post*, 11/10/98, p. A-3.

229 *JAMA*, May 27, 1992, v. 267:2800.

230 ARRB testimony J. Thornton Boswell, College Park Maryland, 2/26/96, p. 50–54.

231 See memo by ARRB staff member, Doug Horne.

232 Mike Feinsalber, "JFK Autopsy Files Are Incomplete," *Associated Press*, August 2, 1998, 11:48 a.m. EDT.

233 ARRB MD # 252; ARRB contact report of interview with Dr. Leonard D. Saslaw, Ph.D., 4/25/96.

234 Mike Feinsiber. "JFK Autopsy Files Are Incomplete," *AP*, Sunday, August 2, 1998; 11:48 a.m. EDT.

235 ARRB testimony of Pierre Finck, MD, 5/27/96, pp. 16, 20, 24–25.

236 Oral History Interview with Admiral George G. Burkley by William McHugh for the John F. Kennedy Library, 10/17/67.

237 Memo to file by Richard A. Sprague, 3/18/77. HSCA record number 180-10086-10295, agency file number 000988.

238 The letters "DSL" were hand written in marginal notations on internal HSCA memos pertaining to this Burkley affidavit. It is not clear whether these notations appear on the originals, or whether they were added later when retrieved from the files by researchers. If they were present on the originals, it is likely this represents a reference to David S. Lifton, the author of the book, "Best Evidence." For Burkley's memo seems specifically directed at refuting the "body alteration" theory Lifton was propounding to the HSCA. He finally published his theory two years later, in 1980.

239 Affidavit of Admiral George Burkley, 11/28/78. HSCA record number 180-10104-10271. Agency file number 013416.

240 Henry Hurt. *Reasonable Doubt.* New York: Henry Holt and Company, 1985, p. 49.

Photographs, Illustrations, and Tables

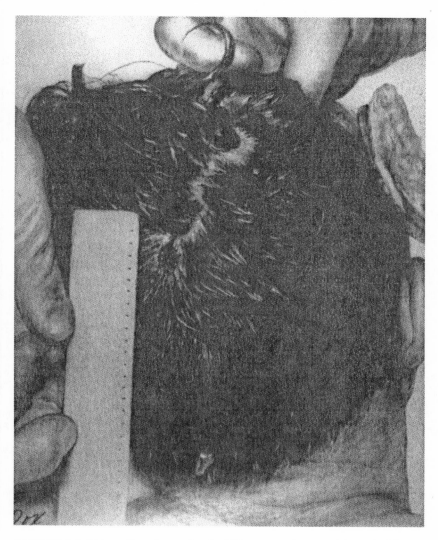

FIGURE 1 A: This replica of an authentic JFK autopsy photograph by artist Ida Dox was originally published by the House Select Committee in 1978 (vol. 7, p. 104). It is accurate, except for one detail. The small spot visible just to the right of the top of the ruler is exaggerated in this diagram. It is significantly smaller in the original photograph, as one can see by comparing this image with figure 1 B, a bootleg copy of an actual autopsy photograph. Some authorities have argued that the spot was an entrance wound for a higher shot than was determined during the autopsy, a claim that was emphatically rejected by JFK's pathologists.

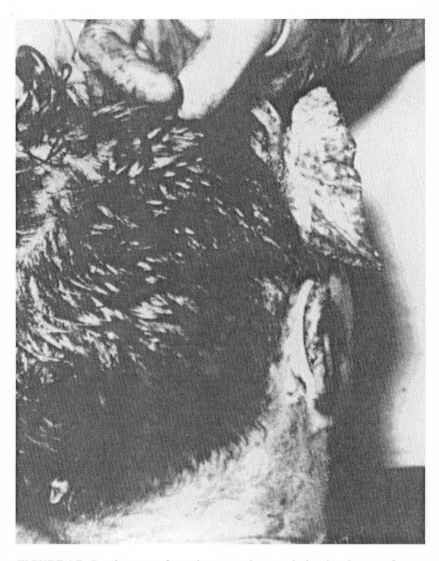

FIGURE 1 B: Bootleg copy of actual autopsy photograph showing the rear of JFK's skull entirely undamaged. Several witnesses claim that this image does not show the large wound JFK had in the right rear of this head. FBI agents who witnessed the autopsy said they believed this image had been "doctored." Autopsy surgeon J. Thornton Boswell reported that this image was taken with a flap of scalp being held over a large area of missing bone in the rear of JFK's skull. Dr. Crenshaw claimed in the early 1990s that this rear area was the site of an exit wound, a claim made in 1964 by Parkland doctors Jenkins, Aiken, Jones and McClelland.

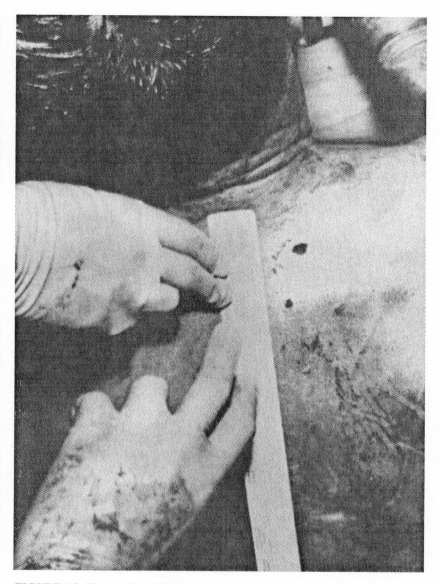

FIGURE 1C: The President's back appears to show two wounds, although in clearer views the lower "wound" appears to be a spot of blood. Neither wound was observed at Parkland because the back was not examined. Dr. Finck testified that he was ordered not to dissect the back wound by someone in the morgue who was not on the autopsy team. As a consequence, potentially valuable clues about the trajectory of the bullet through JFK's body were lost.

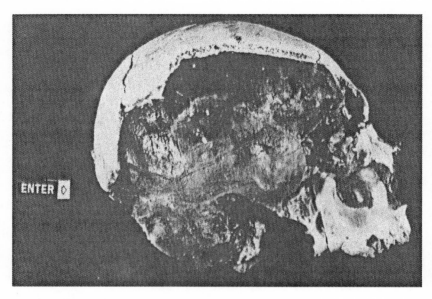

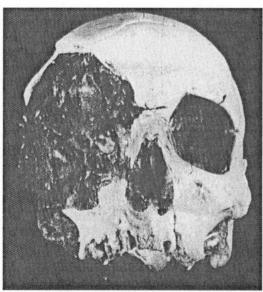

FIGURE 2: Warren Commission's "experimental duplication" of JFK's fatal wound. (Commission Exhibit 861 and 862) This skull was shot during experiments performed by Edgewood Arsenal to duplicate JFK's injuries. The bullet was fired from above and behind, striking the skull in the location specified in the autopsy report. Although it was claimed that the damage was "very similar to the wounds of the President," JFK had no damage to his forehead, to his eye socket, nor to his cheek, which the Commission should have known from the autopsy report and diagrams it reviewed. (See figures 4 and 5) But had Oswald fired a shot the way the Warren Commission believed he had, this would likely have been the result.

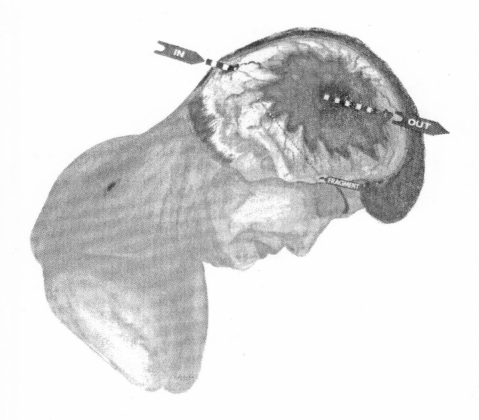

FIGURE 3: Rydberg Diagram, Warren Commission Exhibit 388. Prepared under the direction of JFK's pathologists, this diagram depicts that the greatest bone loss was on the side and rear of JFK's skull. Note, however, that one of JFK's pathologists prepared a diagram on the night of the autopsy depicting greater rearward damage than this image shows (See figure 13), and in 1996 he diagrammed a huge wound with rearward damage for the Assassinations Records Review Board. (See figure 14) Note also that although the Commission knew from this image and from the autopsy report that there had been no damage to JFK's face, it never questioned the shooting tests done on human skulls which, though radically different, were nevertheless described as "very similar to the wounds of the President." (See figure 2)

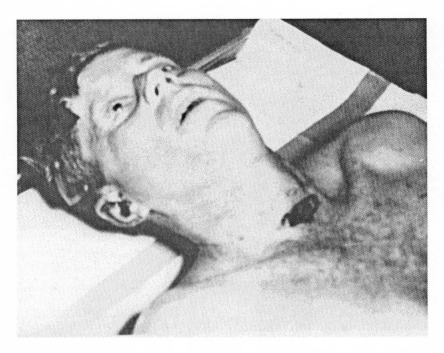

FIGURE 4: JFK in the morgue. This bootleg copy of an actual autopsy photograph from Kennedy's autopsy was first published in 1980. It shows no damage to the forehead, other than what appears in the original image to be a small scalp tear near the forehead. There was a small wound, described originally by all who saw it as an entrance wound, in the President's throat when he arrived at Parkland Hospital. A small incision (tracheotomy) was made to enlarge this wound to insert a breathing tube. Several Parkland witnesses reported that the tracheotomy appears to be much larger than it was when JFK left Dallas.

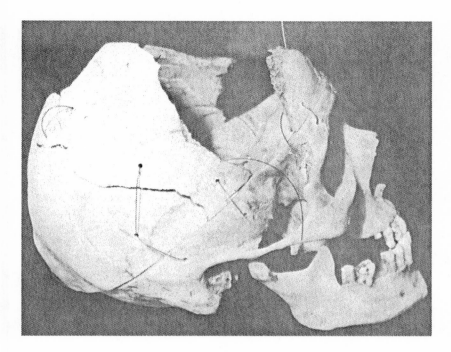

FIGURE 5: "Experimental duplication" of JFK's skull wound by John Lattimer, MD. To correct for the assumed error in the original autopsy report, Lattimer raised the inshoot in his shooting experiments. His bullets struck skulls 10-cm higher than in the Warren Commission's experiments. (See figure 2) Though they were strikingly dissimilar to the injuries Kennedy is known to have sustained, (See figures 3 and 4) Lattimer called his results "strikingly similar" to JFK's.

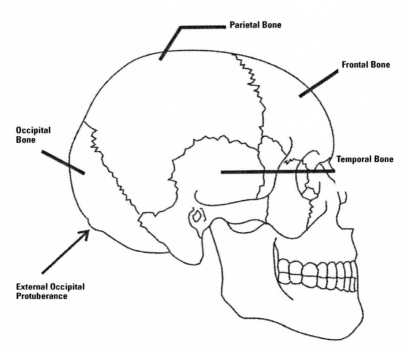

FIGURE 6: Human skull, right lateral view. Note the low, rearward location of the external occipital protuberance (EOP), a small elevation in occipital bone. More than 40 witnesses said JFK's skull wound involved the rear of his head, many of them using the term "occipital" in describing the damage. JFK's pathologists claimed the fatal bullet entered immediately adjacent to the EOP, which was ballistically impossible from Oswald's position given JFK's injuries. (See figure 2) A skull diagram prepared on the night of the autopsy (Figure 13), and amplified upon by one of JFK's pathologists in 1996 (Figure 14), shows occipital bone was missing when JFK arrived at the morgue.

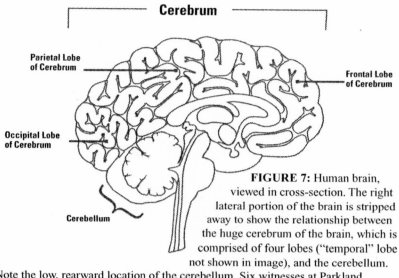

Cerebrum

Parietal Lobe
of Cerebrum

Frontal Lobe
of Cerebrum

Occipital Lobe
of Cerebrum

Cerebellum

FIGURE 7: Human brain, viewed in cross-section. The right lateral portion of the brain is stripped away to show the relationship between the huge cerebrum of the brain, which is comprised of four lobes ("temporal" lobe not shown in image), and the cerebellum.

Note the low, rearward location of the cerebellum. Six witnesses at Parkland Hospital in Dallas claimed that damaged cerebellum was protruding through, or visible through, a bony defect in the back of JFK' skull. Controversial autopsy photographs appear to disprove cerebellum damage. (See Figure 15)

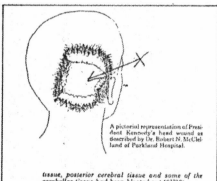

A pictorial representation of President Kennedy's head wound as described by Dr. Robert N. McClelland of Parkland Hospital.

tissue, posterior cerebral tissue and some of the cerebellar tissue had been blasted out (6H33).

This is the clearest description we have of the Kennedy head wound." In reading it we can understand quite readily why neurosurgeon Clark called the wound "tangential." For Dr. McClelland is quite clearly describing an impact on the right side of the head that blasted backward, springing open the parietal and occipital bones [see diagram] and driving out a mass of brain tissue. The precise character of the brain tissue is also important, for only a deep-ranging shot could have blown out cerebellar tissue, which is located very low in the brain. Dr. Marion Jenkins of Parkland remembers how "there was herniation and laceration of great areas of the brain, even to the extent that the cerebellum had protruded from the wound" (17H15; cf. 6H48), and Dr. James Carrico speaks of how the head wound "had avulsed [exploded] the calvarium [skull]" (17H4). A nurse, Pat Hutton, later recalled how "a doctor asked me to place a pressure dressing on the head wound. This was of no use, however, because of the massive opening on the back of the head" (21H216).

140

FIGURE 8: JFK's skull injuries according to Dallas doctors. This diagram of JFK's skull injury was prepared in 1966 with the approval of Parkland Hospital surgeon, Robert McClelland, MD. In 1979, Parkland Hospital's Paul Peters, MD approved this sketch of Kennedy's injuries. (Reprinted from: "High Treason" by Robert Groden and Harrison Livingstone, *Conservatory Press*, 1989.)

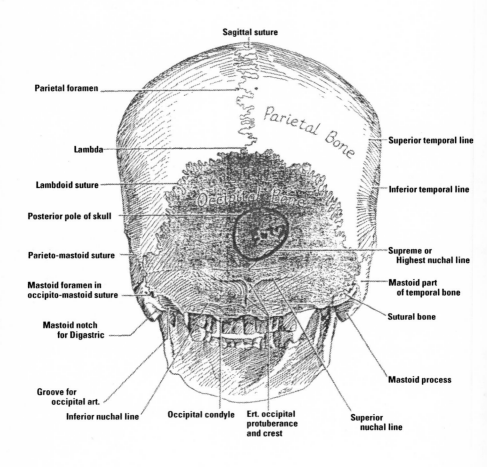

FIGURES 9A AND 9B: Diagrams of JFK's rearward skull wound prepared by one of JFK's treating neurosurgeons, Robert Grossman, MD. Grossman noted two distinct wounds, one in the rear and one on the right side of JFK's skull. The second image is the trajectory Grossman drew on a brain diagram to depict the trajectory of the bullet through the wounds he observed. Note the impossible trajectory for a single shot fired from behind, especially from behind and above.

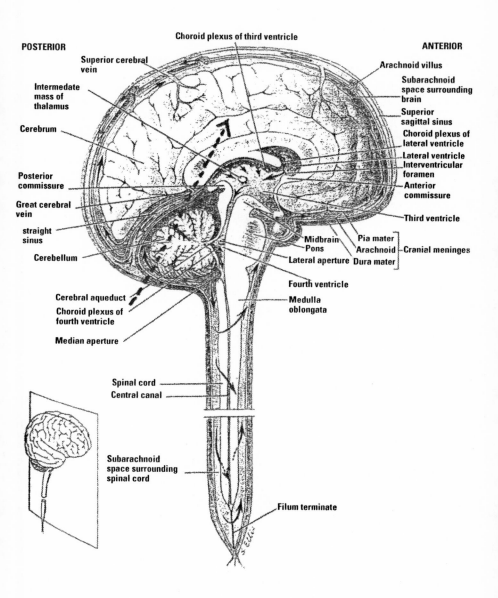

POSTERIOR

ANTERIOR

Choroid plexus of third ventricle

Superior cerebral vein

Intermediate mass of thalamus

Cerebrum

Posterior commissure

Great cerebral vein

straight sinus

Cerebellum

Cerebral aqueduct

Choroid plexus of fourth ventricle

Median aperture

Spinal cord

Central canal

Subarachnoid space surrounding spinal cord

Arachnoid villus

Subarachnoid space surrounding brain

Superior sagittal sinus

Choroid plexus of lateral ventricle

Lateral ventricle

Interventricular foramen

Anterior commissure

Third ventricle

Midbrain
Pons
Lateral aperture

Pia mater
Arachnoid
Dura mater

Cranial meninges

Fourth ventricle

Medulla oblongata

Filum terminate

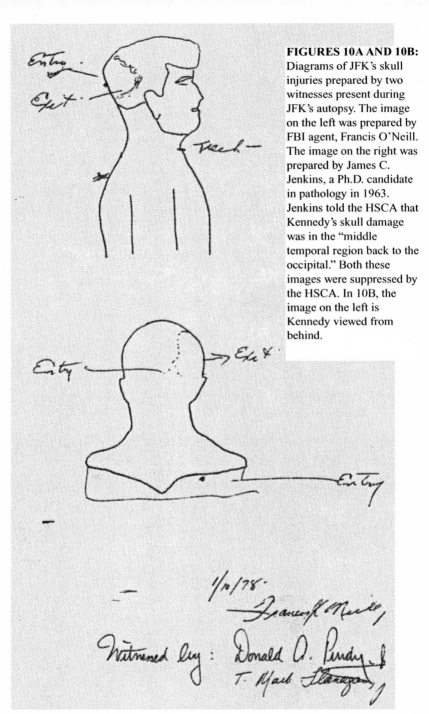

FIGURES 10A AND 10B:
Diagrams of JFK's skull injuries prepared by two witnesses present during JFK's autopsy. The image on the left was prepared by FBI agent, Francis O'Neill. The image on the right was prepared by James C. Jenkins, a Ph.D. candidate in pathology in 1963. Jenkins told the HSCA that Kennedy's skull damage was in the "middle temporal region back to the occipital." Both these images were suppressed by the HSCA. In 10B, the image on the left is Kennedy viewed from behind.

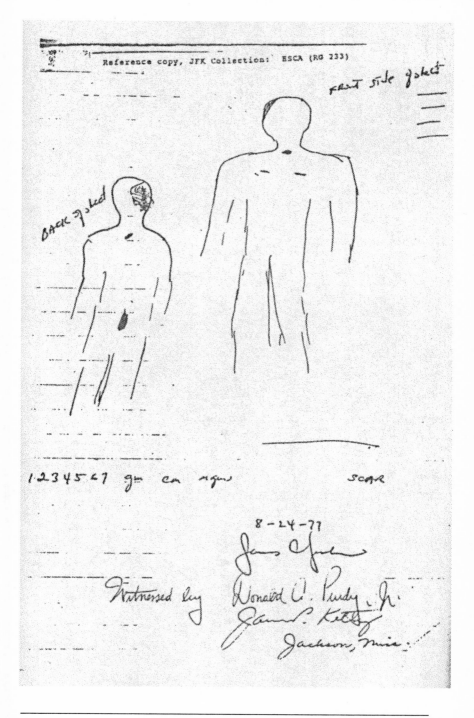

FRONT side goh_et

BACK-picked

1 2 3 4 5 6 7   gm   cm   mgm

SCAR

8-24-77

Witnessed by   Donald C. Purdy Jr.

Jackson, Miss.

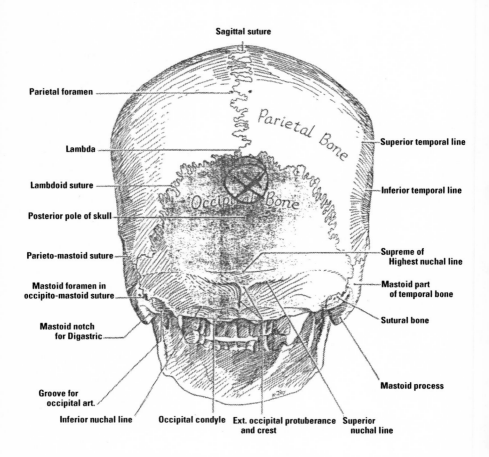

Sagittal suture

Parietal foramen

Lambda

Lambdoid suture

Posterior pole of skull

Parieto-mastoid suture

Mastoid foramen in
occipito-mastoid suture

Mastoid notch
for Digastric

Groove for
occipital art.

Inferior nuchal line

Occipital condyle

Ext. occipital protuberance
and crest

Superior
nuchal line

Parietal Bone

Occipital Bone

Superior temporal line

Inferior temporal line

Supreme of
Highest nuchal line

Mastoid part
of temporal bone

Sutural bone

Mastoid process

FIGURE 11: Diagram of skull wound by NPC photographic technician Saundra Spencer. Spencer testified that she developed some of JFK's autopsy photographs shortly after the assassination, and that one of them showed a wound in this location. No such image can be found in the current inventory. (Note the similarity between Spencer's diagram and Dallas neurosurgeon, Robert Grossman's, in figure 9.)

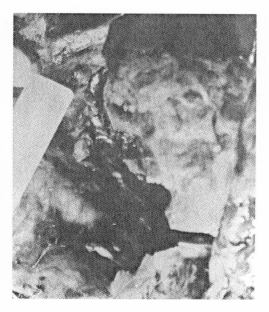

FIGURE 12: Photograph of JFK's skull wound. This is the only image supposedly taken of JFK's fatal skull wound. It is taken so close to the surface of the skull that it is all but impossible to orient as to which side is up or down, left or right. Three witnesses testified that the scalp was reflected to take a photograph of the spot where the bullet struck the skull, but this image does not show that. Nor is there *any* photograph in the current inventory that shows the scalp reflected to demonstrate JFK's skull wound.

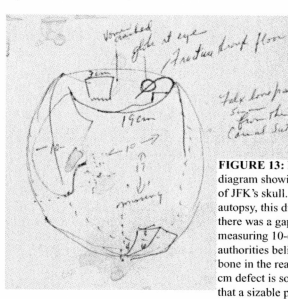

FIGURE 13: Dr. Boswell's face sheet diagram showing the damage to the top of JFK's skull. Prepared during the autopsy, this diagram documents that there was a gaping skull defect measuring 10-cm by 17-cm. Some authorities believe there was no loss of bone in the rear of JFK's skull. But a 17-cm defect is so large in a human skull that a sizable portion of JFK's rearward skull must have been absent for a defect that large to fit.

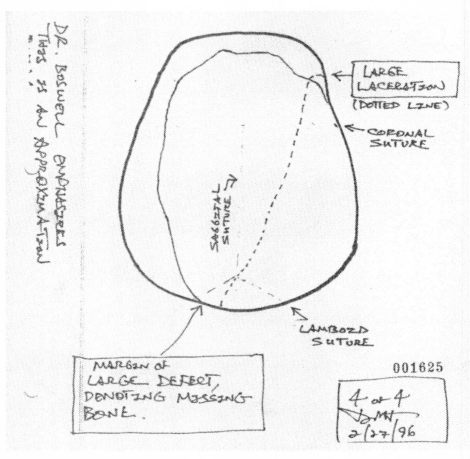

FIGURES 14A AND 14B. Dr. Boswell's depiction of JFK's skull damage to ARRB. These diagrams are two-dimensional drawings prepared by the ARRB to depict JFK's skull damage. They are based on markings made on a three-dimensional human skull model by one of JFK's pathologists, J. Thornton Boswell, MD. Note how closely these diagrams match the face sheet diagram prepared on the night of the autopsy (Figure 13). Note that most of the parietal bone is missing on the right. So also is a large portion of the occipital bone. On the assumption that there was no occipital bone missing, the Clark Panel and the HSCA forensics panel concluded the autopsy findings were consistent with Oswald's guilt.

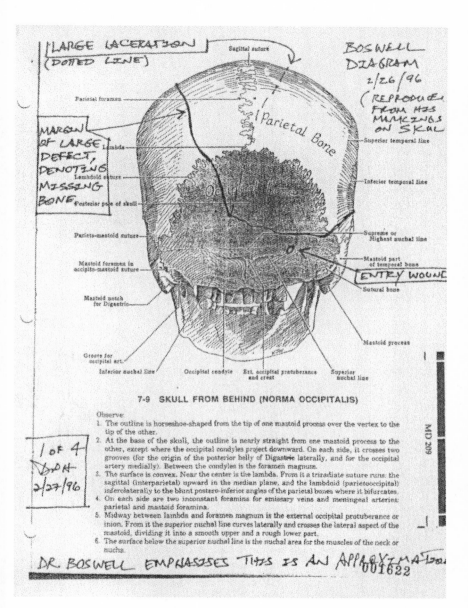

LARGE LACERATION
(DOTTED LINE)

BOSWELL
DIAGRAM
2/26/96
(REPRODUCED
FROM HIS
MARKINGS
ON SKULL

MARGIN
OF LARGE
DEFECT,
DENOTING
MISSING
BONE

ENTRY WOUND

Sagittal suture

Parietal foramen

Parietal Bone

Lambda

Lambdoid suture

Posterior pole of skull

Superior temporal line

Inferior temporal line

Parieto-mastoid suture

Supreme or
Highest nuchal line

Mastoid foramen in
occipito-mastoid suture

Mastoid part
of temporal bone

Sutural bone

Mastoid notch
for Digastric

Mastoid process

Groove for
occipital art.

Inferior nuchal line

Occipital condyle

Ext. occipital protuberance
and crest

Superior
nuchal line

7-9 SKULL FROM BEHIND (NORMA OCCIPITALIS)

Observe:
1. The outline is horseshoe-shaped from the tip of one mastoid process over the vertex to the tip of the other.
2. At the base of the skull, the outline is nearly straight from one mastoid process to the other, except where the occipital condyles project downward. On each side, it crosses two grooves (for the origin of the posterior belly of Digastric laterally, and for the occipital artery medially). Between the condyles is the foramen magnum.
3. The surface is convex. Near the center is the lambda. From it a triradiate suture runs: the sagittal (interparietal) upward in the median plane, and the lambdoid (parietooccipital) inferolaterally to the blunt postero-inferior angles of the parietal bones where it bifurcates.
4. On each side are two inconstant foramina for emissary veins and meningeal arteries: parietal and mastoid foramina.
5. Midway between lambda and foramen magnum is the external occipital protuberance or inion. From it the superior nuchal line curves laterally and crosses the lateral aspect of the mastoid, dividing it into a smooth upper and a rough lower part.
6. The surface below the superior nuchal line is the nuchal area for the muscles of the neck or nucha.

MD 209

1 OF 4
DPH
2/27/96

DR. BOSWELL EMPHASIZES THIS IS AN APPROXIMATION

001622

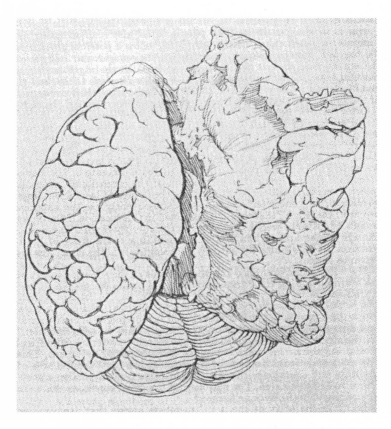

FIGURE 15: Drawing of the superior surface of JFK's brain. Prepared by the HSCA, this is an accurately rendered drawing of a photograph of JFK's brain as captured from above. Because the brain that was photographed weighed 1500 grams, the upper limit of normal for an undamaged, adult brain, doubts have arisen about whether this was actually JFK's brain. The autopsy photographs, and this diagram, support the high weight, for they show disruption of the right cerebral lobe, but no significant loss of brain substance. Witnesses from Dealey Plaza, from Parkland Hospital and from the morgue have all said a significant portion of JFK's brain was blown away. JFK's lateral autopsy X-rays show a loss of tissue from the frontal lobe of the cerebrum, which fits with the witnesses, but conflicts with the autopsy photographs and the measured brain weight. The ARRB's Douglas Horne found compelling evidence that two different "JFK" brains were examined, this, presumably, being the second brain, the one that was not Kennedy's. Note the distinctive, and undamaged, appearance of the small brain lobe at the bottom of the image—the cerebellum, an organ 6 Dallas doctors reported was damaged, including two neurosurgeons.

TABLE 1

Location of JFK's skull wound according to the earliest statements of witnesses at Parkland Hospital.

	RIGHT REAR	RIGHT SIDE	RIGHT ANTERIOR
1. WILLIAM KEMP CLARK, MD	X		
2. ROBERT McCLELLAND, MD	X		
3 MARION T. JENKINS, MD	X		
4. CHARLES J. CARRICO, MD	X		
5. MALCOLM PERRY, MD	X		
6. RONALD COY JONES, MD	X		
7. GENE AKIN, MD	X		
8. PAUL PETERS, MD	X		
9. CHARLES CRENSHAW, MD	X		
10. CHARLES R. BAXTER, MD	X		
11. ROBERT GROSSMAN, MD	X	X	
12. RICHARD B. DULANY, MD	X		
13. ADOLPHE GIESECKE, MD*	X	X	X
14. FOUAD BASHOUR, MD	X		
15. KENNETH E. SALYER, MD	X	X	X
16. PAT HUTTON, RN	X		
17. DORIS NELSON, RN	X		
18. WILLIAM GREER	X		
19. CLINTON J. HILL	X		
20. DIANA HAMILTON BOWRON, RN	X		
21. WILLIAM MIDGETT, MD	X	X	
22. PATRICIA GUSTAFSON	X		

*Claimed JFK's skull damage—occipital to frontal, he said—was on the left side, the only witness to mistake the side of JFK's skull injuries.

TABLE 2

Location of JFK's skull wound according to earliest statements of witnesses present at JFK's autopsy.

	RIGHT REAR	RIGHT SIDE	RIGHT ANTERIOR
1. GODFREY McHUGH	X		
2. JOHN STRINGER	X		
3. WILLIAM GREER	X		
4. ROY KELLERMAN	X		
5. CLINTON J. HILL	X		
6. FRANCIS O'NEILL	X		
7. JAMES W. SIBERT	X		
8. TOM ROBINSON	X		
9. ROBERT KARNEI, MD	X		
10. PAUL O'CONNOR	X		X
11. JAMES C. JENKINS	X		
12. EDWARD REED	X		
13. JERROL CUSTER	X		
14. JAN GAIL RUDNICKI	X		
15 JAMES E. METZLER	X		
16. DAVID OSBORNE, MD	X		
17. JOHN EBERSOLE, MD	X		
18. RICHARD LIPSEY	X		
19. CAPT. JOHN STOVER	(?—"TOP OF HEAD")		
20. CHESTER BOYERS	X		X
21. JAMES HUMES, MD	X		X
22. "J." T. BOSWELL, MD	X		X

ABOUT THE CONTRIBUTORS

Gary L. Aguilar, M.D., is an ophthalmologist specializing in plastic and reconstructive surgery in San Francisco, California. His is also assistant clinical professor of ophthalmology at Stanford University and at the University of California, San Francisco. Dr. Aguilar is a leading authority on the medical aspects of the assassination of JFK, having conducted many inquiries and interviews with physicians and witnesses to the crime.

D. Bradley Kizzia, J.D., is a lawyer in Dallas, Texas, where he specializes in general civil litigation. A graduate of Austin College and of the Southern Methodist University School of Law, Kizzia has been admitted to practice before all of the U.S. District Courts in Texas, the U.S. Court of Appeals, Fifth Circuit, and the U.S. Supreme Court. He has a special interest in the JFK assassination and assisted Dr. Crenshaw in his successful suit against the *Journal of the American Medical Association.*

J. Gary Shaw is a self-employed architect in Cleburne, Texas and is a former director of the JFK Assassination Information Center in Dallas. He is considered one of the world's leading authorities on the Kennedy assassination. Shaw is the author of one previous book on the subject, *Cover-Up*, and was co-author with Dr. Crenshaw of *JFK: Conspiracy of Silence.*

Cyril Wecht, M.D., J.D., is chief of forensic pathology and legal medicine for Allegheny County, Pennsylvania and is widely recognized as one of America's premier forensic pathologists. He has performed over 13,000 autopsies and reviewed another 30,000. His extensive experience and medical-legal expertise have made him a sought-after authority in many of America's most controversial cases. He gained national prominence for disputing the Warren Commission's version of John F. Kennedy's assassination. Dr. Wecht is author of *Cause of Death, Grave Secrets* and *Who Killed Jonbenet Ramsey?*

Printed in the United States
1463400002B/192